MY DAYS WITH
ERROL FLYNN

"I had a friend, Buster Wiles..., a stuntman and a daredevil, one of the best in movies."

—Errol Flynn
My Wicked Wicked Ways

My Days With
Errol Flynn

The Autobiography of Stuntman
BUSTER WILES

With a Special Appendix,
THE FLYNN CONTROVERSY
by *William Donati*

ROUNDTABLE PUBLISHING, INC.
Santa Monica California

ROUNDTABLE PUBLISHING, INC.

933 Pico Boulevard
Santa Monica, CA 90405

First Printing, 1988

Library of Congress Catalog Card Number—88-061235

ISBN No. 0-915677-36-9

All photographs are from the personal collection of Buster Wiles, unless otherwise indicated.

PRINTED IN THE UNITED STATES OF AMERICA

To Mollie Wiles,
who taught me the gift of laughter.

ACKNOWLEDGMENTS

Special thanks to the following for their generous help in making this book possible:

Budget Films of Los Angeles, the Library of the Academy of Motion Picture Arts and Sciences, the Turner Entertainment Co., the Warner Archives of the University of Southern California, the Warner Bros. Legal Department for permission to quote copyrighted material, the Wisconsin Center for Film and Theater Research.

A debt of gratitude is owed the following individuals for their kind assistance: Franklin Roosevelt, Jr., for granting permission to quote from correspondence in the Roosevelt Museum; Jerry Hill, director of the Howard Hill Museum in Wilsonville, Alabama, for permission to publish photographs from the collection of his great-uncle.

Also: Morris J. Alhadeff, Leith Adams, Basile Courtel, Bette Davis, Rick Dodd, Don Donati, Albert C. Drebin, Josef Fegerl, Ben Harrison, Olivia de Havilland, Johnny Longden, Ida Lupino, Dennis Morgan, Trudy McVicker, Bill Nanez, Ann Perrett, Mickey Rooney, Tom Scalzo, Phyllis Searles, Peter Stackpole, Chris Walker, Don Wiles.

CONTENTS

Have you ever seen a kid win a fight and said
   Wish it were me
Have you ever stared at the silver screen and said
Wish it were me
Have you ever seen a gorgeous gal marry a happy guy
      and said
Wish it were me
Have you ever stood next to a winner at the race track
      saying
Wish it were me

I have, my friends, I have
I've wished for all of these things
And sometimes
The lucky fellow **was me**

Prologue

"The train rolled through the night."

The casket was placed in a large wooden crate for the train ride to Los Angeles. Inside a baggage car, it was lifted onto a table used for sorting mail. I sat alone, emotionally exhausted. Two days before, I had been in a bar when a guy walked up and said, "Your buddy just dropped dead."

"Who?"

"Errol Flynn had a heart attack."

It was hard to comprehend that fun-loving Errol was gone. A porter brought me a bottle of Seagram's V.O. I had lifted many a cocktail in company with Flynn, but now I toasted him alone. I glanced inside an envelope, which contained the personal effects he had been carrying when he died. There was cash, too —seventy-six dollars in a gold money clip, depicting a couple in a "69" love embrace.

As the train rumbled along, an eerie creaking suddenly pierced the quiet of the railway baggage car. It was a spooky sound, and it seemed to be coming from behind me. For a few seconds I thought that perhaps another prank was being played.

"Flynn," I said aloud, "if you're pulling another gag on me, I'll kill you."

I hoped to hear Errol's familiar laugh, but all I heard was the eerie creaking. I forced myself to turn around. The strange sound was emitted by the squeaky hinge of a locker door, which had slipped open.

As the train rolled through the night, I leaned back in my chair, propped my feet on the table, and took a swig of whiskey. I closed my eyes and reminisced about my days with Errol Flynn. . . .

It was a windy autumn afternoon in New York City, and Flynn and I were expected for cocktails at a chic gathering of socialites. We briskly walked through Manhattan, dressed in our new tuxedos. On my head I wore the latest model toupee, to cover my bald pate. We were on our way to a reception given by Countess Mercati, wife of the Grand Marshall of the Court of Athens.

We entered a luxury apartment building and were escorted to the residence of the Countess. As we made our way down the hall, Flynn glanced at the bulge under my starched white shirt. He grinned. I was secretly carrying a black fright wig that had a silver streak down the center. The wig was a cherished memento from *The Return of Dr. X*, when I had doubled Humphrey Bogart in a fight scene. Flynn and I were out to do mischief.

As we approached the entrance of the apartment, we were greeted by a servant dressed in the tradition of centuries past. He wore an ornate silk coat, knee breeches, and white silk stockings. Flynn handed him the invitation. The servant stepped inside. From within, we heard him announce in a loud, high-pitched voice: "Mr. Errol Flynn!"

Errol squared his shoulders and strode into the reception area. A few minutes later, the high voice rang out again: "Mister Buster Wiles!"

I entered a large room, where elegantly dressed people were milling about and quietly conversing. A butler, with his jaw in the air, circulated with a tray, politely offering glasses of champagne to the guests. I spotted Flynn, chatting with a regal-looking matron. She was decked with diamonds. I introduced myself and joined the conversation. I'm sure it was the first time the Countess had ever met anyone named "Buster."

After chatting a few moments, I drifted off and mingled with the elite. I conversed with a short, fat stockbroker. When I saw the Countess unengaged, I went over and spoke.

"I beg your pardon, ma'am, but I've got ten thousand head of cattle coming into Chicago today, and I want to see if they were placed on the train. May I use your telephone?"

"Why certainly. Go down the hall, second door on the right."

I followed her instructions, but of course made no phone call. I removed my regular toupee and put on my "skunk wig." I glanced in the mirror. Man, did I look bizarre, like something out of a horror movie!

I returned to the high-ceilinged reception room, where the glittering guests sipped champagne in a casual and easygoing atmosphere. As I drifted among the elite, heads turned and mouths dropped. The party chitchat died, and a puzzled buzz swept the room.

Flynn wore a grin as wide as the Mississippi, reveling in the bewilderment that suddenly changed the ambiance of the high-society gathering. The stockbroker glanced at me strangely as I approached the Countess. She turned, and her face registered a surprise.

"Thank you so much for letting me use your telephone, ma'am. I'm expecting a person-to-person call at any moment. May I use the room again?"

"Yes," she said, obviously perplexed by my appearance.

I returned to the room and pulled off my fright wig. I emerged absolutely bald. Conversation halted, and an audible hush fell over the room. I heard a voice whisper, "He's lost his wig and doesn't know it." There were snickers, embarrassed faces, and puzzled looks. Flynn was about to explode with laughter, but played it cool, pretending not to notice. I was all polite smiles, as I mingled with the socialites.

"Hello, I'm Buster Wiles," I said, all warmth and innocence. The fat stockbroker came over. We began chatting, then he eyed me curiously. He squinted.

"Say, buddy, didn't you have hair when you came in here?"

I ran my hand over my slick head, expressing astonishment.

"Why . . .why yes," I stammered.

"Hey, Flynn!" I yelled, "what kind of party is this? Somebody has stolen my hair!"

Errol's head shot back, and he convulsed with laughter. The onlookers, realizing that we had played a joke, laughed too. Even the Countess enjoyed our mischief: "You fooled me at first," she said.

Whenever Flynn and I got together, we always created something for which I have a profound respect—fun! I have always believed that laughter is the best medicine in the world. The prank we played in New York in the autumn of 1941 was just one of many wonderful times we had together. I knew Errol for twenty-four years. He has sadly been gone for nearly three decades, but I still believe in laughter. I still believe in people.

For me, people are the most fascinating elements in the universe. You can have an expensive mansion, but if no one shares it with you, it can become a lonely dwelling. Life is people.

I've often wondered if there is a pattern or destiny in our brief existence. How is it that certain directions are laid out for us? How is it that a country boy who was born in Missouri and raised in Tennessee came to rub elbows with world-famous celebrities? How did Vernon "Buster" Wiles, a kid who sat in many a movie theater, wishing to be up there on the silver screen, manage to land a job as a stuntman in Hollywood?

I truly believe that there is a certain road each one of us was meant to follow. Things happen that were just meant to be. Looking back on my life, I can see how so many of my wishes and dreams did come true.

PART ONE

THE MEMPHIS
KID

Little Buster and Captain Billy. We won a race at the county fair. Our prize — a barrel of flour.

Below: Big Buster and Snake in *Charge of the Light Brigade*.

ONE

From Caruthersville To Memphis

"I lived so far back in the hills it took two birds to sing one song."

I was born in 1910, in Pemiscot County, near Caruthersville, Missouri. When I made my entrance, my father, Huston Wiles, had a farm. The Wiles family had deep roots in Missouri and Tennessee.

We were country people, and I grew up in a large house, which was surrounded by cotton fields. Near our place was a log cabin where my grandmother resided. She positively refused to leave her rustic dwelling. Stubbornness is a genetic trait in the Wiles family. Longevity is another family characteristic. Grandmother was eighty-six when she passed away. She was trying to catch a rabbit with a piece of stove wood, when her kind heart gave out. That lucky rabbit was one of the few who escaped from Grandma.

My father, Huston, was a quiet man, but once in a while he would have a little nip (or more) and ride his horse into a saloon. Then he would magnanimously order a round for everyone. When I was six years old, Dad gave me a cigar and a shot of whiskey, hoping that the taste of both would be eternally unfavorable to my young palate. The cigar made me sick, but the alcohol.... Well, the reverse of Dad's wish occurred. I liked it.

My mother, Mollie, had the sunniest disposition in the world. She enjoyed a laugh more than anything else. The Wiles family, each and every one, enjoyed a hearty joke. We enjoyed other pastimes too. Now, every country family has a skeleton in every log cabin closet. Ours had a story that I heard in bits and pieces over the years, and I finally put the parts together. It seems that one Wiles member had carried on the favorite pastime in the arms of a lady who belonged to another. The husband surprised them together. He aimed his pistol. The Wiles member did not rise again. The scandal that ensued wasn't due so much to the romantic liaison as to the place where the indiscretion occurred: they were discovered in a cotton field. Well, there were preachers in the Wiles family also.

* * * * *

As a kid, I certainly got into my share of mischief. That's how I acquired my nickname: somebody was usually yelling at me. "Buster" was a name that seemed to fit me like a glove. "Mischief" was my middle name. One of my principal delights was parading through Caruthersville, tooting my alto horn—at 6:00 a.m. My pal, B.F. Rogers, accompanied me in my early morning concerts. Our musical delights consisted of our blasting away on the alto horn outside someone's bedroom window. I got a real thrill when the screeching notes echoed through the alleys and the eardrums of the sleeping citizens of Caruthersville. When they started yelling, we knew our concert had been recognized. B.F. and I took off running. B.F. ran so hard that he eventually became the mayor of Caruthersville.

We would often pick up spare change at the train station by carrying suitcases: "Oh, please, mister, let me help you," I would plead. Occasionally we would fight over some harried business-man's luggage. The poor devil would see his expensive suitcase pulled in every direction, and he would eventually scream, "Here's a quarter! Now get the hell out of here, you little bastards!"

On the farm I had another friend with whom I shared many an adventure—my pony, Captain Billy. He and I would spend hours exploring the countryside. When I was nine, I entered a race at the county fair. Captain Billy and I shared the excitement and thrill of winning! I proudly took home my prize—a barrel of flour.

As a child, my greatest fascination was with the Mississippi

River. I never tired of going down to the river and watching the boats sail by. I can close my eyes and see the *Delta Queen* and the *Island Queen* out on the muddy river, blowing thick black smoke from their stacks. It was the mighty Mississippi that inspired a young writer from Hannibal, Missouri, to pen books that will never die. Mark Twain had once been a riverboat pilot. He knew the river and its cities well. His novels, *Tom Sawyer* and *The Adventures of Huckleberry Finn*, capture every boy's hope for excitement and adventure. I was no exception. I had dreams of seeing where those boats were going.

The showboats often stopped in Caruthersville. I was mesmerized by the plays that were performed aboard these sailing theaters. The performances on the showboats gave me my first dreams of being an actor. There were other dreams of boyhood— fighting pirates on a burning ship, joining the circus, being a cowboy, fighting Indians.

When I was nine years old, the family decided to move to Memphis. This was "The big city." Mayor E.H. Crump was running the town at that time. "Boss" Crump ran Memphis for almost fifty years. He was a politician's politician. He had been swept to power as a reform candidate, intending to eliminate the vice dens filled with gambling, dope, alcohol, and prostitution. Because of his flaming hair, he was nicknamed "The Red Snapper." Mayor Crump was quite a figure—in his white suit, Panama hat, and owlish glasses. He was well-known for his ability always to recall a citizen's name. He would meet you once on Main Street and *never* forget who you were. Years later, I saw the great vice reformer at the Santa Anita Racetrack. By then, the red locks had turned snow white.

"Why, Mayor Crump, what are you doing here?"

"Why, *Buster Wiles*, what are *you* doing here?"

When we arrived in Memphis in 1918, it was a town known as "the murder capital of the world." But I found the city exciting. It was rough too. I learned how rough it was the first day I arrived. I also learned a good lesson.

The Wiles family moved into a house at 367 Union. We had arrived in the city late at night. When I awoke the next morning, I was anxious to see our new town. I remember that morning as if it were yesterday. Mama was getting ready to go to her new job. She had found a position as a saleswoman in the bargain basement of Bry's Department Store. She was earning the grand sum of ten dollars a week. I dressed and stood by the door, ready for action. Mama had other plans for Buster.

"Don't you leave this house. You might get lost," she told me.

I watched her disappear down Union Avenue. Then I followed her to see where she was going. As I walked down the busy thoroughfare, I noticed how tall all of the buildings were becoming. I soon found myself in the downtown area.

In the heart of the city was Court Square. Mama disappeared into the department store nearby. Court Square was a beautiful park, with huge trees and a fountain where Hebe, the goddess of youth, towered above the spraying water. I heard a loud commotion near one of the park benches. Two kids were fighting. One boy was several sizes larger than the other. This violated a cardinal rule I had been taught in the Wiles family: "Pick on somebody your own size." I sauntered over to the big kid and expressed the cardinal rule. He spit right in my face.

I tore into him like a hellcat. I was a pretty big farm boy. Hard work had made me strong. My opponent soon gave up. I have never been one to run from a fight. I've always been a peaceful man, but once I'm riled—watch out!

I learned that the small kid who was getting a licking was a Jewish boy named Nathan. He and Tom had been fighting about who was going to get that territory to sell newspapers. I asked Nathan if I could sell some of the papers in his huge stack. I shouted at the top of my lungs. That day I earned eighty-six cents. I was rich.

At 4:30 p.m., expecting Mama to get off work, I returned to the entrance of the department store. She almost died when she saw me. There stood her little Vernon. Not only had I disobeyed her, but she could tell I had been fighting.

"What are you doing out of that yard, boy!"

I had to do some fast talking. I told the truth. "Why, Mama, I was working. I made eighty-six cents, selling papers."

She softened. The Wiles family always respected work. Sometimes I think work is all I've ever known. Well, Daddy soon decided that Memphis was too big for him. He returned to Caruthersville with my older brother, Vernice. My sister Hazel and I stayed in Memphis.

I soon became a full-time paperboy for *The Commercial Appeal* newspaper, starting with selling papers around Court Square. Sometimes I would be so hungry in the park that I would watch the squirrels bury their peanuts and then go and dig them up. Selling newspapers was a wonderful experience for me. I came in contact with all kinds of people. I learned how to chat with everyone, and this undoubtedly contributed to developing my outgoing personality. Talking to people became fun.

I would meet the milkman every morning across from the publishing company. If I drank a quart of milk without stopping, he would let me have it for free. I made it appear to be a big effort, but I could have downed two quarts without stopping. Food was a big source of interest for me. It always seemed as if I spent a lot of my earnings on food.

The Sunday paper sold for a dime back then. We hustlers would get it for six cents. I would start hollering early in the morning, making so much noise that people couldn't sleep, so they often purchased a paper just to have me go away.

I recall selling extras announcing the death of President Wilson. The extra came out on Sunday morning. I went around to different churches, stuck my head in the doors, and whispered: "Wilson dies!" Then I waited outside for people to run out and buy the papers.

Around 11:30 every Sunday morning, I would take my mother and sister to lunch, and maybe a movie later. During the week, I was attempting to garner an education. My unfortunate ability to get into fights made me shuffle from one school to another like a deck of cards. One school I attended was Leath Elementary, on Linden Street. A girl in my class was Wilma Wyatt. She later married one of the most successful singers in the world—Bing Crosby. Being from Memphis, she had picked up the nickname "Dixie."

My nickname "Buster" was appropriate too. When we had arrived in Memphis, I had attended Christine Elementary School. This place had the reputation of being one of the toughest schools in Memphis. I was determined not to be pushed around. I soon decided that the best way to avoid trouble in the long run was to confront it in the short haul. In other words, find the school bully and beat the living daylights out of him. It didn't take me long to put my theory into practice.

My first day in school was the opportunity that came so unexpectedly. Walking down a hall, I spied this big fellow taunting a smaller Chinese boy with a grasshopper. This was my chance to earn my reputation: whip this bully, and I would be left in peace. I stuck my nose in the fracas. Once again I elicited the cardinal rule: "Why don't you put that on someone your own size?"

He did. The grasshopper was thrust in my mug.

We decided to tangle in a vacant lot across the street. After we started trading punches, I realized that this bully was tough. The fight eventually resulted in a draw, mainly because some teachers appeared and broke it up.

The next morning, the little Chinese boy came to school with a five-pound sack full of apples and peaches. He did this every morning for a week. I readily appreciated this treat. My family ate so much oatmeal at home I had begun to neigh at horses. The Chinese boy had recently come to Memphis from Shanghai, China. His father had a restaurant on Union.

Years later, when I was between pictures, I returned to Memphis for a visit. I took eight or nine people to a Chinese restaurant for dinner. When I asked for the check, the waiter told me it was all taken care of by someone else. The waiter pointed to a man in a uniform, sitting in the rear of the restaurant. It was my Chinese friend, Shu-Wong. He never forgot the small favor I had rendered years before. He was dressed in the uniform of a Chinese aviator, getting ready to depart for the war in China. He emerged from the conflict as a high officer. His Chinese restaurant on Union is still there today.

My school friend had been taught to fly by a well-known Memphis pilot named Vernon Omlie. He was married to the legendary Phoebe Fairgrave Omlie. Together they formed a team that dazzled the nation. They were incredibly daring barnstormers of the air.

Tiny Phoebe was a wing-walker and parachutist. She had once dangled above the earth from an airplane, supported only by a bit between her teeth. Now that was something to see! I was enthralled by her exploits. She once stepped from the wing of one plane to that of another. This stunt was shot and used in *The Perils* of Pauline.

Vernon Omlie died in a plane crash in 1936, and Phoebe later became an aviation consultant in Washington.

The idea of appearing before a crowd was appealing to me. I pulled a stunt of my own when I hitched a ride to the Millington Airport and hid in the rear seat of a biplane about to take off. Once aloft, I tapped the pilot on the shoulder, and he practically snapped his neck, so sharply did he turn around, with disbelieving eyes staring through his goggles. I was thrilled as the plane climbed, dipped, and buzzed low over Memphis and the Mississippi River. Until then I had never realized how curved is the path of "the Father of the Waters."

My usual view of the muddy river was from the downtown cobblestone wharf, where I often caught the rope of the docking showboats. If I had any spare money, I would watch the dramatic or musical presentations aboard these "floating palaces." I followed the performers around like a puppy. There was a fabulous trumpet player who always got loaded as soon as the boat landed. He would grab his trumpet and, if the mood was right, place it to his lips and play for the bar patrons. Sometimes, on his way back to the showboat, he would amaze bystanders as he continued his improvised concert on the downtown sidewalks.

I often wandered about Beale Street, where it was "always Saturday night." Mr. Crump had, somehow or another, forgotten to close the saloons and gambling houses that flourished there. While living in Memphis, the immortal W.C. Handy had written "St. Louis Blues" and "Beale Street Blues." He was responsible for this form of music becoming recognized the world over.

I can still smell the mouthwatering aroma of barbecued ribs being cooked in the dives along Beale Street. No place in the world has better barbecue than Memphis. There were a lot of ribs cracked on Beale Street too. With all the bars, fights were commonly held inside or on the crowded sidewalks.

As I got older, my primary interest in school became sports. Football and boxing were my areas of expertise. I played a rough game of football, as part of a sandlot team at Morris Park. There were some great Italian boys on our squad. Lou Chiozza was my fullback. He later played professional baseball for the New York Giants.

Sometimes, I would play three games in one day. I would start out at Morris Park in the morning, then head for Forest Park for a romp, and end up playing for Messick High School! After my football days and stunt work in Hollywood, it's a miracle I can still walk.

One day I was hawking my papers at the top of my lungs, when I noticed a man staring at me. I had been shouting about my favorite football team's latest victory—the "Tennessee Docs" was the greatest team in the world. The man came over and asked me how I knew so much about the Docs. I explained that they were *my team*. As I looked at him closer, it dawned on me that this man was the quarterback for the University of Tennessee physicians, who were tearing up the turf with their victories.

"Aren't you Dr. Sam Sanders?"

"Yes....How would you like to sit on the bench at our next game?"

I couldn't believe it. I couldn't have been more honored if President Coolidge had invited me to the White House for dinner. I became the squad's mascot. Led by Dr. Sam Sanders, the team had an incredible series of wins from 1920 to 1926. The Docs even beat Ole Miss. In November of 1926, a Fort Benning Army team triumphed over the Docs. An Army play that day broke Sam's leg. I ran out on the field with a bucket of water in my hand. I was ready to demolish the perpetrator of such a foul deed. I merely cursed up and down the field for a while, but, man, was I hot! Dr. Sam was my hero. He still is. Today he is eighty-six, and still a practicing physician in Memphis. What a tiger! What a great humanitarian! All of Memphis loves that guy.

Another sport that captured my interest was golf. I was a caddy at Overton Park. I had some good "loops." In those days, you got a quarter for nine holes. Most golfers knew I was taking my money home to Mama, and they gave me fifty cents. Once in awhile, I would get a dollar for a loop. Big money in those days.

Between loops, I devised a method of earning extra pay. On the fifth hole, there was a blind spot where the golfers couldn't see exactly where their ball was headed. When I heard voices teeing off, I prepared for action. When that little white ball came sailing through the air, I would make a dive. Selling golf balls was my line for a while. One day I made a superb catch. Out from the bushes stepped my supervisor, Norman Kelley.

"Nice catch, Buster. Catch yourself a week off this job."

Another rule to remember: "Crime doesn't pay," or "Don't get caught."

I always enjoyed a good laugh, but invariable somebody would start a beef. One day at Overton Park, my party was ready to tee off. A guy showed up, asking for Buster Wiles.

"What do you want with him?" I asked.

"I walked six miles just to whip him."

"Gee whiz."

I debated which I should carry out first—my loop or my fight.

"Wait just a minute. I'll see if Mr. Wiles can accommodate you."

I turned to Gene Price, who years later was a scenic designer at Warner Bros., and explained the situation.

"Could you get another foursome to go ahead of us? I don't think this will take long."

"You bet," said Gene, "I'd like to see this myself!"

I asked the guy who had walked six miles to walk with me to the number one fairway, which was uphill. I stayed uphill the entire battle, so I could punch down. As we fought, I could feel something sharp pierce my skin. My opponent was no fool. He was wearing a bent horseshoe nail around each hand. I let him have it for all I was worth. After slugging it out for about thirty minutes, my opponent said he had enough. I was almost done-for myself. He slumped off.

"I'm sorry to disappoint you after you've walked six miles just to whip me." I picked up one of the horseshoe nails and threw it at him. I told Gene to get someone else to caddy my loop, staggered to the number-two hole, and collapsed in the bushes.

Memphis was a city very enthusiastic about prize-fighting. I was no exception. One year, I won the Golden Gloves award. I later boxed against a fighter named Eddie "Kid" Wolfe, in a three-round amateur match. Eddie later turned pro and fought light-weight champ Tony Canzoneri. The more fights I got, the better I learned a fighting technique. My style was jab and dodge. I never dove. Today, my hands are swollen with knots. I didn't get those broken knuckles from squirting perfume bottles.

Fighting, football, and golf were my favorite sports. I met some real characters in all three fields. One of the first sports hustlers I ever met was a guy named Titanic Thompson. One of his main sources of income was betting people he could hit a golf ball half a mile. He would find a sucker for a bet, then take him to a frozen lake. The golf ball would sail across the ice.

He had an assistant called "Tubby," who worked with me as a caddy. Titanic would often wait on the golf course for a prospective client. He would usually ask a lone golfer to join him. As they got deep in the wooded area, Titanic would make his pitch. What team would win a baseball game being played at that very moment? What football team would be victorious? The wager was placed, as they leisurely played their game of golf. At a predetermined point, Tubby would be in the woods. The winning team's name would be on a card.

One time, he made a bet with a bookie about an out-of-state horse race. Here comes Tubby, leaning out of a car window, with the card reading "#6." When they returned to the clubhouse, Titanic was surprised to learn that he had lost the wager! How could Tubby have possibly gotten the winning horse wrong? Titanic finally realized that his partner-in-crime had held the card upside down. Number "9" had won! Sometimes you win; sometimes you lose.

Besides selling papers, I had a job as a delivery boy for Dr. Gregorio's Pharmacy. I was given a fast bike to deliver anything and everything. I could deliver a tray of Cokes by balancing them with one hand. As I got better, I started doing stunts on the bike. I found a place where kids congregated on a hilly street. Each day I impressed them with a superb jump across an incline. Each day I got further. One day, I pedaled as fast as I could and made the leap. When the bike hit the pavement, it just disintegrated. I found myself on the sidewalk amidst a dozen pieces. Dr. Gregorio nearly had a fit when I came into the pharmacy, carrying the bike in a box. Sometimes you lose.

I later got a job delivering for another drugstore. Every afternoon, when school recessed, I rode my own bicycle from our house at 657 Kent, in the Buntyn section, to downtown Memphis. This was a ride of about seven miles to Goldfarb's Drugstore, at Manassas and Adams. At this place, I got to jerk the sodas and make the milkshakes. After we closed at 11:30 at night, I was usually too exhausted to pedal home. I devised a method to make it with a minimum of effort. I would grab a car fender and coast alongside the vehicle. Sometimes, we would reach a speed of forty miles per hour. During classes at school, I would sometimes doze off. My teacher knew I was working, so she would whisper to the class "Shhh, be real quiet, and don't wake Buster."

The janitor at Goldfarb's was a big, muscular black fellow named Brooks. He was a swell guy and a hell of a fighter. One night on Beale Street, he whipped eleven men in a pool-room brawl. He saved my hide one afternoon, when three kids came to the store looking for me. Brooks asked what they wanted.

"We're gonna whip him."

"You are? Well, I've got to see that. But I'm going to tell you one thing right now. You've got to line up. All three of you aren't going to jump him."

About this time, I rode up on my bike and heard Brooks dictating the sporting rules. He smiled at me.

"Here comes Buster. Now, which one of you is first?"

I dropped the first one, and the other two disappeared.

Who took my scalp?

My mother Mollie and son Don pose with me alongside my hotrod that set a speed record.

I've got more hair as an Indian than as a cowboy (on the right) in *The Plainsman*.

Two

Florida Sunshine, Color It Green

"He who asks faintly begs a denial."

In 1924, there was a real-estate boom in Florida. Mama decided that our future would be in the Sunshine State. We soon found ourselves in Tampa. I happened to be returning from the beach one day and passed a crowded bank. Only a few clerks were in sight. I saw an opportunity. Here I came, barefoot, looking for the manager. I spotted a harried fellow behind a teller's cage. Mr. Ashley Gibbons was his name.

"Can I help you, son?"

"Yes, sir. Buster Wiles is my name. With all of these people, it seems like you need some assistance."

He raised his head and pursed his lips.

"What do you do with all the money you earn?"

"I take it home to my mother."

"Sit down."

We had a brief discussion about a position.

"Can you be here at 8:00 tomorrow morning?"

"Yes, sir!"

He glanced at my feet.

"By the way, uh . . . . Do you have any shoes?"

At age fifteen, I was in the bank business. The next day, I came all dressed up to begin work. Mollie Wiles had the best time explaining my new job to everyone.

"My son's a bank teller. He tells everyone where to go."

I felt I was J.P. Morgan, being around all the money. I picked up a lot of information about the business world by being around bankers. I also got a chance to chat with the customers. This was just as rewarding. I was moving up.

After several months in the Sunshine State, Mama reconsidered our situation. It was decided that Florida would not be our destiny. Back to Memphis we went. I was determined to remain in the banking profession. I liked being around those greenbacks. In downtown Memphis, I strutted into the Bank of Commerce. I barely had a chance to open my mouth before the bank manager chased me out.

"Go away, and don't come back."

I was mad as hell. If he had merely said that there was no work, I would have searched elsewhere. His rudeness was intolerable. It was a violation of Southern courtesy and manners. Politeness was ingrained in my soul. It's still there. My feathers were ruffled, so I huffed over to *The Commercial-Appeal* newspaper building. I asked to see Mr. C.P.J. Mooney, the editor. When I walked into his office, he appeared surprised to see me.

"Buster, where have you been? My golf game has gone to pot."

I explained my absence to him. I stated my case.

"I'd like to get a job, Mr. Mooney."

"Where?"

"The Bank of Commerce."

I could have mentioned any bank or any company in town, but I really intended to show the manager who chased me out.

"Okay."

He buzzed his secretary. The editor told her to address a letter to Mr. T.O. Vinton, president of the Bank of Commerce.

Mr. Vinton:

I'm sending you a man who is well-equiped to handle work in the banking business. I would appreciate any favors . . .

The letter in my hand felt like a gold bar. My caddying had paid off beyond my wildest dreams. I confidently reentered the bank. The manager came over immediately.

"Didn't I tell you to . . . ."

"I'm not here to see you. I'm here to see Mr. Vinton."

"Oh?" He looked puzzled.

"I have a letter from Mr. Mooney to Mr. Vinton."

"Yes?"

"Yes!"

I handed him my passport to employment. After a little while, the president called me into his office. We discussed conditions in Florida—the real estate situation, banking, and so on. I tried to make myself appear as knowledgeable as possible. He buzzed for the manager, and he sauntered in.

"I'd like for you to meet Mr. Wiles."

"I've met him," he sniffed.

"Mr. Wiles is joining us."

He looked incredulous.

"What? We've already promised Mr. Fry that his grandson could work here this summer."

"No, he was only *considered* for the position. Mr. Wiles *has* the job."

The manager stood with his mouth gaping like a fish. It was a stroke of luck that I happened to choose the Bank of Commerce to land a job: my position there eventually led me to Hollywood.

I started off at the bank as a runner. I collected money and delivered cash for the bank's customers downtown. One of my favorite routes was Front Street, where the wealthy cotton merchants found a tip for young Buster. I was happy, but my goal was to be an actor. Has anyone else ever thought about that? Only everyone!

The world of show business had always filled me with excitement. When Will Rogers came to Memphis in 1928, I crept backstage. I just had to meet him. The noted humorist was kind to me. He even gave me a lariat, which I treasured for years. One of the greatest jugglers in the world came to Memphis with a vaudeville troupe. W.C. Fields performed feats of agility that had the audience on the edge of their seats. I got to know his assistant, Midge Fately. Her stories of life as a stage performer were entrancing.

Motion pictures had always been one of my passions. At the Lyric Theater, or the Palace, I spent many a night watching the silver screen. I saw every film that played Memphis. The big names in those days were Valentino, Douglas Fairbanks, John Barrymore, Richard Dix, William Haines, Ramon Novarro. Lillian Gish and Mary Pickford were beauties beyond compare. I wanted to be an actor—just like everybody else did.

I've never been shy. I enjoy talking to everyone. I worked at the bank for three years and got to know everyone well. One day, I was conversing with the vice-president, Abe Lewis, and I casually told him of my dream to be in pictures. He told me he had a friend at Universal Studios. I almost fell through the floor. Mr. Lewis kindly arranged for me to travel to Los Angeles: I would try my luck with a screen test.

I was seventeen, and going to Hollywood was a dream come true. I stayed at the Biltmore Hotel, as if I were a star already. At that time, Universal Studios was one of the most successful motion picture companies in the world. The guard waved me through the gate, as if I were already working there.

My exhilaration was short-lived. To my dismay, I discovered that my contact was gone. He had unexpectedly been sent to Europe on business. I met Carl Laemmle, president of Universal, and was allowed to wander about wherever I wished. For hours, I watched as a film was being shot. I tried to figure out how everything worked. But without someone to really open the right doors for me, I was only viewed as a visitor. I never got my screen test.

I was disappointed, but I was only seventeen. I told myself that there was still time to secure some type of work in motion pictures. I didn't realize that it would be several years before I worked in a film.

After being in Hollywood, my bank job seemed boring, and after three years, I had to move on to something less sedate.

I got a job working for a man who revolutionized the grocery business. Clarence Saunders was a genius. Instead of having clerks running around the store filling orders for customers, Saunders initiated the concept of the self-service supermarket. He gave shoppers a basket and let them make their own selections at their leisure. Clarence Saunders made millions with his Piggly Wiggly chain of stores. I was a grocery checker. In those days, the checkers had to remember the prices of *all* the items!

I enjoyed chatting with the customers, whom I got to know, and I became well-acquainted with Saunders. He was a nice, down-to-earth guy. When he let me ride with him in that fabulous sixteen-cylinder Cadillac, I felt like a Rockefeller. Due to complex stock manipulation, he lost his fortune and his Piggly Wiggly chain of stores. He came back with another line of supermarkets called "Clarence Saunders, Sole Owner of My Name." He secured another fortune.

Saunders had his own professional football team called the "Sole Owner Tigers." Once, he paid all expenses for the Green Bay team to fly to Memphis for a charity match with his Tigers. When the Depression hit, he lost the Sole Owner chain, too. Did he give up? No, sir. He developed an even more innovative operation for fast-food service, which he called the Keedozzle. The concept behind this was, "a key does it all."

Once when I returned to Memphis for a visit, I went to see Saunders. He had just opened the Keedozzle stores. He and I wandered through one of the places late one night after it had closed, and he showed me how everything worked. Customers purchased a key for a dollar. They used it to select items behind small glass enclosures. As Saunders told me about his plan, he grew enthusiastic. It's the American Dream—to think up some scheme to become a millionaire. He did it, not only once but several times. I started wondering how I could make some money too.

One night, I finally got a brief taste of "show biz." The newspaper advertised a one-hundred-dollar prize for the winner of "The Twist Dance Contest." This was a modified version of the Charleston. Since I loved to dance, this challenge was right up my alley.

"Man, I'm going to pick that up!"

Each night there was a winner, and then there was to be a grand finale. I was chosen for the finals. I sized up my main adversary. She was a beautiful girl named Nellie Wilson. She was well-known around town, since she carried the lobby card advertisement across the stage at the Pantages Theater. Everybody was certain she would win. I started to think about my chances, and it looked pretty dim.

The one-hundred-dollar prize would go to the person who received the most applause. I spread the word to all of my friends that they were invited to the Lyceum Theater. They would even be permitted to come inside at no charge.

"I'll have all the exit doors unlocked," I told my pals.

The night of the finale, all the exits were open. Backstage, I spread the word that Mayor Crump had sent censors out front to arrest anyone who got out of line. I watched from the wings as my competitors declined to go all out. When my turn came, Buster shook it for all it was worth—I twisted like a man on fire.

When the judge's hand hovered above the head of Nellie Wilson, you would swear no greater applause could be given. Then the judge put his had over me. My pals didn't let me down. The theater shook until I thought it would collapse.

"Buster Wiles is the winner!"

I went out front to collect my prize money. The theater manager looked at me. He gave me a twenty-dollar bill. I waited for the rest, but what I got was a surprise.

"We can't give you one-hundred dollars. That was just publicity."

"Where's my hundred dollars?"

"I'm telling you, son, there ain't no hundred dollars."

"You don't think so? Just a minute."

I gathered all of my pals and explained the swindle. I shouted, "Hey, gang, he's trying to cheat me out of my prize money!"

I pointed to the box office. My indignant allies picked up the entire box office—with the cashier in it! The poor girl's eyes were as big as half-dollars. My friends headed toward the street, carrying the box office. The manager came over yelling. You should have seen the expression on his face, as his cashier moved along the sidewalk!

"Give me my money," I demanded.

"Here," he yelled.

I took all my pals to a restaurant called Foppiano's. I bought everybody chili and root beers: they deserved it. Never try to hustle a hustler.

THREE

Hollywood:
Take Two

*"He who would climb the ladder must begin at
the bottom."*

Memphis was getting less appealing every day. I decided that I
had to return to California; I just *had* to make another try at being
in motion pictures. My desire to depart was prompted by a touch
of bad luck. One day, Mama sent me to pay the gas bill, and I lost
the money in a craps game. Now was the most opportune moment
to sever the cord with my native city. I grabbed a handful of
boxcars. At the first place the train halted, I called Mama and told
her not to worry—I was on my way to Hollywood.

Arriving in Los Angeles was a thrill. Hollywood was where
people came to fulfill their dreams. "Go west, young man!" are
words Americans have lived by for years. You can't get much
further west than Santa Monica Beach, unless you end up in the
Pacific Ocean. I found a boarding house where the landlady gave
me words of encouragement: "You look just like William Boyd!"

Now, my landlady had known William Boyd back in Utah,
before he gained fame as a cowboy motion-picture star. Gee, if I
looked like him, maybe I *could* break into pictures. I bummed
around Los Angeles awhile, trying to figure out how to get my foot
in the door. I eventually did what thousands of others have done to
get into films: I registered with Central Casting.

Meanwhile, I found I could make some money at MGM.

Around midnight, the alleys on the MGM lot filled with guys looking for work. One could be hired for set building or set removal during the night. I was beginning to see how the studios looked at movie-making—as a business, rather than a glamorized means of getting rich.

Central Casting called me for crowd work, but I was seldom informed the titles of the picture I was working in. We extras were just cattle. I worked in a Laurel and Hardy film, where I donned dark make-up and played an Arab. I later found out that the picture was called *Beau Hunks*.

I thought maybe my luck would change when I met a guy at a party who saw talent in *me!* Singing had always been a favorite pleasure of mine, and I had a strong voice too. I was vocalizing at a party one night, when a fellow named George Meeker came up to me.

"Friend, you've got quite a voice."   He was a professional voice coach, and he couldn't believe that I was just an amateur, without any real training. He was a concert singer himself and a close friend of opera star Lawrence Tibbett. He compared my voice to Tibbett's powerful tones and suggested that I study with a famous teacher who resided in New York.

"Go and see him," said Meeker. "With formal training, there is a chance you could get a musical scholarship to study in Italy."

Why not? Nothing was happening for me in Los Angeles. Mr. Meeker wrote a glowing letter to his associate, informing him of my immediate departure. After a train ride to New York, I hastily knocked on the door of his studio. His secretary handed me a letter. It informed me, rather apologetically, that my prospective coach had been suddenly called to Europe. I was asked to return in a few months. What a predicament. I was practically broke. I reverted to my old trade of hawking newspapers to earn some fast cash.

While I was hustling papers on a busy Manhattan streetcorner, a thunderstorm broke overhead. I scurried under a narrow canvas awning to keep from being drenched. Soon, an elegantly dressed woman came running down the sidewalk, seeking a place to keep dry. I called her over, and we huddled together under the small awning, but is wasn't enough for two, so I gallantly stepped out in the rain.

She protested: "Oh, no. We can both stay here." She gently

pulled me back under the shelter, and we stood close to one another. Her fragrant perfume was intoxicating. We chatted, and the rain poured down.

"I'm Canadian," she said, "I'm unfamiliar with New York...Do you think you could show me around?"

"Gee, I think I could do that."

Young Buster was always eager to assist a lady. Well, we didn't see too much of the city, but we did spend five unforgettable days admiring the New York skyline from her plush hotel room. I learned that she was a prominent woman, a Canadian senator's wife. After our brief time together, she sadly told me that she had to return. I never even learned her last name.

I considered attempting to discover her identity but decided not to. It was simply one of those brief romances that had come and gone. After she departed, though, New York seemed cold and empty. I was flat broke and didn't feel like hustling papers. There was nothing to do but ride the rails back to the Coast. As I walked to the rail yards, the scent of the unknown woman's perfume returned to me. It has never left.

With my pal Harold Menjou. Gee, it must
have rained hard. My pants have already
shrunk to my knees.

Where's my jockey?

FOUR

Buster Joins The Circus

"He who has not silver in his pocket must have honey on his tongue."

Riding the rods could be a dangerous business. Many a bum and unticketed traveler has frozen to death in a boxcar. I hopped a freight train out of New York, but jammed a piece of wood in the sliding door to prevent it from permanently shutting on me. I was half-dozing when the train pulled into the Chicago freight-yard. I rolled over, trying to sleep amidst the aisles of wooden crates, dimly conscious that unloading on the nearby rail was in full swing. Then, a piercing blood-chilling roar made me sit up. Tired though I was, I pushed open the heavy freight door and dropped to the ground. Gazing beneath my rail car, I could see a tiger in an iron cage. Moving closer, I read the colorful words emblazoned on the side of the boxcar—"Ringling Brothers Circus."

One of my childhood dreams had been to work under the Big Top. There was the exciting anticipation of setting off on an unknown adventure, when I fell in with the advancing line of men and animals. There was also the pleasurable thought of a square meal. I hadn't tasted hot food in days. As the heavy, iron-wheeled tiger cage rolled along, I leaned behind it to help a guy who was pushing and sweating.

"Say, buddy, who's the man to see about a job?"

"Mr. Wink. You cain't miss him. He's only got one eye."

I proudly walked along several blocks, until the circus parade arrived at an enormous canvas tent. After a few more inquiries, I came face to face with Mr. Wink. He was in charge of the concession stands.

"What is it?" he asked, letting fly a stream of brownish tobacco juice.

"I'm looking for work."

He screwed up his one good eye and sucked in his lips, with the air of a man making a weighty decision. His eye began fluttering as he looked me over.

"Mister, can you really hustle?"

"Why, you're looking at the greatest hustler you've ever seen in your life."

He paused, then said: "All right, go get a jacket and start with the 'drys.' That's souvenirs."

I was in the circus. I spent long hours walking up and down the aisles, hawking magazines, banners, dolls, and cheap toys. Every chance I got, I flopped in a seat and sat spellbound watching a guy get shot through a cannon. I especially admired the lion tamer. These were my kind of people. I knew right then and there that, if you could do something different, risking your neck night after night, people would pay to see it. Meanwhile, Mr. Wink was impressed by my sales ability. As a reward, he moved me to the "wets"—soft drinks.

Later, I joined the roustabouts, who assembled the tent rigging. These guys were a tough lot, especially Peanut Bill. He had joined the circus as an orphan kid. Now, in middle age, he was a gruff, hairy brute, who acted as if he owned the circus. He had a sarcastic tone that grated against me, and we nearly came to blows a few times.

But if Peanut Bill was someone who angered me, there was another fellow whom I positively idolized—Alfredo Codona, the first man to ever perform a triple somersault on the trapeze. He headed a family act known as "The Flying Codonas." It was a dangerous life. In fact, his wife Lillian had died in a tragic fall in Copenhagen. With all the boldness I could muster, I asked him to teach me some of his tricks. Alfredo graciously made me his pupil. He explained the technique of body control while sailing through the air, stressing the importance of head movement. I was enthralled by swinging from one trapeze to another. At the time, I didn't realize that I was indeed preparing myself to be a stuntman.

Since I'm crazy about animals, the circus provided time to admire all of the exotic creatures that one only sees in a zoo. I never tired of watching the chimps, tigers, bears, and horses. I even fell in love with Betsy—the sweetest elephant I ever met. Every morning, I got in line for my breakfast. Betsy would be nearby, and I would always give her a piece of my roll. Every time she saw me, she let out an ear-splitting trumpet yell.

Betsy was certainly a lot nicer than Peanut Bill. He and I finally came to a showdown one night in Lincoln, Nebraska. Mr. Wink had given me the night off. I was strolling down the midway with a cute blonde on my arm, when my arch-enemy passed by. He stopped dead in his tracks and glared at me. In a sneering tone, he provocatively asked, "How come you ain't working?"

I ignored him. Being with a lady, I wanted to avoid trouble. We kept right on moving, but he came up behind me and bellowed, "Where are you going, Buster?"

I turned sharply on my heel, with my blood boiling. "Peanut Bill, that's none of your business!"

We faced each other with hands clenching into fists. His huge frame tensed. He telegraphed what was coming.

"You're a smart little so-and-so!" he spat out. He threw a punch, but I jerked back my head, and he missed.

My right hand shot out with all the power I could muster. Down he crumpled. I was never so surprised in all my life. I had thought we were in for a bloody scrap. In all my fights, I tried to get the first punch at my adversary, but this time, since I had a girl with me, I hesitated. It was the last time I would ever wait for a fist to come at me.

After several months with the Ringling Brothers Circus, I decided to leave. As much as I loved the Big Top, there was still a yearning to make a career in motion pictures.

* * * * *

Once again, I hopped aboard a freight train to save some dough. Near Indio, California, I left the train in search of food. I walked into a residential neighborhood and approached a lady who stood in her front yard. Since this was the middle of the Depression, it was common to see destitute men seeking any type of work in exchange for a meal. I asked her if she had anything for me to do. She shook her head.

Sitting on the curb, I saw a dry cleaner making a delivery across the street. I asked him if he knew where I could find work in exchange for a meal. He kindly gave me four sandwiches, two of which I gave to a Mexican guy who happened by. I had an expensive gabardine suit that needed cleaning. The delivery man said he would take care of it and leave it at a pool room in town. He took off in the opposite direction to make his rounds.

I began my trek into the city. Coming to a huge estate, I walked inside the gates and up the winding road. Before me was a mansion, and off to one side was a glassed-in breakfast room. I noticed that a bearded man was eyeing me curiously. He stepped to a door.

"Can I help you?"

"Yes, sir, I'm looking for work."

He invited me inside and offered me a seat in his expensive-looking room. He gave me a cup of coffee.

"I really don't know if our foreman needs anyone, but when he comes in I'll ask him."

While the man was talking, I felt I had seen his face before.

"What's your name, son?"

"Buster Wiles. What's yours?"

"King Gillette."

Then it hit me like a ton of bricks. He was the guy who manufactured Gillette razor blades: his picture was printed on each box!

I instinctively ran my hand over my stubble

"Guess I need a shave," I said.

"Me too," laughed Gillette.

Later in the evening, the cleaner showed up with the freshly-pressed gabardine suit. We had a chat in the pool room. He told me he had been pistol-whipped and robbed a few weeks earlier, and he still suffered from dizzy spells. I volunteered to take over his route. He not only gave me a job for two weeks but he let me stay with his family. A few years later, when I was making some money, he asked if I could help him out with a loan of five-thousand dollars. I didn't hesitate. Wally Taylor had helped me when I was down and out. You don't forget things like that. In the Depression, many people were worse off than I was. There were no jobs, and families really suffered. Those sandwiches he had given me tasted better than any meal I've ever had.

***Objective Burma* was one of the toughest pictures I ever worked on. I'd just been blown out of a bunker when this photo was taken.**

My days as a distributor of fine spirits earned me a Pierce Arrow.

Buster the bootlegger.   I was legit with this place.

GRanite 7444   GRanite 8591   BUSTER   VERNON

"BUSTER"
INSURANCE BROKER

B & M
CLEANERS AND DYERS
1646½ WEST 11TH STREET
"We Clean the Stars"

REPRESENTATIVE

___ _____   DAY AND NIGHT
                              SERVICE   PHONE EXposition 9665   FREE DELIVERY

BUSTER WILES   JIMMIE HOLMES

Yᵉ LITTLE BROWN JUG
7231 SANTA MONICA BLVD.

BREAKFAST   LUNCHEON   DINNER

FIVE

Laurel Canyon Moonshine

"If at first you don't succeed...get a still and bootleg whiskey."

Back in Los Angeles, I convinced the manager of a new Clarence Saunders store that I was qualified to work as a grocery clerk. With my new position, I rented an apartment on the corner of Doheny and Sunset. The area was still rustic, and I would walk up Doheny into the hills to hunt jackrabbits. One of our regular customers at the store was a young guy named Harold Menjou. He was a friendly fellow, with a zest for living. He and I became pals. His mother, Kathryn, was the former wife of screen star Adolph Menjou. Harold and his mother shared a beautiful beach home in Santa Monica.

They were very kind to me, and even invited me to live with them. I readily agreed, since my salary was rather small—just temporarily, I promised them, until I could save some money. At night, Harold and I caroused together. I was somewhat surprised to learn that he had no movie aspirations. Quite strange, I thought. Didn't everyone want to be in pictures? And with his connections! But Harold wasn't the least bit interested. He *was* curious about my ability to survive while out on the road. I once made a bet with him that I could leave Los Angeles with two dollars and travel to Memphis without spending a cent of it. I proved it by riding free, courtesy of the railroads, and Harold lost his bet.

I didn't stay with the Menjous for long, just until I saved enough money to buy a car; then I was gone. Soon I had my own apartment and was sporting flashy clothes. I was no longer a grocery clerk. Harold was puzzled. I merely told him that I was "in business." After awhile, he learned my secret. One afternoon, in April, 1932, we were speeding down Laurel Canyon toward Ventura Boulevard. The rain the previous night had washed sand onto the road, but we zoomed along anyway.

"I'm gonna make the curve at fifty-five miles per hour!" said Harold.

"You'd better step on it, partner, because you're only doing fifty!"

Harold stomped on the pedal. When we neared Laurel Terrace, the car skidded on the slippery sand and flipped over. Harold was uninjured, but my chest had smashed against the door. I was spitting up blood as I lay on the sidewalk. A police car screeched up.

"Harold," I whispered, "don't tell them anything about me."

An ambulance soon whisked me off to a hospital, where I lapsed into blackness. From faraway, I heard my mother's voice. She was talking to a doctor. I opened my eyes to see only whiteness. I was covered by a sheet. In a blind panic, I blurted, "Mama, I ain't dead! Don't worry, I'll be all right!"

The sheet was thrown back, and Mama reassured me that she was aware I was very much alive. The next day, a somber-faced doctor revealed to me that I had punctured a lung in three places. My voice had lost its amazing power. All hopes of being a professional singer vanished. Not long after, a policeman came into my hospital room, took down a report of the accident, then asked, "Son, what do you do for a living?" I hesitated, then, with the first thought that came to mind, I replied, "I'm a costume designer."

"Uh-huhh," he murmured, then disappeared.

I couldn't tell him my real profession. I was a bootlegger. Harold learned the truth while I was recuperating in the hospital, but he wasn't surprised. I was a young man in a hurry. I had grown tired of being poor.

In the era of the Great Depression, not everyone was poverty-stricken. Some guys were making big money. Al Capone was doing all right. Al said, "You can make more money with a smile and a gun than just a smile." I never admired Al, but I saw bootleggers making cash hand over fist. By 1932, it was apparent that the Eighteenth Amendment was a failure. The 1919 law was being ignored by everyone but the federal officers who made a half-hearted attempt to enforce it. Prohibiting the sale and manufacture of alcoholic beverages didn't do anything but make a lot of bootleggers wealthy. I was going to be one of them.

I prepared to deal in "wets" again by locating a guy who could set up a booze plant for me. I then found four "after-hour spots" to distribute my product. My main places were in Hollywood. I found a big mansion in Laurel Canyon after things "got cooking," so to speak. I didn't live there, but I had my manufacturing plant there. My next-door neighbor said I was the best milkman he ever had.

I eventually bought a restaurant in Redondo Beach called "The Streets of Paris." It was a fancy place, with murals of Parisian scenes situated about the dining room. I had a partner in this project, to whom I eventually gave a half-interest. Not long after, he told me not to bother to come to the restaurant since "you're no longer involved." I couldn't believe he was trying to steal my place. I sent a group of guys in one night, and they wrecked the restaurant. Sure it was crazy, but people learned never to cross me.

At the plant in Laurel Canyon, we made our product twenty-four hours a day. We didn't waste time aging our whiskey in oak barrels—we aged it overnight by inserting electric needles. Our biggest seller was "Green River," but I could provide any brand a customer wanted, since I manufactured my own labels too. At my four speakeasies, patrons had to say the magic words: "Buster sent me."

One of my main spots was the "B&M Cleaners and Dyers" at 1646 1/2 West Eleventh Street—"We Clean the Stars; Free Delivery."

Green River started the money flowing into my pockets. I bought a sleek 1932 Pierce Arrow, with two French horns on the fenders, and I rented an expensive bungalow on Fountain. My standard uniform was a camel-hair jacket with pearl buttons. I was on top of the world. I soon discovered that other hustlers were out there, lurking like sharks in the ocean.

One of the standard methods for entrepreneurial advancement was to hijack the goods of someone else. I knew a guy named Oscar Lund. He was shrewd, and he had guts. He bought a garage on Wilshire just to store the whiskey, expensive stuff, that he had hijacked from a mother ship unloading alcohol from Canada. Oscar was "big time." I never wanted to get deeply involved in that type of situation. All I wanted was for my little speakeasies to keep on churning out those greenbacks. Still, I didn't want to have my plant hijacked either. I bought some defensive weapons. I gave my Arab assistant, George, a Luger, and I bought a sawed-off shotgun.

You never could tell when a weasel might try to sink his teeth into you. One came into my place one night. I entered my after-hour spot in Hollywood and heard a guy jabbering away with a heavy Southern accent. I was able to pinpoint exactly where a Southerner came from by his twang. I asked him where he was from.

"L-L-Louisiana," he stuttered.

"No, that doesn't sound right," I responded.

"M-M-M-M-Missouri."

"Now you've said it."

He told me he was from Caruthersville.

"Did you ever know Buster Wiles?"

"Y-Y-Yes, I . . . I grew up with him."

I recognized him. It was Julian. His old man had stolen my father's horse and buggy. My daddy wanted to have him arrested, but I intervened and begged him to forget it. Poor Julian was broke. He didn't have anything, so I gave him a job and advanced him some dough. He stayed with me awhile, working in "wets." One day, he said he was going to quit. After he had disappeared, I learned that he was selling booze to my customers. I found where he was living and made an appointment to meet him on the Santa Monica Pier. I confronted him with the evidence.

"I gave you a job, never prosecuted your old man when he stole from my father. Now look what you've done." He had been judged guilty. I hit him so hard he turned three flips. I never saw him again. Julian was just one of many rats looking for a way to cash in on the times.

One of the standard techniques of shrewd swindlers was to raid your joint, steal your alcoholic products, flash a phony badge, and "arrest" you. The "marshal" would shove the unsuspecting bootlegger in a car and actually drive him to the police station. On the way down, the "marshal" would offer release for a certain remuneration. I've known of swindlers getting into the elevators in the police department and putting the squeeze on the poor devil, right then and there! I can imagine how much cash was coughed up for immediate release. I was just hoping to earn my dough before Prohibition ended. Everyone saw it coming.

I got a call once to meet a Hollywood police inspector for a golfing date. The inspector told me, after teeing off, "Buster, we know all about your sales, but we haven't touched you because your places don't cause any trouble. Keep it that way."

I tried to, but I made a mistake. I was in my car making a delivery one day; in the passenger seat was old Green River. Pulling to a stop, I saw a guy awaiting me. I reached for my product, and he flashed a badge. It looked real, but I wasn't sure, so I popped him in the jaw and screeched off. Looking in my rear-view mirror, I could see him sprawled in the driveway.

Back at my place, I wondered if I had really struck a federal law officer or some phony crook. I learned soon enough. That night, four guys burst into my place, stating that they were law officers. They beat the you-know-what out of young Buster. I was taken downtown and charged with possession and manufacture of booze. I *had* struck a federal marshal!

When I was released, I went to the plant on Laurel Canyon, accompanied by a young lady named Dolly. When I approached, I saw one of the federal officers—one who had whipped me—in the house. I bolted. From the bushes, I could see them loading my product into trucks. I had a suspicion that the stuff wasn't going to the Pacific Ocean to sweeten the salt, but was being hijacked. I told Dolly to wait in the car. My next-door neighbor was a musician who worked at Paramount Studios. I sneaked inside his home, while he was waving off some guests. As he re-entered his living room, his "milkman" stepped from behind the drapes. I scared the hell out of him, and he jumped sky-high. I was pretty excited myself.

I made a call to Oscar. I explained to him that my stuff was being hijacked.

"Put men at the Laurel Canyon exits on Sunset Boulevard and Ventura Boulevard," I told him.

He did it. Sure enough, the product was delivered to a

mechanic's garage. I was mad. A crooked marshal had gotten wind of my situation and had gone for my plant. Never swindle a hustler. George got his Luger, and I got my sawed-off shotgun. I didn't intend to use it. All I wanted was to get even.

In front of the garage, I saw a guy standing near the truck. When he saw the shotgun in my hand, he stepped back. I spoke up, consumed with anger. "Buddy, I've never bothered you or your partners, but you stole my whiskey."

"Oh, please, mister, please!"

"I'm looking for my stuff."

He showed me where it was, and I made him load it. I saw other cases of alcohol, and I took them too. I had to get something for my trouble.

My arrest and trial resulted in a suspended sentence. Soon after, one of the worst laws ever passed disappeared. Prohibition had been a big mistake. Citizens never stopped drinking. The Eighteenth Amendment only spawned disrespect for the law and created more problems.

On December 5, 1933, the Repeal of Prohibition was implemented. I decided to remain in the "after-hours" business. I kept one of my places, at 7231 Santa Monica Boulevard—Ye Little Brown Jug. It was just across from United Artists Studio. This stretch of the boulevard was called "Little Tijuana," due to it's wild atmosphere.

During the day, the studio employees would jam the Brown Jug, downing Coors Beer for lunch. At night, gays frequented the bar. I had a guy running the place for me, who had been down on his luck and had been sleeping on a mattress above a garage. I trusted him. I only came by to have a drink and check the books. I helped get him back on his feet. Then I discovered that he was stealing from me. I had bought the place for only $756, and it had brought in big money, but that slowly diminished to a trickle. I confronted my manager one night as he was leaving nearby Barney's Beanery.

"A-a-ah, Buster, you don't understand. It's just that the books are all wrong."

"I know. They're all wrong because you screwed them up!" Wham! I dispensed justice so hard that he brought down an entire chain-link fence when he careened backwards. Do guys a favor, and they backstab you; I've never understood it.

When word came my way that half-crocked gays were being rolled as they left my bar, I set up a stakeout and caught the culprit. I beat the hell out of him. I detest seeing defenseless people taken advantage of.

Oh, the charming blonde who was left nervously sitting in my Pierce Arrow near my Laurel Canyon plant became my wife. Dolly Dee Spore was a beautiful woman, a professional dancer who had toured the country with Johnson and Olson, appearing on-screen in many films. Dolly had a great sense of humor. She joked that she had fallen for me because of "those broad shoulders of yours— from picking cotton no doubt." We rented an apartment on Franklin Avenue, in the heart of Hollywood.

Though now married, I had no intention of becoming a nine-to-fiver. The dreams of my youth drove me on.

Aboard the *Sirocco* with the legendary archer Howard Hill.

Flynn's yacht the *Sirocco* was a wonderful place to have fun. Sharing a laugh with Errol. (Photo: Peter Stackpole)

Errol with his first wife Lili Damita. (Photo: Jerry Hill Collection)

Flynn and Howard shooting Marlin with bow and arrow. (Photo: Jerry Hill Collection)

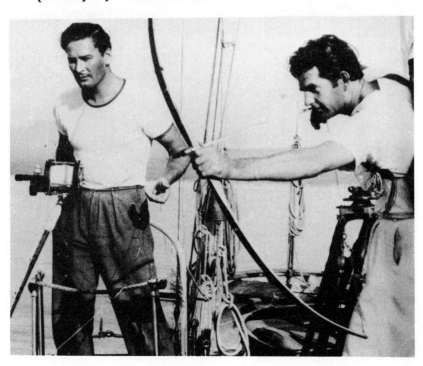

Flynn and I take a break on the set of *Desperate Journey*. We burned the candle at both ends, and in the middle too.

Doubling Pedro de Cordoba in *The Sea Hawk*. I'm about to be thrown overboard. (Photo: Courtesy of the Academy of Motion Pictures Arts and Sciences. © 1940 Warner Bros. Pictures, Inc. Ren. 1968 United Artists Television, Inc.)

Chatting on the set of *Dodge City*. When Flynn and I got together we made the prairie look small. (Photo: Courtesy of Rick Dodd. Property of Warner Bros., Inc. Used by permission.)

The crew of Robin Hood assembles for a charity baseball game. Far left, kneeling, "Friar Tuck" — Eugene Pallette. Above him, Howard Hill. I'm next to Howard. In the center, director Bill Keighley and lovely Olivia de Havilland. *(Photo: Jerry Hill Collection)*

On one of hunting trips to Catalina Island, Errol caught a boar piglet. He shows it to his Schnauzer, Arno. Flynn later gave it to Bette Davis as a joke. *(Photo: Jerry Hill Collection)*

While making Dodge City, the crew played a charity baseball game. I listen attentively as my teammates Victor Jory (with baseball) and Big Boy Williams argue a point with Freddie Graham. *(photo: Courtesy of the Academy of Motion Picture Arts and Sciences. Property of Warner Bros., Inc. Used by permission.)*

Below, Errol's bedroom. Many a lady dreamed of a night with Errol Flynn. Many a lady had her wish come true.

Flynn's Mulholland House. My residence for three and a half years.

The famous scene in *High Sierra* where lovely Ida Lupino cries over the body of Bogart. I doubled Bogie and, of course, only my better half was shown. *(Photo: © 1941 Warner Bros. Pictures, Inc. Ren. 1968 United Artists Television, Inc.)*

Errol relaxes in the dining room.

The living room. Flynn's portrait by John
Decker and Gauguin's painting on the far
wall were cherished possessions.

In this scene from *Dodge City*, I doubled Douglas Fowley. Flynn helps me make a quick exit. (photo: *Courtesy of the Academy of Motion Picture Arts and Sciences.* © *1939 Warner Bros. Pictures, Inc. Ren. 1967 United Artists Television, Inc.*)

Custer's Last Stand. Howard Hill and Flynn rehearsing the exciting climax of *They Died With Their Boots On.* (Photo: *Courtesy of Motion Picture Arts and Sciences. Property of Warner Bros., Inc. Used by permission.*)

The reign of falling stars kept me on the go, but besides stunt doubling, I often played various roles in each film, as shown by these photos from *Desperate Journey*.

Perched on a telephone pole as an enemy lineman. *(Photo: Courtesy of Warner Bros. Archives—USC's School of Cinema-Television. Property of Warner Bros., Inc. Used by permission.)*

Portraying a German soldier, I'm about to be decked by Alan Hale. *(photo: Courtesy Warner Bros. Archives--USC's School of Cinema-Television.)*

On location in Palm Springs for *Objective Burma*. Errol and I cool off with ice cream. Man, it was scorching. (Photo: *Courtesy of Warner Bros. Archives—USC's School of Cinema-Television. Property of Warner Bros., Inc. Used by permission.*)

On the set of *Desperate Journey*. From left, Ronald Reagan, Flynn, me and Ronald Sinclair. (photo: *Courtesy of the Academy of Motion Picture Arts and Sciences. Property of Warner Bros., Inc. Used by permission.*)

During the filming of *Objective Burma,* Flynn sent this photo and a heated, yet witty, letter to Warners complaining about his "dressing room." The scrawled MEN conveys its former use. *(Photo: Courtesy of USC Archives of the Performing Arts. Property of Warner Bros., used by permission.)*

A merry party at the Decker-Flynn Art Gallery. From left, Ward Bond, John Decker, Phyllis Decker, Errol, Mrs. Alan Mowbray, Harry Hays Morgan, Red Skelton, Mrs. Skelton and Will Fowler, Jr. *(Photo: Courtesy of Phyllis Decker)*

PART TWO

A STUNTMAN AND A DAREDEVIL

You mean there's an elevator
in this place?

I never had much luck with cars.

Six

A Stuntman
At Last

"He who stays in the valley shall never get over the hill."

Though discouraged by my dismal luck in attempting to break into the motion-picture business, I never gave up hope. Out of the blue, Central Casting notified me of extra work for *The Last Days of Pompeii,* an epic starring Preston Foster as a blacksmith who becomes a gladiator in the doomed Roman city.

Early one morning, in the cold dark of the pre-dawn hours, I hurriedly dressed and made a beeline for the RKO-Pathe Studio in Culver City. There was already a mob of men and women gathered near the main gate. As the slanting light of the rising sun cut across the sky, I joined the other hopefuls shivering in the cold morning wind. As time passed, more would-be extras huddled behind me, and I grew colder just standing still in the chill air. Thoughts of retreating to Ye Little Brown Jug for a steaming cup of coffee crossed my mind. I took out a coin, flipped, and it landed *heads,* so it was my fate to remain at the studio gate.

A list of names was shouted at the entrance. Luckily, I was called. The men were shown to a dressing room, where we donned togas; then we were led to outdoor sets representing Pompeii in various degrees of destruction. Day after day, director Ernie Schoedsack herded us from set to set, telling us to display fear and panic as an imaginary Mount Vesuvius exploded, spewing forth hot, thick ashes and lethal fumes, which asphyxiated the unlucky. Carefully hidden behind the elaborate columns and porticos were dozens of inky smoke-pots, which emitted dark fumes that seemed to envelope everything. The grimy smoke smudged our faces and costumes and smelled horrible.

One afternoon, during our lunch break, I was wandering around the set with a sandwich in hand, when I spotted a grip crew, rigging a net.

"I'd hate to be the guy who falls in that," I said aloud. The supervisor eyed me curiously, dressed as I was in my flowing toga.

"Yeah? What's wrong with it?" he gruffly asked.

"The tension is way too tight. You're gonna bounce somebody off the net and into the dirt."

"How do you know so much, buddy?"

"I used to be in the circus."

"I bet you did," came the response, with dry sarcasm in his voice.

I let the comment pass and proceeded to explain how I had seen the rigging set up in the circus. The supervisor listened attentively, then told me, "All right, you're in charge of the net. You can also be the first one to fall in it."

"Mister," I shot back, "you got a deal."

He looked a little surprised. I guess he thought I would slink away, but he didn't know Buster very well. He called Ernie Schoedsack over and explained the situation.

"You know how to fall in a net?" asked the director.

"Yes, sir."

"All right, Buster. Be here bright and early. You can do the stunt."

That evening, I excitedly told Dolly of my good fortune. This was a stroke of luck that I had been hoping for. There was no doubt in my mind that the stunt was an easy one, but I was overwhelmed by anxiety just the same. I tossed and turned before falling into a fitful sleep.

Long before sunrise, I was dressed. I ran a few blocks, as the first gray streaks of dawn crept through the sky. Feeling limber, I drove to the studio, brimming with excitement. The backlot was vacant when I climbed atop a two-story building, with the net far below. I had a magnificent view of distant mountain ranges etched in golden sunlight. I pondered making a practice leap, but thought better of it.

"Hell, if I break my neck, at least make them pay for it."

Down below, I spoke with the assistant director, who told me they had other scenes to film before mine. I returned back atop the building and watched the lot begin to hum with activity. The morning warmth lulled me into a drowsy half-sleep. I stretched out, as cries of anguish floated upwards, the same cries I had heard for days: Pompeii was once again in the throes of death. I was dreamily conscious of someone tugging at my arm. It was the assistant director.

"Come on, Wiles, everything's all set."

I felt somewhat stiff, but peering down, I saw upturned faces, surrounding a camera, aimed in my direction. After slipping on my toga, I hastily went through a few stretches to loosen my tight muscles. I listened carefully to the director's voice, rising through a megaphone.

"Buster, the volcano explodes, the building shakes, you wave your arms and fall. Got it?"

I perched on the edge of the building, my heart thumping wildly.

"Action!" yelled the director.

I plunged into space. To my great relief, the rigging held me with its warm embrace. I hopped down, and the director signaled me over.

"All right?" I asked.

"That was fine, Buster. I've got something else for you. Go and talk to Yak."

I felt light-headed. I had not only survived, but I had obviously made a good impression. I was a *stuntman*. I was in excellent company, too—the best. The fellow who gave me instructions for my next stunt was the legendary Yakima Canutt, a former rodeo champ who had entered pictures in 1923. Yak, as he was nicknamed, was supervising the dangerous stunt sequences.

He also performed stunts, most notably the exciting chariot race. He and stuntman Cliff Lyons were doubling the principal actors. But this was simply a day's work for these guys. They had worked together in the silent version of *Ben Hur*. As a kid, I had thrilled to the sight of Francis X. Bushman whipping around the

Circus Maximus. Now I learned that it was Yakima who was the unsung hero of that chariot race.

As I came to know him during the production, I fully understood why he was the best. He had more guts than anyone I've ever met. It was rather unfair, I thought, that the stars received the accolades, while Yak and his crew went unrecognized by audiences. But that was the life of a stuntman.

Yakima and I staged an arena fight-scene that was taking place during a slave revolt. We rehearsed in strenuous bouts. Yak taught me a great deal about the art of making it look real without getting hurt. He was a taciturn fellow, but I listened carefully to his carefully chosen words, because he was truly a master stuntman.

While Yakima was friendly toward me, the other stuntmen were cool. As a newcomer, I was viewed as something of a threat to their livelihood. But the first stunts I ever performed whetted my enthusiasm. The sheer excitement was only curbed by my inability to find further work. I wandered from lot to lot, eagerly selling my skills as a daredevil, but it was readily apparent that the brotherhood of stuntmen was a tight clique of professionals, closed to interlopers.

Ye Litte Brown Jug was providing a living for me, but I was losing interest in the bar. I just *had* to be a stuntman. My dream of becoming an actor was slipping away, along with my hair. Though only in my mid-twenties, I was rapidly going bald. As a child, I had suffered several serious illnesses, and I thought these might have contributed to my disappearing hairline. I was philosophical about my plight. "Hair today, gone tomorrow," I thought when I looked in the mirror.

But my shiny scalp didn't interfere with my plans to be a stuntman. I excitedly read that Warner Brothers was producing an action film about pirates. The newspaper story mentioned that director Mike Curtiz was conducting screen tests for the leads. *Captain Blood* was undoubtedly going to be a lavish production, with lots of fighting. I hustled over to Burbank, brimming with enthusiasm, quite confident that my silver tongue would get me a job.

I got as far as the Main Administration Building, then encountered a human roadblock. A young guy sat behind the reception desk, guarding the electric buzzer that permitted the mighty to pass into the sacred temple.

"I'd like to see Mr. Curtiz. I want to talk to him about working in his picture."

"Sorry," the kid said, "I can't let you in without a pass."

I did all I could to convince the receptionist to let me inside. "If I could just talk to Curtiz, I know he'll hire me."

But the kid wouldn't budge. "I could lose my job if I let you inside."

I was determined though. The next day, I came back and stated my case as eloquently as possible. He still wouldn't press that damn buzzer. I tried another approach. "Partner, you better take care of me, because I'll be a star one of these days."

Well, sure enough, *that* got him to laughing. The ice melted, and he became sympathetic to my pleas. "If I let you in, do you promise never to tell anyone how you got inside."

"I swear," I said.

He pressed the magic buzzer. I scampered inside, wandering the halls until I found the right office. I took a deep breath, then casually entered. As luck would have it, one of filmdom's most powerful and talented directors sat alone at a desk, a sheaf of papers before him. His high forehead raised upwards, and he frowned at me, obviously disturbed by my intrusion.

"Who are you?" he asked, in a thick Hungarian accent.

"I'm Buster Wiles."

"Who?"

He started to rise, so I made my pitch as fast as possible. He looked somewhat exasperated on hearing what I wanted, but softened a bit as I hustled my expertise as a stuntman.

"So, you're a good stuntman?"

"Man, I'm the toughest damn stuntman you're gonna meet."

He stared at me. "Good huh? I like a man with balls."

"Yes sir, I've got two."

"Write your name. Maybe we call."

A few weeks later, I received a telephone call to report to Warner Brothers to play a pirate in the battle scenes of *Captain Blood*. The kid behind the reception desk had given me a real break. Mort Lickter was his name. He eventually worked his way up to become the Director of Still Photographs at Warners. We became friends for life, and I can never thank him enough for risking his job and pressing the magic buzzer.

Doubling Flynn, I make the escape over the castle gate.
(Photo: Wisconsin Center for Film and Theater Research. ©
1938 Warner Bros. Pictures, Inc. Ren. 1965 United Artists
Television, Inc.)

*Rare still, taken during The Adventures of Robin Hood. I
await on the gallows as Howard Hill takes aim at the
hangman.* (Photo: Jerry Hill Collection)

SEVEN

Captain Blood

*"When Flynn and I got together we made the
prairie look small."*

Errol Flynn and I became great friends. Flynn is now one of
Hollywood's legendary figures. I met him on the set of *Captain
Blood,* in August of 1935, while he was still a virtual unknown. He
had played a few small parts in minor films, but his dynamic
portrayal of Peter Blood, a physician turned pirate, would
skyrocket him to international stardom.

A lot has been written about Flynn. If he had done everything
attributed to him in print, he would have been dead by the age of
twelve. However, his life was an exciting adventure, which began
in Australia in 1909 and ended in Vancouver fifty years later.

I distinctly recall how we met. A group of pirates and crew
members was shooting dice during lunch. I noticed Flynn
watching us from the other side of the sound stage. A couple of
technicians began mumbling about him. They found him rather
aloof. He didn't fraternize with the crew, and after a scene, he
would immediately retire to his portable dressing room.

"I bet he's all right," I said.

I had always been at ease meeting people. I walked over and
began chatting with him. The next day, there was another craps
game when he strolled nearby.

"Hey, Flynn," I said, "come on in and get lucky!"

He joined the gambling, and from that day on, he was one of the guys, quite an admired and well-liked star on the Warner lot. I don't remember if he won or lost in the craps game, but he sure got lucky with his first starring film. Errol later told me how it had happened. He had been walking toward the studio commissary, when Mike Curtiz suddenly stopped and pointed at him.

"That's Captain Blood," Curtiz said.

Earlier, Curtiz had directed Errol in *The Case of the Curious Bride,* but it had been an insignificant role that had failed to impress Curtiz. Flynn said that it was just luck that Curtiz chanced to see him, but he always credited Jack Warner for making the final decision to put an unknown in a starring role.

From the beginning though, Flynn and Warner Brothers were at odds. Flynn had signed a standard contract. He bitterly resented the fact that he only earned two-hundred dollars a week for *Captain Blood,* while the picture brought in millions for the studio. After the premiere of *Captain Blood,* Flynn's agent told him to "disappear" while he negotiated a new contract. By January of 1936, he was making $750 a week, which was still a paltry sum by Hollywood standards. Errol felt he had a bad deal, but Warners had the contract, and any increase was at the studio's discretion.

After our initial meeting, Flynn and I became fast friends. We had similar interests, particularly a strong attraction to sports and gambling. We began attending the local fights together. Flynn was quite a boxer himself. He told me of his rowdy youth in Hobart, Tasmania—how he had gone to New Guinea in search of gold, eventually becoming a government cadet whose job was to supervise the primitive tribes. The latter position was fleeting, and Errol struck out as a recruiter of native labor and captain of an old yacht called the *Sirocco.*

Though only twenty-six, Flynn had indeed lived an adventurous life. He was enthused by my background and listened attentively to my stories of riding the rails, bootlegging, and working with the circus. As we exchanged details of our early years, we discovered that we shared one definite trait—a sense of humor and love of laughter. I always had ready jokes on hand, some of them corny, but I usually had everyone laughing. Flynn shared the same penchant for laughter and mischief-making.

Errol introduced me to his lovely French wife, Lili Damita. They had met abroad, before Flynn arrived in America. Lili was already an established actress, who socialized with the international film aristocracy. She had a fiery temper, and one night she cracked Flynn over the head with a champagne bottle. I was glad that she was fond of me. Errol and Lili lived at 8946 Appian Way, in a home that commanded a magnificent view of Los Angeles. Errol and Lili were a stunning couple. They told me it had been love at first sight.

On a warm autumn afternoon, I arrived at their residence wearing a swimsuit. Errol had asked if I wanted to go to the beach. As I leaned on the horn, Flynn came outside.

"Lili's coming too—and one of her friends," said Errol, with a sly smile. Lili always had a bevy of beautiful girls around her, so I was eager to see what this one looked like. We stopped at a home on Sawtelle Boulevard, and I leaned on the horn again. I seemed to recognize the young woman who walked toward the car. No, it couldn't be, I thought to myself. I glanced at Flynn, who was smiling broadly. Our passenger hopped into the back seat, next to Lili. I casually turned around to see if I was mistaken.

"Booster," said Lili, in a heavy French accent, "thees ees Greta Garbo. Greta, thees is Booster Veels, Fleen's friend."

"Pleased to meet you," I told her.

"I'm sure," said Errol with a wink.

I drove down Sunset to the ocean, and we had a wonderful afternoon picnic. Garbo was lively, not the least bit shy as I had expected her to be. Flynn told me that Lili and Greta often swam together on this stretch of beach. As they frolicked in the shallow surf, I marveled at the two beautiful women.

By January of 1936, Flynn's face was known to millions throughout the world. He took his good fortune in his stride, almost as if he had expected the phenomenal success to occur. Fans, especially women, mobbed him wherever he went. Flynn was hardly the typical husband, being a hotly-pursued film idol. Lili was quite possessive, wanting him to stay home at nights, but Flynn wasn't ready to be domesticated. I wasn't either.

We pretty much did as we wanted. In the afternoons, I would accompany Flynn to the Hollywood Athletic Club, where we would box. I was surprised by how good he was. Flynn's image was that of the debonair romancer. When women turned their heads in his direction, their boyfriends and husbands got jealous.

If somebody made a crack, Errol tried to ignore it. If a guy insisted, well, Flynn didn't back down. He was tough as nails and wouldn't take abuse from anyone.

At a lavish party at Mary Pickford's home, Flynn had heated words with a well-known athlete. Errol chased the guy out of the house, and he dove under a car, trying to hide.

"Come on out, old chum," said Flynn coolly.

But the guy wouldn't budge, and Errol left him cowering in the shadows.

We were in the Seven Seas Restaurant one night, when a redhead kept coming on to Flynn. He ignored her. Then she began talking loud, quite abusively, about Errol. Finally, Flynn had listened to enough of her jabbering. He rolled a newspaper, dipped it in the fireplace, held the flaming paper high in the air, and marched toward her. The girl's eyes almost popped out of her head.

"How would you like that red hair of yours a bit more flaming?"

She bolted like a rabbit, as laughter filled the bar.

Captain Blood was a turning point in Flynn's life, it was a lucky break for me, too. Said Flynn: "My next film's going to be *The Charge of the Light Brigade.* You can ride a horse, can't you?"

"Sure."

"Then, you're going to work in the picture. There's going to be lots of action, Buster."

I did some horseback riding out in the San Fernando Valley, and I was in fine shape for what was to come—or so I thought. I should have rehearsed on something a little larger—like an elephant!

The Charge of The Light Brigade

The Charge of the Light Brigade was scheduled to begin production on March 30, 1936. About a week before the cameras rolled, I got a call from the production staff to report in the morning to the fountain near the Administration Building, a popular rendezvous for Warner crews. I stayed out late drinking, and when I arrived at the fountain, my head felt like a balloon. A guy introduced himself, then told me that I was to go to Mission Park.

"Why?" I asked.

"To check the elephant."

"The elephant?"

"Yeah, you used to be in the circus, didn't you?"

"Yeah, sure, sure."

He finally got through to me that I was to test the elephant that would be used in the leopard-hunting sequence of the film. I was specifically requested to make sure that the elephant could work with the "howdah," or riding canopy, on its back. The guy pointed me in the direction of a waiting car, I got in, and the driver sped off. I felt so ill I had to ask him to stop three times.

As we drove along, I thought to myself that Flynn had certainly done a hell of a good sales job on my behalf.

"I'm on my way to test an elephant," I mused.

When we got there, I stared at the gigantic creature in front of me. The elephant stared back, then let fly an ear-splitting trumpet blast. I turned to the trainer. "Has it ever worked with one of the riding canopies before?"

"No."

I smelled trouble. I suggested that we lower the howdah onto its back. I would then sit behind the elephant's ear for a short walk, to determine the response. Simple enough. The howdah was slowly lowered.

The trainer wanted me to get inside. I declined. I got on a ladder and gently sat behind the huge ears. You never realize how tall elephants are until you sit on one. The trainer tightened the straps, and the elephant took off! It ran for a low shed that had a tile roof. Just before we got there, I jumped. The elephant tore that shed to pieces, trying to knock the howdah off its back.

I turned to the trainer. "And you wanted me to sit there!"

"I'm not a stuntman," he whined.

But he was right. If I wanted to be a stuntman, I had to expect the unexpected. It was my job to risk my neck. "Get used to it," I mumbled to myself.

The Charge of the Light Brigade was to be a baptism by fire for stuntman Buster Wiles. For three months, I worked as one of the Twenty-Seventh Lancers. The script was a simple tale about the British in India and the revenge they exact against Surat Khan, an evil fanatic who has massacred innocent women and children.

Flynn and Patric Knowles were cast as brothers who vie for the love of beautiful Olivia de Havilland. On-screen and off, Olivia captured the hearts of every guy she was around. Flynn fell for her, but, like an idiot, he hid a dead snake in her costume underclothes as a gag. It was hardly a romantic gesture.

A major portion of the film was shot on location at the Lasky Mesa, in Agoura. This was where the Chukote fort had been constructed. I spent most of the picture on a horse. In fact, to offset boredom between scenes, we riders would amuse ourselves by forming elaborate pyramids of horses and men. Our steeds would prance along in a tight line, then guys would straddle from horse to horse, and other fellows would climb atop their shoulders, moving along until we collapsed in a heap of human bodies.

Mike Curtiz drove the production along with a firm hand. He knew exactly what he wanted. As a native Hungarian, he had a difficult time with the English language. Sometimes he couldn't express himself, and he would get frustrated and start yelling. But beneath the bluster, he was a fine man. While filming interior scenes back at Warners, I used to amuse everyone by singing. Even though my voice wasn't as powerful as it once was, I could still carry a melody. I used to sing to Olivia de Havilland, "Light's out sweetheart." When she replied, "You make my day, Buster," I was elated. One day I was crooning and noticed that Curtiz was staring appreciatively. He dubbed me "Singing Marie," and in later years, I became "Vagon Veels," after one of his favorite tunes.

Often, when we had completed our designated scenes for the day, Curtiz would call me over to croon a song. He positively beamed as the set grew silent and my voice filled the sound stage. Once, a crewman approached me after a final scene: "Buster, sing something." He pointed to the clock. "Another fifteen minutes and we get overtime." I launched into a song, and Curtiz sat back in his director's chair, telling everyone to be quiet. I would stop halfway through the tune, then start again. Sure enough, the crew got overtime pay.

Segments of the final charge were shot on a wide plain in Columbia, a small town near Modesto. Flynn asked me to drive his station wagon to the location. I readily agreed, since I wanted to leave early to do some hunting. The station wagon was perfect for transporting a pal's four hunting dogs; besides, it had a built-in bar. The dogs were uncaged, and unfortunately, they made a real mess of the car. We drove into Modesto before I could have it cleaned. Flynn took one look inside his car and said, "Buster, just keep it. You can have it."

I paid a guy to clean it, and it looked like new. Man, it's a good thing Lili didn't see it. There would have been fireworks for sure.

While working on *The Charge of the Light Brigade,* I rode a horse I insisted on using for years. "Snake" was a born actor. When Curtiz yelled, "Action," he would take off on cue; then, once the scene was over, he would return to his exact position without the least bit of prompting from me. I was delighted. Horses are unpredictable: they are smart in some ways, and they can learn tricks easily, but they can also panic unexpectedly. If a horse gets caught in a fence, it can tear itself to shreds in the blind rush to escape. As we galloped daily, I saw guys thrown right and left. But Snake was a superb creature.

When it came time to film the final assault of the Lancers against the Russian cannons, I rode Snake with complete confidence. The Lancers advanced over an area of planted explosives. As our trot developed into a full gallop, the hidden mines began exploding and the earth suddenly opened up with a violent shake. Dirt slapped against my face. Puffs of whitish smoke filled the air. I saw a horse rear its head and throw a rider when a mine exploded, but Snake just kept going like a champion.

Don Turner was doubling Flynn in the picture. Besides Don, Warners employed a standard contingent of stuntmen comprised of Sol Gorss, Alan Pomeroy, Freddie Graham, and others. These fellows were all daredevils, frequently called on to double Warner stars. In the final dramatic sequence, where the Lancers charge the cannons of the Russian army, I took numerous "saddle falls" rigged by "the running W." A cable was strung from an old car axle, driven in the ground, and then tied to a horse's forelegs. The designated length of cable let a rider know exactly where the horse would topple. The fall area was over a camouflaged pit of soft dirt and turf. Unfortunately, horses would often be injured, with snapped legs, due to the fierce jerk of the cable. It was a dangerous stunt for both man and horse. Riders were breaking limbs daily. I cracked three ribs, but I merely taped myself up and kept on tumbling.

On film, "the running W" provided a realistic image of a horse being shot from under a rider, but humane groups complained, and rightly so, about the harsh method of bringing a horse down.

One morning, I greeted Clyde Hudkins, the fellow who furnished all the wagons and livestock for the picture.

"I'm in a hell of a spot," he said worriedly.

"What's the matter, Clyde?"

"I've got these two good jumpers who are balking at leaping the cannons. Man, we're supposed to do the shot now."

"I'll jump it with Snake."

"No kidding?"

"Sure."

I rode up to where the camera crew had a low-angle shot prepared, right beneath the cannon. There were two other riders who would follow me. I had confidence that Snake would make it. If he balked or struck the heavy metal cannon, the riders behind me would crash into us. I walked him away from the crew. As the cameras rolled, I gave him a stinging slap on his rump a few times, and he shot off like a rocket with the others on our tail. Closer and closer we came; then Snake gracefully sailed in the air in a smooth leap. Clyde Hudkins ran up to me.

"Buster, you saved my life."

When word spread of my improvised leap, my stock shot up, both in the eyes of Warner Brothers and my fellow stuntmen.

Another Dawn

Being a stuntman was not only a precarious profession but a very different one as well. When the film ends, you are out of work. Consequently, one had to keep sharp ears tuned to the forthcoming productions that required stunts. Then you had to convince a production official that you were the top guy for the picture.

I thought about keeping Ye Little Brown Jug as a safeguard against starving, but eventually I sold it for a profit while I could. It was too hard keeping tabs on the guys who were running it for me.

In October, I was signed to work in *Another Dawn*, a film starring Flynn as an army officer in love with Kay Francis. I played an Arab and also doubled Flynn in a battle scene in which marauding tribesmen attack a military outpost. I was now earning about two-hundred dollars a week, but the money wasn't that important. I was happy just to be working in motion pictures, a boyhood dream come true.

I was always willing to take a chance, and betting was a source of income. Errol was an excellent athlete, six-feet-two, lean and muscular, and I discovered I could make a profit by betting on Flynn in tennis matches. As Errol's popularity grew, he circulated among the celebrities whose homes boasted tennis courts. Very few expected Flynn to be so expert with a tennis racket. In later years, tennis champ Bill Tilden said Flynn could have turned professional, had he wished.

Valley of the Giants

When people learn of my years as a stuntman, they often inquire what my most dangerous stunt happened to be. Without a doubt, it was the leap I made in *Valley of the Giants.*

One afternoon in June, I received an urgent telephone call from Frank Mattison, a unit manager at Warners. Frank often hired me for stunt work. He was a tough company man, who rigidly made certain that the studio's money was well spent. My usual arrangement was a fee each time I performed a stunt. If the cameraman didn't get it right or the director simply wanted another take, well, too bad. I expected to be paid for each time I performed the stunt. But I earned it.

Frank Mattison knew I delivered the first time, seldom having to repeat a take because of a mistake. Now he was in a jam.

Said Frank: "One of the stuntmen was hurt in a fight. We're on location, and I need you to jump from a boulder into a pool of water. The boulder's about fifty feet above the water line, and the pool's about four-and-a-half feet deep."

"Four-and-a-half feet?"

"That's right."

"When do you need me?"

"This weekend."

"Just give me the directions, partner."

Immediately after hanging up the telephone, I knew I was in for a tough fall. Four-and-a-half feet deep! But on my kitchen table was a slip of paper that forced my acceptance. It was a tax bill, and it was overdue. By this time, Mama had moved to Los Angeles. With my savings, I had purchased an apartment building, which she managed. I didn't realize that the taxes would be so steep. I now needed money in a hurry, or else I would lose the property.

Money was so tight that I decided to leave my auto at home and hitchhike my way to northern California. I had a few days to make the journey, so I packed a suitcase and thumbed a ride up the Pacific Coast Highway. In Eureka I found a hotel room reserved by the studio. Boxing champ Freddy Apostoli was in town for a rest. Being a fight fan, I struck up a conversation. Freddy was intrigued by my work.

"You're gonna jump in a little pool of water from fifty feet? I was leaving tomorrow, but now I'm gonna stay, just to watch you commit suicide."

Early the following morning, a studio driver sped me to the company location, about five miles from Bridgeville. In the afternoon, I met with director Bill Keighley, who explained the stunt to me. I was handed a script and learned that the film was about lumbermen. My scene took place on a dam that is about to be blown up. After my brief conference with Keighley, I borrowed a car and drove to the exact location to see the spot for myself.

One thing I had discovered long ago was that life was most rewarding in the excitement of taking chances. But as I gazed at the enormous boulder and the river below, an uneasy feeling began to churn my stomach. I got in a rowboat and probed the spot where I would splash into the river. Mattison had been exactly right: the depth was four-and-a-half feet. I made certain there were no hidden rocks or submerged objects, but I knew I was going to be pushing my luck.

Saturday evening, the night before the leap, I returned to the site. Low clouds hovered about the sky, except for a small space where distant stars were visible through a patch of midnight blue. The mist soon enveloped the tips of the towering redwoods, and the jewel-like stars vanished. The boulder assumed increasingly fearful proportions. An eerie feeling came over me, and I hurriedly drove back to town. I placed a telephone call to Los Angeles. There must have been a note of apprehension in my voice.

"Buster, what is it?" asked Mama.

"Oh, nothing, I just wanted to say hello . . . , just wanted to say I love you."

As I lay my head on my pillow that night, terrifying images came before me: I was falling endlessly, without control. Suddenly, I lay crumbled in a heap, my limbs unable to move. I awoke with my heart racing, sadly conscious that panic was beginning to overwhelm me.

Night melted away, but my uneasy feeling did not. At 6:30 a.m., I was at the location. As the day wore on, hundreds of people lined the river bank. Word of my attempted leap had spread, and about a thousand faces scanned the river site to watch Buster succeed—or else leap into eternity. I propped myself against a tree stump and waited, as three cameras were set up at various angles. Mattison was only going to pay me for one leap, that was certain.

Freddy Apostoli came walking toward me. He glanced at the massive boulder, then fixed an awestruck gaze on me: "Buster Wiles, you are crazy."

"So I've heard," I said.

The question of "would I make it?" weighed heavily on me. My heart was fluttering in my chest. Keighley and a handful of assistants came over. I casually wiped the beads of perspiration from my forehead, but something must have shown in my eyes. Keighley pursed his lips, then said:

"Buster, if you have any reservations about doing this, it's not too late. There are some guys here . . . ."

"No, I'm ready as I'll ever be."

"All right," he said. "Everything is set. Now, when you hit the water, stay under. Slowly count from one to ten, then let your body rise and float down river."

On my way to the boulder, I passed actors Wayne Morris and Charles Bickford. They bid me good luck. From high atop the boulder, I could see clouds floating across the sun. I peered straight down at the shallow pool, mentally positioning my body. Then the sun broke forth and illuminated the exact spot where I would hit.

The assistant director came up and went over the action: a sentry, played by me, is about to shoot at Wayne Morris, who is planting a dynamite charge on the dam. Alan Hale slides down a cable and boots the sentry off the boulder. Doubling Hale would be veteran stuntman Cliff Lyons.

From the edge of the precipice, I spied the sun's reflections glinting off the three cameras. A multitude of faces craned upwards to see me make it or break it. An air of fatalism swept over me.

It was now around 3 p.m., and my nerves were unraveling. I breathed in deeply. Then, with a surge of resolution that bordered on defiance, I impatiently told the assistant director: "Come on, man, let's go!"

He scurried down from the boulder. Bill Keighley waved at me and raised a megaphone: "Remember, Buster, count to ten!" The cameras were rolling.

"Action!" yelled Keighley.

From behind, I heard Cliff Lyons sliding toward me. Just before he kicked his leg out, he shouted, "Go!"

I thrust myself over the boulder and turned a half-gainer, orienting my fall to hit on my side, since that's the toughest part of the body. Just above the water, I straightened out so the impact would slow me.

With sickening force, I splashed into the shallow water. A spasm of pain shot through my back, and my left hand oozed into the slimy riverbed. Frantically, I tried to stay beneath the water, but a sudden onrush of pain forced me to count "nine and one is ten," and up I came, rolling over, gasping for breath.

I staggered to my feet, clasped my hands together, and raised them in a symbol of victory. Cheers went up from the crowd. The impact had knocked the breath from me, and I had strained a back muscle, but each sweet mouthful of air resuscitated my confidence.

I slumped on the bank, exhausted but triumphant. I stared up at the boulder, and I felt as if I had beaten the toughest opponent of my life.

In later years, the scene showing my leap was lifted from *Valley of the Giants* and used in the 1952 Warner film, *The Tall Trees*. The studio never missed a chance to save a buck. They could have asked Buster to perform the leap again. I would have done it . . . maybe.

My reputation as a stuntman was growing with every picture. As a measure of my success, the studio asked if I would like to appear in a special interview. At first, I thought the questions would be for a newsreel interview, but then I was informed that it was for something called "television." This was still the late thirties, and I was unaware of the burgeoning phenomena. A publicist said: "They're doing a special broadcast and they want to talk to a stuntman. Interested?"

"Sure."

I drove downtown, quite excited to be participating in such a unique event. I spotted a mob on Seventh Avenue, and I knew this was the location. A prominent car dealer name Earl C. Anthony was giving instructions to the crew. Anthony was sponsoring the experimental broadcast. He pointed me in the direction of a huge camera, and I was interviewed about my life as a stuntman. I later learned that the signal was beamed only as far as Wilshire and Fairfax, very close, but the broadcast made a big publicity splash, which was Anthony's idea. I would give anything to see this early broadcast. Yes, sir! Buster Wiles was a television pioneer.

Not only was I making history with the experimental TV broadcast, but I was about to perform stunts in a film that would become a part of motion picture history.

The Adventures of Robin Hood and Gold is Where You Find It

One afternoon, Flynn telephoned me with the news that he would star in *The Adventures of Robin Hood*. He was excited about the role. Not long after, on the Warner backlot, Errol introduced me to Howard Hill, a tall, firmly-built fellow with dark, wavy hair and a warm smile.

"Howard's the greatest archer around," said Flynn.

Errol raised his bow and let fly an arrow aimed at a straw-filled target. Hill frowned as the arrow clipped the target's corner and sailed into the earth. He raised his own bow and instructed Flynn how to shoot. His arrow struck the bull's-eye dead center. Pretty soon, a small crowd had gathered to watch in awe as Howard's archery lesson became a demonstration of his remarkable skill. He lay on his back and, placing the bow between his legs, fired. Another arrow struck the center. He stood up and pointed to a nearby telephone pole.

"Well, I could hit that," I thought.

But Hill pointed the bow skyward. The arrow sailed high in the air, then curved in a downward slope. It struck dead center—on top of the telephone pole! Over the years, I was to see other amazing archery feats by Howard. He could shoot coins out of the air. Once, I saw him fire an arrow high, then—reaching over his shoulder—he withdrew another feather-tipped arrow and split the descending arrow in mid-air!

Howard became a close friend of both Errol and me. He was a native of Wilsonville, Alabama, and spoke with a rich Southern drawl, a characteristic that hindered his screen test to play the role of Robin Hood. Howard told me how he had come to Warner's a few months earlier to audition for the archery work in *The Adventures of Robin Hood*. Although he enjoyed a superb reputation, he had been made to join an assembled group of professional archers, all vying for the coveted assignment.

On the studio lot, a gallows had been erected. Most of the archers were good enough to pin the noose to the wooden structure. Toward the end of the day, Howard's turn came. He declined to shoot, simply stating that he would return the following day.

"What's wrong?" asked the director of the competition.

"I would just rather shoot tomorrow," he said.

That evening, he took a hunting broadhead point, reversed it to where it was a V-shape, then sharpened the interior to a razor-fine edge. He practiced late into the night. The next morning, a snide voice greeted him.

"Well, Mr. Hill, are you any better today?"

Replied Howard: "How many times do you want me to cut it, and how much are you paying?"

He then shot an arrow that actually sliced the gallow's noose. He had won the job of supervising the archery in *The Adventures of Robin Hood*. Due to Howard's expert instructions, Flynn became a master with a bow and arrow. While the company was on location in Chico, California, Flynn and Howard spent hours hunting, and Basil Rathbone filmed their hunting expertise with a sixteen millimeter camera.

While the crew was in Chico for the Sherwood Forest scenes, I was on location with the company of *Gold Is Where You Find It.* Always a hustler, I would jump from one picture to another, often not even knowing the titles of the released films. I would stage a fight here, wreck a car there, fall off a cliff or into a pond. I worked in the Warner Brothers lake so much, I asked for a bar of soap.

In *Gold Is Where You Find It,* I took some hard, hard knocks. The film was shot on location in Weaverville, California. The story was about gold-rush prospectors and their fight with ranchers. We began filming around the La Grange Mine, and I was assigned an important stunt along a one-way road leading to the mine entrance. We were filming in a narrow section of the road, close to a twenty-five-foot drop. The script called for Tim Holt to serve George Brent a subpoena. Tim rides up and confronts a guard at the barricade. In his attempt to leap the obstacle, he is shot in mid-air.

Tim rode up, and was filmed as if he were ready to jump the barricade. Now Buster goes to work. Tim's mount was a fast thoroughbred, which had run professionally. The first thing I noticed was that the horse was very fidgety and hard to handle. Then I realized something that made my heart sink. I had forgotten to bring my thick pads, which protected my elbows and knees from injury. In the picture business, the first lesson you learn is never to waste a minute of the company's time. I couldn't say, "Hey, guys, let me run down the hill and get my pads, and, by the way, I don't like this horse, so get me another one." The director, Mike Curtiz, would have raised hell. Besides, it was my mistake, and I had a reputation to maintain.

I managed to calm my unruly horse, and we sailed over the barricade. In mid-air I fell, as if struck by a bullet. I braced myself, but it wasn't enough. A sharp pain stabbed through my knees and elbows as I struck solid bedrock and actually *bounced* out of camera range toward the precipice. All that saved me from tumbling over was my foot striking the sound truck, parked near the ledge.

"No good," said Curtiz.

The crew could see the look of agony on my face, but I simply remounted and did the scene again. Thank heavens the second take was usable. I could barely rise. I had burst the cartilage in my elbows and knees, and my joints swelled like balloons. I limped away in absolute agony. Later in the picture, back at the studio, I broke three ribs in a bar-fight when a guy's knees smashed against my side. But that was nothing. I merely taped myself up and kept right on working. But the day I bounced on solid bedrock! Oh, Lord, I can still feel it.

That evening, I was hobbling around our location living quarters when I heard someone mention my name. I recognized the voice as that of our sound technician, Dick Williams. "That Buster Wiles is the toughest man walking." Dick didn't know that I felt like crawling. I guess when you bounce off bedrock you are tough—or stupid. Maybe both. Later in the evening I regained my spirits, and we began whooping it up. I rode a mule into prop-man Limey Plew's tent, rousing him from a sound sleep. Unexpectedly, the mule let go right in Limey's shoes. We made a fast retreat, as an angry Limey chased us away. The next morning I was so sore, I could barely get out of bed.

I doubled black actor Wille Best in a fierce gun battle and was nearly trampled to death by frightened horses. I rubbed black makeup on my face and entered a corral where Wille was supposed to be watching the horses. The scene called for a dam to be blown sky-high, and at the sound of the gunplay and explosion, all hell broke loose as the terrified horses panicked and began kicking me. A hoof grazed my head, then a strong kick got me in the rear, and I was sent sprawling in the dirt. I yelled in pain as another horse stepped on my thigh. Fortunately, I was able to crawl under a horse and scramble under the fence to safety. My thigh wasn't broken, but through my ripped pants, I could see the outline of a hoof imprint in my bleeding skin. I didn't even have time to recuperate from these stunts, but had to rush to Warner Brothers to double Flynn.

The Adventures of Robin Hood is now considered one of the greatest action films ever made. I had a feeling back then that it was going to be a spectacular success. I doubled Flynn in Robin's escape from the gallows. First, we filmed the scene where the hangman is toppled from the high ladder by a well-aimed arrow, fired by Howard Hill. Then I escaped from the gallows with my hands loosely tied behind my back. I leaped on a horse and, ouch, you guys know what I mean. I galloped through the streets, with Prince John's men in hot pursuit. My scenes were filmed by a second unit crew, with Mike Curtiz directing the escape with his usual keen eye for excitement. When the time came to film Robin scrambling over the castle gate, Curtiz waved me over to his director's chair for instructions.

"Singing Marie, you pretend to cut rope, hold on, go up. Show lots of energy!"

When "*Action!*" was yelled, I withdrew a sword from astride my horse, then chopped at a thick rope attached to the drawbridge. I grabbed the rope and held on, shooting upwards to the castle parapet. We got the shot in one take. On the other side, I lowered myself down a rope, then dropped about ten feet. Flynn stepped in for the closeup of Robin fleeing to freedom. "I'm sure bushed from that escape," said Errol.

Howard Hill had a roll in the picture, as Captain of the Archers. The publicity department released the story that Howard had actually "split the arrow" in the famous tournament sequence, filmed at Busch Gardens in Pasadena. But, as great as Howard was, the publicity story was off the mark by a long shot. Howard was indeed able to strike another arrow, but the notch deflected a direct split, and it didn't photograph well. A wire was rigged in front of the Administration Building, and I fired the arrow down the wire. Now it can be revealed—Buster Wiles split the arrow!

Wild Boar Hunt and Elizabeth and Essex

The Adventures of Robin Hood was a tremendous success. Flynn was so impressed by Howard Hill's uncanny expertise with a bow and arrow that he financed "the world's greatest archer" in a series of action shorts, released by Warner Brothers.

Howard had previously been featured in exciting film shorts— in *The Last Wilderness,* he is shown dispatching such "outlaw animals" as a rattlesnake. Howard and I had become fast friends. He was a down-to-earth guy, quite modest about himself, but he possessed a truly adventurous spirit—and tough, too. He was the only man I ever knew to have been bitten by a rabid dog, become infected, and *live,* after going mad for a brief period.

Over the years, the Flynn-Hill shorts would exhibit his amazing ability with a bow and arrow. I appeared in a few of the early productions. Howard, camerman Al Wetzel, and I went to Catalina Island to shoot *Wild Boar Hunt*. I played a farmer (good casting) who is "on the case of the missing chicken." I meet Howard, who kills a hawk that has been menacing my chicken coop. Howard then does some trick shots. He hits a rock in mid-air and shoots a mushroom off the end of my rifle. A "killer boar" makes off with my prize hen, leaving four orphan chicks. To revenge this dastardly act, we set off on his trail, in company with lion hounds "Mr. Bill" and "Mickey the Finn."

We cornered a boar in the thick underbrush, I got as close as possible, then the furious beast lunged at me, I fell, tumbled, and the boar came after me. Getting close to an angry boar is extremely dangerous, for its six-inch tusks could rip open a man's guts. The ugly brute was right behind me, chasing me across a clearing, when Howard brought him down with one shot.

During the filming, we stayed at the Eagle's Nest Lodge where, on a Sunday afternoon, Flynn met us and introduced his father, Professor Theodore Flynn, a distinguished marine biologist who taught at Queen's College in Belfast, Ireland. Professor Flynn was on the quiet side, displaying a scholarly demeanor. Errol greatly admired him.

Flynn was in the midst of *The Private Lives of Elizabeth and Essex*. I had worked on the film and knew that he and Bette Davis weren't getting along. In fact, Errol would place a piece of garlic in his mouth before they did a closeup together. Now, Errol was unhappy over missing all the fun we were having filming *Wild Boar Hunt*.

"I'd rather be in your film," said Errol.

We were sipping cocktails as we talked, and before long, Professor Flynn and I emptied a bottle of Scotch. Errol suggested that we go in the brush in search of wild boar.

"We killed this bottle of Scotch, Flynn, that's good enough for me."

Errol insisted that we start off on the boar trail.

"Flynn," I said, "one of those creatures might tear your nuts off."

"Couldn't be any worse than some of the fans who come after me."

Undaunted, Errol led the way, with his bow in hand. Stealthily, treading like cats in the thick brush, we crept soft-footed. I was behind Flynn as we crouched along the barely-visible trail. Then, in the dead silence, I grunted like a boar. Flynn shot up like a rocket, his head swiveling from side to side, searching for the charging beast. I rolled over with laughter. Realizing who the boar was, he broke up too.

"Buster, don't so that!" he chided.

All we managed to catch that afternoon was a boar piglet, which Flynn gave to Bette Davis as a gag.

While working on *Elizabeth and Essex,* I met one of the greatest all-around athletes in sports history. During lunch, I was chatting with a few American Indians who were working on a short-subject film. In their midst was the legendary Jim Thorpe, former all-American football star and Olympic champion. In 1912, Thorpe had won the decathlon and pentathlon in the Olympic Games at Stockholm, but a year later, an investigation by the Amateur Athletic Union revealed that he had played semi-professional baseball before the Olympics. As a result, he was stripped of his gold medals. In later years, he was a pro football player and excelled at several sports, but his personal life was marred by alcoholism and marital problems. As a kid, I had marveled at Thorpe's athletic prowess: he could throw a football from one goal-post to the other. When we shook hands, his grip was powerful. It was a handshake I've always remembered.

In *Cavalcade of Archery,* I again assisted Howard in one of my most dangerous stunts. The film opened with unused archery footage from *The Adventures of Robin Hood.* The narrator said that Howard Hill was better than both Robin Hood and William Tell. Howard performs some shots, striking a swinging light bulb; and, looking through a mirror, he shoots backwards, striking a target dead center.

I arrived at Lakeside Country Club in such an outlandish outfit that golfers were staring right and left. I was the guinea pig for a William Tell shot. Yes, Howard intended to shoot an apple atop my head. I sauntered down the fairway in a medieval costume left over from *The Adventures of Robin Hood.* I wore boots, tights, a balloon-sleeved white shirt, and a period jacket. On my head was a shoulder-length page-boy wig. I had more hair on my head than I ever had in a lifetime.

Beneath the wig was a thin metal helmet. Howard insisted that

I wear this to protect myself. As good as he was, there was always the possibility that the unexpected would occur—a sneeze, an insect sting, or the bow-string might break. A misfired arrow, even by a fraction of an inch, could result in instant death. I would be gone, and Howard's career as an archer would be over.

I knelt, facing the camera, as Howard placed an apple on my head. I had absolute confidence in his skill. From about sixty yards behind me, Howard—all in one swift movement—raised the bow and, without hesitation, fired. In slow motion, the arrow is shown slicing the center of the apple. Next, he placed a *prune* on my head. This shot was extremely dangerous. If Howard somehow missed and struck the back of my head, the arrow could easily pierce the thin metal.

I again knelt, trying not to think about the sharp broadhead point that was coming my way. Zap! Audiences around the world could see the arrow coming at me in slow motion, then striking the prune atop my head. It was an amazing archery feat, and I'm glad I lived to tell the tale.

Hell's Kitchen

Another harrowing experience was in a film I did with the Dead End Kids. In *Hell's Kitchen* I doubled Grant Mitchell, who was playing the vicious superintendent of a correctional school. He locks Bobby Jordan in a freezer as punishment. The mistreated kids rebel and decide to give Mitchell a mock trial and a taste of his own medicine. But he escapes. This is where Buster stepped in. I crashed through a window in a two-story leap. That was easy enough, but the next scene had me jumping in a car and driving through the structure with the barn doors open. I was ready, or so I thought.

The special effects men started the fire, and I stomped on the gas. But once I was inside, the flames and smoke hid the exit doors. I smashed through off-center and clipped a wagon, which spun around and smashed into the side of the car. I could see crew members diving for cover, as shards of wood burst in all directions. I managed to keep control of the car and came to a screeching stop with my heart racing. I caught my breath. About an inch from my eye was a sharp piece of metal, attached to the toppled wagon. I could have lost an eye, or the spike could have possibly pierced my skull, resulting in instant death.

One afternoon, I was with Flynn in a dressing-room as he was about to go before a live audience for Cecil B. De Mille's *Lux Theater.*

"What can I do to get a laugh, Buster?"

I thought for a few moments, then told Flynn to sit down. I took off one of his expensive loafers and, with a pen knife, cut off the end of a silk stocking, exposing a naked big toe.

Flynn was introduced, to loud applause, then sat onstage with the other players. In the dead silence of the auditorium, an announcer began the show. Flynn casually slipped off his shoe and pretended to be engrossed in his script. A twitter of laughter started, then peals rolled across the theater as the audience noticed Flynn's big toe. He played the scene straight-faced, then rubbed his foot and replaced his shoe.

During the broadcast, I was handed an urgent message from Howard Hill, who was filming an archery short aboard the *Sirocco.* Howard relayed that a young crewman was in critical condition from a burst appendix. The ship was moored in a remote area off the coast of Mexico. Howard said to send an airplane in right away. Flynn telephoned Bud Ernst, a first-rate pilot and a good friend. When we met him at Burbank Airport, the weather was extremely bad: thick fog limited visibility. The control tower made it clear that no planes were to depart until weather conditions improved. Flynn's brow furrowed.

"We've got to help that kid," he said. "Right now."

Bud and I readily agreed. An airport official came over and tried to convince us to wait a few hours, until the fog would lift. Flynn forcefully argued that our flight was a crucial emergency mission. "You'll be taking quite a chance," said the fellow with apprehension. We finally convinced him that every minute counted in our attempt to get the boy to a hospital.

As the plane taxied down the runway, I discovered I was sitting on five cans of gasoline. No wonder Errol was so eager to sit up front! Before the plane arrived in San Diego, I pulled out a cigarette and match. I called out to Flynn and pretended to light the cigarette. What a shout he and Bud made when they saw those matches!

Bud made a superb landing in a desolate area near the beach. After getting off the plane, we bumped around in pitch-black darkness until I rolled some newspapers and made torches—the five gallons of gas came in handy. Howard Hill and I stayed on the *Sirocco*. The boy was carried to the back of the plane, and away it went. He reached a hospital, where he was operated on, and his life was saved. Ironically, the kid's mother later sued Flynn. She claimed they were Christian Scientists, whose religious beliefs had been violated by the use of medicine. Flynn ended up settling out of court with the family, all for saving the boy's life.

Tear Gas Squad

I had many close calls in my stunt career, but none so frightening as what occurred on *Tear Gas Squad*. The picture was a B-programmer, featuring Dennis Morgan as a cop fighting mobsters. I doubled Dennis in the action shots. Everything was fine until I stepped in to work in a scene where machine-gun bullets were to tear into a wall. It was a simple set-up. The special-effects men rigged explosive charges, implanted under the stucco wall, to create the impression of a hail of bullets ripping in front of me.

I had always dismissed a serious accident as, "It won't likely happen to me." But this time it did. About a year earlier, I had been playing a fur robber in *Heart of the North* when the unexpected happened. I was sitting in a canoe that had been wired with charges to resemble bullets. When they went off, splinters went into the side of my neck and face. It was a harbinger of what to expect on *Tear Gas Squad*, but I ignored the similarity.

The scene was so easy that I was taken by surprise at the ferocity of the machine-gun effects. As they exploded, each charge was more deafening than the last. Then, with devastating suddenness, there was a booming sound, and my face was peppered with stucco. I clutched my head and stumbled to the ground with my ears ringing. Awful thoughts crossed my mind as I crumpled in agony, my face searing with pain. I tried to focus, but one of my eyes was awash in blood. I had the horrendous thought that I might be blinded.

Just a few seconds earlier, I had been a capable, cocky stuntman. Now here I was, flat on my back. Shadowy figures hovered above me. A light was shone in my face, and I immediately asked that someone check my eye. Fortunately, it was clear. My cheek and forehead were bloody, though. I took a handkerchief and wiped the streaks of blood that oozed from my forehead.

I wiped my face the best I could until the first-aid man arrived. He bandaged me up and wanted me home, but I insisted that I was all right. As usual, my face wasn't being shown so I did the scene again. Apparently, the powdermen had rigged the charge with too much punch, to say the least. I pretended that I was really quite all right, but I was soaked in sweat from the terrible thought that I could have easily damaged my eyesight.

From then on, I carefully checked any explosives that were placed near my face. By day's end, I was drained. But my ordeal wasn't over. The stucco that had peppered me festered in my cheek, leaving tiny scars, constant reminders of my perilous profession.

There was another accident during the picture, but this one was my fault and occurred out of camera range. In the cast of *Tear Gas Squad* was George Reeves, in later years to achieve star status as television's Superman. George was absolutely enthralled by the hot driving I did in the picture. He would stare in awe as I tore around the backlot, with tires squealing, and he asked me if I would teach him to drive like a stuntman. We met at the Fog Cutter and downed some hefty cocktails, then I jumped behind the wheel of his car.

"Just watch how I do it, George."

I tore off down Hollywood Boulevard, weaving through the traffic at high speeds. Near Laurel Canyon, I approached a stoplight and gunned the accelerator to squeeze between a car and a parked bus. In a flash, the car pulled into our lane. Swerving sharply, I clipped the rear end of the bus, and our front bumper was pulled out and around the car, where it twisted up in the air, just like it was waving to us. As George surveyed the damage, he nearly broke into tears.

"What's my mama gonna say?" he whimpered.

Years later, whenever I saw "the man of steel" on television, the scene came to mind. I just had to laugh.

Dodge City

Dodge City was Flynn's first Western. Errol was somewhat hesitant about playing a cowboy, but audiences loved him as the tough hero who cleans up the rowdy cattle town. Production began on location, about forty miles outside of Modesto, California. I was on horseback as the wagon train, led by Flynn, crosses the wide prairie. In Modesto, the publicity department decided to present a charity baseball game. I was called on to organize the teams. There was a quiet fellow who was hanging around the production. Though he was reserved and remained in the background, he was recognized, and whispers went around—America's richest man was courting Olivia de Havilland. When I spied him watching the filming, I walked over, mentioned the baseball game, and asked what position he wanted to play.

He thought for a moment. "Buster, I'll be umpire," said Howard Hughes.

It was a lively game, and Hughes did a fine job as first-base umpire. I doubt if any of the spectators even recognized the shy billionaire.

Back on the Warner lot, a rip-roaring brawl was filmed in the Gay Lady Saloon on Stage 16. Flynn's adversaries were his real-life friends, Bruce Cabot and Victor Jory. His cronies in the picture were another duo of pals—Alan Hale and Guinn "Big Boy" Williams. Hale was as jovial off-camera as on-screen. He gave me his membership card to play golf at Lakeside Country Club, and I still keep it in my wallet as a memento of this wonderful man. Also working on the picture was an actress whom everyone adored. Ann Sheridan was a dream. She was not only gorgeous, but down-to-earth as well. She was from Denton, Texas, and as natural as honey. I felt that, when she and I got together, it was like cornbread with cornbread.

Ann was singing "Marching Through Georgia" in the saloon when we cattlemen launched into "Dixie" and a gigantic brawl began. I smashed through a bar window onto the wooden sidewalk. Cagney's double, Red Breen, worked with me in a fight scene on the second-floor bannister. On the first take, the balsa wood didn't break. Then I told him, "Watch out, Red!" I gave him a punch in the chest, and over he went onto five or six guys. We then crashed through the second-level floor in another fight.

I realized by this time that I could earn more money if I doubled the culprit that Flynn demolishes, rather than good guy Errol. In the barber shop where Clem Bevans shaves Flynn, bad guy Doug Fowley pulled a gun. I doubled Fowley, and Flynn heaved me through the door into the street.

Whenever life got dull around the set, I would think of ways to brighten the day. After a morning of hanging around, waiting and waiting to film, I had a make-up man who was a pretty good artist draw a face on my bald head. My fringe of hair served as a beard. I put a jacket on backwards, knocked on dressing room doors, and turned around. Either a shriek or a laugh let me know that the joke was a success.

I guess I was always clowning around. I was a good ventriloquist, with a knack for imitating female voices, young and old alike. I would often call a pal—or an enemy—and in a delicate, lilting voice ask for him.

"He's not here," came the expected reply.

"Who is this?" I demanded to know.

"This is his wife."

"Oh, my goodness, he didn't tell me he was married!"

It was a great prank.

Once, Flynn and I were in a Wilshire bar when a loud-mouthed fellow began introducing himself rather boastfully. An attractive woman entered and sat nearby. "And give that beautiful lady a drink!" he bellowed. She sipped her cocktail, thanked him, then left. I slipped to a pay phone and called the bar, asking for Mr. Big Shot. Using my female voice, I identified myself as the just-departed lady and asked to meet him. "And I'll meet you at the bus stop out front. Now watch for my big white Lincoln."

I rushed back to the bar in time to catch his farewell: "Yeah, boys," he chuckled, "I've got some sudden business to attend to." I watched him through the glass door. Every fifteen minutes, he would jump out in the street. When we left the bar two hours later, he was still there.

Virginia City

On November 25, 1939, I was sitting on a horse on the Hopi reservation in Arizona. We were near Flagstaff, filming a covered-wagon scene for *Virginia City*. I was calmly sitting astride my horse, waiting for the cattle to be cleared so marauders, led by Humphrey Bogart, could attack the wagon train. Bogart and George Regas were standing near me, when Bogart suddenly pointed to a trail of dust coming over the horizon. A crew member in a station wagon pulled up in a swirl of dust.

"Hey, Buster, your wife's just gone to the hospital to have the baby!"

I did a back roll off the horse's rump. "Buster's leaving!" I shouted to everyone.

Man, was I excited! I rushed to the train station and purchased a ticket to Los Angeles, then I rushed to a bar, where I bought drinks for every patron in sight. The porters had to practically carry me into my sleeper compartment. I soon passed out, but exactly at 9:30 p.m., I awoke as sober as a judge. I glanced at my watch, opened the shade, and stared out at the dark landscape. Then I was out again. Later that evening, I arrived at the hospital and asked Dolly what time our son had been born.

"It was nine-thirty on the dot."

The very moment I had awakened, Don had made his entrance. Our son was named after Don Swimly, a wonderful friend, who was an official at the Bank of America. He had provided innumerable favors, especially the kindness of arranging loans when money was tight. Don Swimly later became an accountant for restaurateur Dave Chasen. I knew Dave from the time he had a tiny place with six stools. Chasens became one of the foremost restaurants in the nation. Dave was a fine host, making everyone feel at home. He would let Flynn and me use his private steamroom; then we would enjoy a great meal.

Not long after the birth of my son, I saw Jimmy Cagney on the Warner lot. When I told him the good news, he reached in his pocket and gave me fifty bucks.

I had worked with him in *The Fighting 69th,* an action picture about soldiers in World War I. During the filming, he had planned to buy circus tickets as a gift for his sister, Jeanne. That night, I went down to the Ringling Brothers tent and found Mr. Wink. On spotting his former employee, that one eye of his brightened. "If it ain't Buster Wiles! The man who knocked Peanut Bill on his ass!"

When I told him that I was now a stuntman he beamed. "Boy, I always knew you'd make it. You were the best hustler I ever had."

Mr. Wink gave me six complimentary tickets for Cagney. The next day, when I gave them to Cagney, he couldn't believe it.

Later in the week, Mr. Wink did another favor. After the lights dimmed, a circus attendant lifted a canvas flap, and Flynn, Bruce Cabot and I slipped inside and were shown to front-row seats. Before the circus left town, I sent Mr. Wink a case of booze.

The new addition to our home at 5740 Franklin made me a happy man, but it didn't slow me down. Dolly complained that I was seldom around, which was true. I was a father, but Daddy Wiles was still running wild. When Flynn and I got together, we made the prairie look small. We could really have fun. Flynn had a truly exciting presence that ignited fireworks wherever he went. We considered ourselves free spirits, pursuing wine, women, and song.

After Flynn acquired his yacht, *Sirocco,* we were always at sea. He had named the ship after his earlier boat, which held fond memories for him. He loved the ocean tremendously. He was a born mariner who could have sailed a piece of bark around the world. Flynn purchased the sixty-foot yacht in Boston, for $25,000. The great times we had aboard the *Sirocco* are memories of incredible fun and laughter. Errol kept the yacht moored in Balboa's Lido Isle Channel. Dick Powell and Joan Blondell lived nearby and often came aboard for cocktails. There was also a speedboat we used for waterskiing. The yacht was mine to sail whenever I wished. I had many a romantic moonlight cruise aboard the *Sirocco.*

High Sierra

One of our favorite outings was a weekend at Catalina Island. We would moor the ship, then take the speedboat out for a day of adventure. One of Errol's special areas of fun was Fourth of July Cove. If it was morning, a stick of dynamite over the side would bring up fresh fish for breakfast. Then, Flynn and I would be lazing aboard the *Sirocco* when the sound of giggling and splashing would be heard around the boat. Peering down, I would see a group of girls who had paddled out from the beach to catch a glimpse of Flynn.

"May I help you aboard?" I would ask.

"Oh yes!" they would squeal, practically jumping out of the water like penguins.

A familiar sight in the area was Humphrey Bogart's tiny boat. At this period, he was married to Mayo Methot. They were known as "the battling Bogarts." We would pull alongside their little boat for a morning cocktail, and he would have a black eye or Mayo would look as if she had just fought several rounds. Pretty soon they would start arguing.

When Bogart did *Virginia City*, he had yet to achieve stardom. By 1940, he was moving toward major success. The picture that put him over the top was *High Sierra*. I worked with Bogart in May of 1940, on *They Drive By Night*. Bogart and George Raft portrayed two brothers, trying to make it as independent truckers. Ida Lupino's performance as a scheming wife infatuated with George Raft stole the picture from everyone. I doubled Raft in a dangerous stunt where the two brothers lose control of their truck before it went over a cliff. I jumped from the truck before it went over the side. That stunt was child's-play compared to my work a few months later.

High Sierra remains one of Bogart's most popular films. His role of the violent gangster with a heart boosted his career. Previous to *High Sierra*, Bogart was primarily known for his portrayal of "heavies." The picture was directed by one of the best directors in motion-picture history—Raoul Walsh. His talent gave audiences memorable films that are still admired today. Raoul became a good friend of mine.

He was a guy who had quite a life. During the period of silent movies, Raoul had been a successful actor. He had appeared in D.W. Griffith's masterpiece, *Birth of a Nation*. His acting career ended when a jackrabbit smashed into his car windshield in Arizona. As a result of the accident, he lost an eye. The black patch he wore became a memorable trademark.

Raoul's method of directing was different from his equally-talented contemporary, Michael Curtiz. Raoul managed to develop an intimate rapport with the actors and actresses. He would kid and cajole the reluctant stars into doing the scene the way the director wanted it. Curtiz was another great director, but he gave explicit orders the way he wanted the scenes played.

Mike could lose his temper very easily. Raoul stayed calm. Raoul's close friends, such as Ida Lupino and Errol Flynn, had an affectionate nickname for him—"Uncle." Raoul got excellent performances from the stars of *High Sierra*. Bogie played "Mad Dog" Roy Earle, a Dillinger-type convict, who plans to rob a plush resort. Mad Dog falls in love with a young girl with a clubfoot. He pays to have an operation, but afterwards she rejects the gangster's love, and he turns to a girl who used to work at a "dime-a-dance joint."

Ida Lupino's performance as the loyal Marie was captivating. Roy and Marie were more than just criminals; they were real people who loved animals and pitied bankrupt farmers, yet they were two people destined to fail. After the robbery, Marie and Roy try to escape, but the police trap Roy in the High Sierra Mountains. The police shoot Roy from atop a high crag, where he tumbles to his death.

In September of 1940, the film company traveled to Lone Pine to shoot the dramatic climax of the picture. Raoul Walsh chose me to double Bogie in the mountain fall. He and I searched the area around Mount Whitney, the highest point in the U.S.—14,494 feet above sea level. Raoul was a quiet, pensive man, with a keen sense of humor. He was constantly visualizing how to make a scene come to life. As we peered up at the steep crags, Raoul smoothly rolled a cigarette. His one eye, searching in a sweep of his head, scanned the mountain range. His black patch not only gave him a buccaneer aspect, but accentuated his serious demeanor. His finger shot out.

"There! Can you fall off there?"

"Yeah, I can fall off, but I would be dead when I landed."

Raoul laughed; and, at my suggestion, we walked along the rugged terrain. Raoul pointed again.

"Can you tumble down that slope?"

"If I can't, I'll eat my Whitney."

That was it. I had made my commitment to the director. Now I had to deliver. The scene was to be filmed at the Whitney Portals.

At our hotel in Lone Pine, I asked Bogie if I could borrow his car to drive to Bishop. He reached in his pocket.

"Don't you give him those keys!" came his wife's sharp voice. Bogie tossed me the keys, and they began arguing like cats and dogs. I made a fast exit and jumped in the car. As I pulled away, I spotted Mayo glaring after me with her hands on her hips.

When Mayo wasn't around to make him nervous, Bogart was relaxed and easy-going. He and Flynn were good pals. He admired the way Errol didn't let the studio step on him. After he became a star, he emulated Errol's tough stand with Warner Brothers.

In a feat of cinema magic, I got shot off the mountain by *me*. The scene called for a marksman to climb the mountain behind Roy Earle and shoot him in the back. A special team of mountain-climbing mules and horses was loaded with equipment for the ascent up a steep path. I doubled the rifleman and stood precariously on the edge of the precipice, aiming down at Bogart. This was extremely dangerous, due to strong downdrafts circulating amidst the crags. Bogart seemed nothing but a small figure far below.

After the crew had filmed me firing the telescopic rifle, I descended and donned Bogie's clothes. We moved to the slope where Roy Earle was to topple after a bullet strikes him. This last section was a very steep area, near a precipice. Raoul insisted that not one, but three lifelines be stretched across the section, with three crewmen on each line, to prevent my tumbling over the edge. At the shout of *"Action!"* I began the descent, rolling on a slope and dropping off nine feet, then rolling over a smooth white rock that was almost a straight fall.

The first line impeded my speed, but I couldn't grab it, I was rolling so fast. I grabbed the second rope, which further slowed me, but it slipped from my hand, leaving a rope burn on my skin. The third rope, about six yards away, stopped me. I rose to my feet, scraped, bruised, and disappointed. Raoul came over, and I told him:

"I didn't feel like it was a real good fall. Let's do it again."

He slapped me on the back and replied, with a wide grin, "Buster, it's good enough for the twenty-five-cent customers."

I also doubled Bogart lying dead in the dust. Marie, played by Ida, runs to her dead lover and strokes his hand. She cries and expresses a simple but poignant thought, "He's free...."

I'll never forget the tears streaming from Ida's beautiful blue eyes. I really felt she was crying for me.

After my fall on *High Sierra*, I never had to worry about finding work again. The more dangerous the stunt, the faster you built your reputation. As a stuntman, you had to be your own press agent. You sold yourself to a director, and if you delivered, you were in the select clique of stuntmen who worked regularly.

It's interesting that most stuntmen seldom studied acting. The director merely depended on the stuntman's natural ability to mimic the characteristics of the performers he doubled. I had a good eye for exciting stunts. On the set, I would always try to suggest a good action stunt for the director to use. This meant more work—and more money for me, of course.

My main training was running. Jogging is the rage today for healthy well-being, and it was for me too. I used to run seven miles a day. My body was my livelihood. You might call me a "Method Stuntman." The Stanislavski Method of Acting was named after the famous Russian director of the Moscow Art Theater, Konstantin Stanislavski, who devised a technique for actors to give a more realistic performance by actually *being* the character. I always tried to do the same thing when I was working on a stunt. I studied the script and learned the motivation for the action being performed by the actor I doubled. Prior to a fight scene, I would work myself into a frenzy and get my adrenalin flowing, to make it look real.

In November, I was down from the heights of the Sierra Mountains and back at Warner's Stage 21 for *The Sea Wolf*. The cavernous sound-stage was an architectural wonder. It held a specially-built ship, a three-masted schooner, 130 feet long with a thirty-two foot beam. The ship rested in a huge tank, five feet deep. I was a crew member aboard the *Ghost*. An expensive rocking mechanism made it seem as if the ship were truly being bounced around in the ocean.

Our captain was "Wolf Larsen," played by Edward G. Robinson. The real captain, of course, was Mike Curtiz. I had sailed with Mike on the same ship back in February, only then the vessel was called the *Albatross*, commanded by captain Errol Flynn, and the picture was *The Sea Hawk*. Flynn was as romantic and dashing as ever. I doubled Pedro de Cordoba in a scene where I was heaved over the side of a Spanish galleon. Several takes had to be filmed, and each time I had to fall very carefully to avoid hitting the thick oars.

As we were shooting *The Sea Wolf,* I was once again amazed by the ability of filmmakers to transform a movie set into a real image on the screen. Jack London's story made a great picture. I had read the book as a child and always remembered the scene of the brutal captain throwing a man over the side of the *Ghost* as punishment. A shark snaps off one of his legs. Barry Fitzgerald was the unfortunate guy who went over the side. Watching this wonderful actor convey the anguish of having a shark take off his leg was agonizing. I could feel its sharp teeth too!

In February of 1941, I was given my most unusual stunt task. *Out of the Fog* starred John Garfield and Ida Lupino, and Stage 21 had been made to look like Sheepshead Bay, on the East Coast. The waterfront set depicted a huge wharf and fishing bay. The scene called for Thomas Mitchell and John Qualen to pull in some live fish. Director Anatole Litvak gave me my assignment.

I slipped on a pair of pants with lead weights in them, hooked a live carp onto a fishing pole, and slipped under the water. On cue, when the line was pulled, I let the fish go. Litvak drove Jack Warner crazy with his curious technique of shooting numerous takes of the same scene. Thank heavens we got my underwater assignment wrapped up in three takes.

I never will forget my work in *Blues In The Nights.* The picture, directed by Litvak, was about the tempestuous lives of jazz musicians. There was a fight scene with Richard Whorf and Lloyd Nolan. Another guy and I were doubling the two actors for the fight. Anatole Litvak had us doing the fight for over a dozen takes! What he was looking for I'll never know. Maybe he didn't know either.

Whenever I received a call from Warner's or any other studio, offering me stunt-work, I was always ready for action, no matter how difficult or dangerous the assignment. Word spread that I was fast and dependable. I don't think I ever turned down a stunt job in my life. If the salary was right, I was right. One of my friends reported a remark he had overheard on a Warner's set. Director Lloyd Bacon was having problems with a slow stuntman.

Said Bacon: "Come on, man, hurry up and get this right, or we're going to call in Buster Wiles."

Only once did I have second thoughts about taking on a job. The studio telephoned me and asked me to work in the Bogart film, *The Wagons Roll At Night.* I was asked if I wanted to double Eddie Albert in a scene with a lion.

"I'm your man," came the reply.

On the set, the lion was somewhat nervous. He snapped at the trainer. I had been watching from a distance. Gee, I thought, should I refuse? Maybe let the trainer stay in the cage, pretending to be Eddie Albert? It's a sobering thought to know that a lion's jaws can snap a man's head clean off. What the hell—I'll give it a shot.

As I approached the cage, two enormous eyes turned and gave me the once-over. I could smell the lion's bad breath a foot away. The trainer and I got inside the cage together, and he introduced me to the big cat. I felt uneasy the entire time. Once the scene ended, I breathed a deep sigh of relief and got out of the cage as fast as I could. The lion gave a mighty roar, and those two brown eyes stared at me, as if saying, "I could have kept that head of yours."

Manpower had me executing another very risky stunt. This was a Warner A-picture, starring Marlene Dietrich, George Raft, Edward G. Robinson, and Alan Hale. The story involved telephone linemen fighting over the affections of beautiful Marlene. The tension on the set was electrifying too. Gossip spread that Raft and Robinson were vying for Marlene off-camera as well.

I was doubling Alan Hale in his action shots. Just watching on the set, it was apparent that Raft and Robinson weren't getting along. The stars' simmering feud exploded, and they came to blows. A furious Raft told me, "I slapped the hell out of him." A photographer for *Life* magazine just happened to be on the set, and the fisticuffs made Big News. I bought a copy of the magazine; as Raft passed one day, I pointed to the sensational layout.

"George, don't let this happen again."

He visibly stiffened and glared at me. "Look...." he began.

Before he could get any angrier, I jumped in: "Man, you're going to put me out of work."

A smile came over his face.

While the film was under way, Raoul Walsh spoke with me:

"Buster, can you climb a telephone pole seventy-two feet in the air?"

"Well, sure I can."

"Okay. You're going to double Hale in a scene where he climbs up a pole to rescue an injured lineman. You haul him down, but we're not using any dummy." His voice intensified. "I want realism!"

"I'm your man, Raoul."

I didn't know a damn thing about climbing telephone poles, but I could learn. I called the chief studio telephone technician, and he kindly agreed to meet me on the backlot. In those days, linemen used tiny hooks attached to their ankles and hands to "squirrel" up the wooden poles. The next day, George Raft, playing the injured lineman, was filmed on a platform about four feet high. Then I went to work. First, I had to pad my clothing, since Hale was a big guy, and I tried my best to resemble him. Duke Green doubled Raft.

The telephone pole was on a sound-stage, but the atmosphere was realistic, with rain pouring over me as I began my ascent. At the top, Duke was hoisted on my shoulders and I slowly came down. My ankles hurt so much the next day I could barely walk. The special-effects department created a superimposed thunderstorm, which blended well with my stunt. When I saw the picture, I was surprised that much of my pole climbing was a long shot. A dummy could have easily been used. I guess the only dummy was me. But Walsh wanted *realism.* Looking back over my career as a stuntman, I'm surprised that more daredevils weren't killed or injured. But there were many near misses.

River's End was a picture that nearly ended the life of my good buddy Cliff Lyons. Ray Enright directed this adventure story about the Canadian Mounties. We were shooting on location at June Lake, and Cliff and I had a rough fight scene to do. I was doubling Victor Jory, and Cliff was doubling Dennis Morgan. We were fighting near the edge of a cliff.

Somehow or another, Cliff tripped on a rope. He turned a flip, then smashed into a tree growing from the steep hillside. he managed to hold onto it, but I could tell by his dazed look that he was about to lose his grip. I jumped down and grabbed him. I held him tightly until a rope was thrown to us. On the way back, Cliff was driving, and I asked if he was all right. He began some tale about his aunt coming out from New York: he was still dazed from the fall.

"I'll drive, Cliff."

Cliff was a tiger, but sometimes the stunt was tougher.

In *Tugboat Annie Sails Again*, I was asked if I could play a drunken sailor who rides a bicycle off a pier—talk about perfect casting. When I arrived at the pier down in Long Beach, the director, Lewis Seiler, showed me how he wanted me to do it.

"I don't think that looks like he's drunk," I told him.

"Just do it."

I did it—his way. A few days later, I was called to do the shots over again—my way. It hadn't looked like the sailor was drunk the first time. I swore that, if I couldn't imitate a drunk, I would stop drinking. Here comes Buster down the pier, over the side and underwater, up to the surface. The director yelled that we would do another take.

"Why?"

"Your toupee is floating behind you!'

"Oh . . . ." Sometimes I wish I hadn't been scalped.

Warner's bought me four wigs to wear when I needed them. I sometimes wore one to a social event and then would casually let it fall off my head, which got a lot of laughs. It was a great way to meet people, especially women. Once you've got people laughing, you'll be friends in no time.

Bald men weren't supposed to be romantic figures, but I disproved that stereotype. Flynn and I would be driving along, when we would spot two girls walking along the sidewalk. One would be attractive, the other less so.

"Yours don't look so good," Flynn would say.

Well, before long, the ladies would be our guests for a cocktail or ice cream. Of course, they were dazzled by Errol Flynn, film star, but old Buster soon had them laughing, and I would turn on the charm.

"Let me light your cigarette, dear. Can I get you another drink?"

Then Flynn would turn on the courtesy, the charm, and finesse. We vied with each other for the attention of the loveliest, and often I would win a date.

"I guess she just likes those country boys from Memphis," I

would tell Errol.

But he accepted each loss philosophically. "There are many fish in the sea, Buster."

Santa Fe Trail was another Flynn Western with great actors in the cast, like Raymond Massey and Van Heflin. Also appearing was Ronald Reagan. I got to know Reagan when he was in *Hell's Kitchen.* He was just a contract player then, but was beginning to move up in the film world. This was due to his performance as the immortal George Gipp in *Knute Rockne—All American.* I wish Flynn could have lived long enough to see Reagan as President. He wouldn't believe it. I can hardly believe it myself.

The picture was about John Brown's raid on Harper's Ferry. I recall that Brown's granddaughter sued Warner Brothers because of her grandfather's image in the film.

I thought Flynn would get into a legal tangle with the studio also. The studio insisted that Errol was required to work more than eight hours a day. Flynn never liked being bested by Warner Brothers. The production got behind schedule, and the studio wanted the crew to work day and night. Flynn refused to work after 6:00 p.m. Eventually, it was determined that everyone was exhausted from working day and night, so work after 6:00 was halted. But we always worked on Saturdays. The glamor of motion pictures is missing in the actual filmmaking process. It's hard, tedious work.

In *Santa Fe Trail,* I doubled Van Heflin, and Don Turner doubled Flynn in a fight scene. Once, a friend of mine asked why he never saw my name listed in the credits of the movies I worked on. Early in my stunt career, I often asked myself the same question, but I came to realize the rationale behind the decision. Jack Warner and other studio bosses opposed any lessening of the illusion that screen heroes weren't gods. No glory for me. I was just happy to be having a ball, and the money was great.

I was fortunate in having Flynn as a friend, for he informed me whenever his salary rose, then I could expect more as his stunt double. Flynn approached contract renewals like a boxer out for a kill. His opponent, Jack Warner, was a skilful adversary who never gave an inch, unless pressured. He and Flynn would lock horns whenever contract talks were under way. But, deep down, they liked one another.

Jack Warner seldom came to the set when a film was being shot; he didn't have to. He had spies everywhere. These secret informers told him who was drinking or who was stealing props or costumes. Whenever Warner would suddenly appear on Flynn's set, they would banter back and forth. I was present one day when the studio chief unexpectedly showed up. He was "Mr. Warner" to me, but Errol always greeted him as "Spider," or some such term. They exchanged small talk, then Warner turned to leave.

"Oh," said Errol, pointing up at the catwalk, "would you mind taking your stool-pigions with you? They've been leaving their droppings on me all day."

Warner just laughed, but the spies remained.

In July of 1941, we began *They Died With Their Boots On,* a classic adventure film, and one of my favorites. Errol was superb as General George Armstrong Custer. The story was somewhat fictionalized, but audiences loved the action, fighting, and romance. I doubled Flynn as Custer, and played calvary troopers and Indians too. The production called for lots of stuntwork—dangerous stunts.

I almost injured myself, soon after the cameras began rolling. The stunt was "a breeze." We were on Stage 12, where Custer visits Elizabeth Bacon, his bride-to-be. I watched as Errol and Olivia de Havilland met in the Bacon residence, with Hattie McDaniel chaperoning their encounter. He and Olivia were simply wonderful, playing their scenes with humor and charm. Flynn was really an underestimated actor. He made it look too easy on-screen, but who else could wear a uniform with such elegant style or handle a sword or a lady with such magnetic charm? He pretended not to care too much for acting, but, as far as I could tell, he always did his best to make each character he played come alive. In later years, Eddie Albert complemented Flynn on his acting expertise. At first, Errol thought he was kidding, then when Albert made clear the sincerity of his admiration, tears came to Flynn's eyes.

While shooting the scenes at the Bacon home, I was called on to perform what I thought was a relatively easy assignment. The shot required Custer to jump from the bannister of the Bacon home to a tree. He throws a kiss to his lady, then jumps down. In the early morning, before the cameras rolled, I studied the situation. I put a triangular piece of wood in the tree fork to prevent ankle injuries, then I had a thick mattress brought in to break my leap. After lunch, Raoul Walsh explained how he wanted the stunt performed. At the sound of "Action," I ran along the balcony, stepped onto a short bannister, and leaped into the tree. I threw a kiss and jumped. In mid-air, I was aghast to find that my mattress was gone. Instinctively, I doubled in a ball and rolled—I was lucky that I didn't break my ankle or leg. I was lucky a lot in several harrowing near-misses on horseback.

Jack Budlong wasn't as fortunate. On July 30, I was at the Warner Ranch for a dangerous battle sequence. I was doubling Flynn in a Civil War skirmish. Custer was in the lead of a charging group of Union riders, out to seize a bridge. Jack Budlong was riding next to me. He was a nice kid, who had just inherited a large sum of money, at least a million. Jack was a well-known polo player, who had squared off against Flynn in several matches. As we sat astride our horses, waiting for the scene to start, we chatted. I asked Jack what he was doing *working*. He replied that he enjoyed riding and being in films.

"Boy, if I had your money, I would be traveling."

I noticed that his horse was becoming difficult to handle. "Jack," I said, "you're going to be bringing up the rear of this charge, if you don't wake up that horse."

We rehearsed the scene a few times and were ready.

In the distance, a red flag dropped. At this signal, Jack and I led dozens of riders, four abreast, down a dusty road toward the bridge. Beside us, mines began exploding, as if cannon fire were striking. We galloped at full speed, with sabers held aloft. As we neared the bridge, Jack's horse started bucking. I reined in my steed to keep away. Apparently, he expected to be thrown, for he hurled his saber to get rid of it. At that very instant, his stirrup broke, and the horse bucked. Jack slammed against the horse's rump, then was tossed in a complete somersault.

Tragically, the saber he had flung landed on its hilt, and poor Jack was impaled on it. The sharp sword went through his back and out the other side. I sharply veered the men away to prevent his being trampled to death. When I swung around, I saw Jack staggering to his feet. He tottered to the side of the road, where a kid named Jim Snyder gently eased him down, put his knee against Jack's back, and withdrew the saber. Our first-aid man, Roy

"Bullet" Baker, rushed up and helped Jack into the rear seat of an awaiting car.

The driver hesitated. I jumped inside and drove as fast as I could, hitting speeds of ninety miles per hour. I was trying to attract a police car to obtain an escort. It's a wonder I didn't get us all killed. When I hit Yucca and Cahuenga, the traffic stopped. The tires squealed as I made a sharp right turn through the lot of a Richfield gas station. We made it to Cedars of Lebanon Hospital in one piece.

"Buster, when you call my wife, be kind of soft telling her the news . . . . We're going to have a baby."

"Jack, I can't call . . . ."

Bullet offered to do it.

Errol phoned the hospital every day to inquire about Jack's progress. Unfortunately, complications set in, and Jack died August 5.

Jack's passing was a somber reminder of lurking danger, unexpected, swift as lightning. I wonder how many guys have died making pictures. That day, I believe, I shed lightheartedness and eagerness in stunt-work. In my mind's eye, there always remained the image of the tragic death of Jack Budlong.

We filmed the battle of the Little Big Horn at the Lasky Ranch, in Agoura. I was constantly busy, performing several dangerous stunts. I doubled Flynn on horseback, when General Custer and the calvary chase the redskins, then I donned a beautiful Indian costume with a long headdress and led the charge against the cornered Seventh Calvary. My mount was a white horse that had been ridden by Rudolph Valentino in *The Sheik*.

I had many challenging stunts on horseback, including a fierce gallop toward the doomed calvarymen. One set-up had me riding at a furious pace, then leaping from my horse into a group of troopers. I reined in my horse so fast, I was lucky it didn't fall, but I sailed through the air at such a speed that, when I struck the ground—*bam*—my leather moccasins shredded. They just disintegrated.

For the close-ups, Yakima Canutt doubled Flynn, and Cliff Lyons was the Indian who attacked him. I was busy taking arrows in the back from Howard Hill. I doubled Charley Grapewin for Howard to shoot two arrows into the cork padding under my buckskin jacket. The cork was so thick that I couldn't feel anything, so a crewman stood nearby, and as the arrows hit home, he fired a pistol to signal for my jerking reaction. No one seemed to notice that, in the next shot, a close-up of Flynn and Charley, only one arrow was visible. With all the improvised stunt-work, I made quite a sum on this picture, especially the action sequences of the Little Big Horn fight. This was Errol's first picture with Raoul Walsh at the helm, and it turned out to be an enduring classic.

Warner Bros. publicity still for *They Died With Their Boots On*. The leap where my moccasins disintegrated. *(photo: Buster Wiles Collection. Property of Warner Bros., Inc. Used by permission.)*

Exact moment the arrow fired by Howard Hill strikes the prune atop my head. *(photo: Courtesy of Budget Films. © 1945 The Vitaphone Corp. Ren. 1973 United Artists Television, Inc.)*

EIGHT

Laughter

"He who tickles himself may laugh when he pleases."

At the end of September, *They Died With Their Boots On* was completed. The final week of filming had seen me spending long hours in the saddle and in the dust, fighting the Battle of Little Big Horn. On payday, I collected my huge earnings and happened onto an impromptu craps game. Flynn watched as I took off on a winning streak. The dice were hot in my hands, and I cleaned out my opponents. Back in Flynn's dressing room, I counted my profits. There was $10,000 in cash.

"Hey, this week you made more money than I did," said Flynn.

"Yessir!" I cheerfully responded.

"Let's go to New York for three months."

"New York is not getting one nickel of my money, Flynn."

"It won't cost you a cent, Buster."

My resistance faded. "How's that?"

"I'm scheduled to do five radio shows. I get five-thousand dollars for each program. You'll get some roles and some money, then we simply put all the cash in a box, and we spend every penny of it."

"When do we leave?" I asked.

"Go home and pack, and we're off," said Errol.

"I'm ready now."

"Where's your stuff?"

"I'm standing in the middle of my wardrobe."

It was no wonder that Flynn wanted to get away. He had just finished a tough picture, but he had personal problems as well. His marriage to Lili had unraveled, even though a son, Sean, had been born in May. The Myron Selznick Agency was suing him for breach of contract and asking for $58,250. The agency had even attached his salary during the lawsuit. Errol told the court that he needed $14, 595 as "necessary monthly expenses."

Newspapers printed these personal woes, as well as a much-publicized fight with columnist Jimmie Fidler. The week before the incident, Fidler had testified before a Senate committee and denounced Hollywood producers for making "pro-British propaganda" films. This testimony occurred during "the great debate" over American foreign policy. The Roosevelt Administration was determined to throw the might of the United States on the side of Great Britain as soon as it could be sure of public support. Isolationists were out to prove, in the Senate interstate commerce subcommittee hearings, that a few men controlling the motion-picture industry were resolved to plunge the nation into war.

A few days before Fidler testified in Washington, a public uproar swept the country when Charles Lindbergh made a speech accusing the British, the Jewish, and the Roosevelt Administration of being "the three most important groups which have been pressing this country towards war." For various reasons, from sincere pacifist to pro-German, Americans were asked not to support Britain.

As the *Los Angeles Examiner* described the incident: "Reverberations of the Senate committee hearings investigating movie war propaganda echoed early yesterday morning on the floor of a Hollywood nightclub with a flurry of words and blows between Errol Flynn, actor, and Jimmie Fidler."

On the evening of September 21, at the Mocambo Club, Errol approached a table where the influential writer sat with his wife. As Flynn later told reporters: "I didn't like what Fidler said about the motion-picture business, so I went up to his table and told him what I thought about him. I put my left fist against his chin and gave him a slap with my right on the side of the head. I said, 'You're not worth a fist.'"

Fidler went to court, complaining that "I make my living with my mouth, and if he should punch me so hard I couldn't talk, it would cost me thousands of dollars."

Besides the political aspect of the incident, Errol seethed over comments Fidler made regarding the death of Flynn's beloved pet schnauzer, Arno. Poor Arno had disappeared from the *Sirocco* one night while at sea—most probably he went after a flying fish and drowned. We had everybody from the Boy Scouts to the Coast Guard searching for him. The Coast Guard eventually found his lifeless body, returned Arno's collar, and disposed of Arno's remains. Fidler infuriated Errol by stating that he didn't bother to claim his dog's body. Flynn was devastated by Arno's death and brooded over Fidler's cruel comments. If Errol had a pet alligator, you couldn't call it ugly without risking Flynn's wrath. That's how much he loved animals. But he was genuinely angry over Fidler's Washington testimony, and Hollywood rallied around his bold action in confronting the gossip writer.

Lawyers and reporters besieged Errol by the time we packed our suitcases and sped to the airport. We flew to Chicago, then drove to Madison, Wisconson, where Flynn had arranged a romantic interlude. He was meeting a beautiful young woman from an extremely wealthy and prominent family, an aspiring actress who attended the University of Wisconsin. When we registered at our classy hotel, the house detective immediately suspected something fishy.

It was no wonder. Flynn wore fake sideburns and a phony mustache. He spoke with a German accent and gave himself the title of "Professor." It was one of his worst performances. Errol had taken three adjoining suites, so he and his lady could see one another in private. But we couldn't shake the house dick. Everytime I turned around, he was watching us. I decided to confront him. He played dumb, then admitted his curiosity.

"That guy looks like Errol Flynn, but he's too goofy."

He was really confused. Flynn managed to have his romantic rendezvous and treated his paramour like a little queen. We left Madison and were only two miles out of town when I told Flynn to turn around. "I'm gonna drive that guy crazy."

I went back in the hotel and ran up to the detective. I excitedly shouted, "Oh, help me, help me! He's loose! I can't find him. He's a lunatic and dangerous!"

The poor bastard's eyes got as wide as saucers. "I knew it! I knew he was nuts!"

He took off running down the hall, and that was the last I ever saw of him. In New York, Errol and his girlfriend met again. At a chic restaurant, she introduced us to her socialite friends. As part of our inside gag, I now wore the fake mustache and was presented as "the Professor." She soon returned to Madison, eventually becoming a well-known actress and marrying a big star.

After the departure of his wealthy flame, Errol began attending the ballet and introduced me to his latest passion, a gorgeous prima donna who had appeared in a Warner Brother's short. Flynn never lacked female admirers. Never. As Errol was wont to say, "There are many fish in the sea."

The last time I had seen New York, I had to leave town on the bum. Now Flynn and I were sharing a suite on the thirty-second floor of the Ritz Hotel. This was pretty high living for a boy from Memphis. Flynn loved New York. He liked walking down the busy streets. Unfortunately, fans would see him and go wild. As we approached the Ritz at Park Avenue and 57th streets, throngs of people would be waiting. We were pushing through a mob when a girl screamed in Errol's ear, "I saw you in *Robin Hood!*"

"What do you want? You're money back?" asked Errol.

Everyone wanted to meet him. At the Ritz, we became acquainted with Mr. and Mrs. Charles Marcus. He was vice-president of the Bendix Aviation Corp. They were in the upper echelon of New York high society, and very nice people. We were their guests when they had afternoon cocktails.

Flynn and I would often pass the time in the bar at the Ritz. Once, a friend of ours, Pat De Cicco, came in with his future bride, Gloria Vanderbilt. I was feeling in high spirits, and I started biting off the boles of champagne glasses and "eating" them. Gloria was astounded by this trick and said she would do it too. I think she was serious. "Wait!" I yelled. I suppose I did the fashion world a favor. But if someone back then would have told me that Gloria Vanderbilt would be selling jeans today, I would have scoffed, "Sure, and Reagan's going to be president!"

We also met another fascinating heiress. Doris Duke was the daughter of the founder of the American Tobacco Company. Doris had a 2,500 acre home in Somerville, New Jersey, and she had another mansion called Shangrila in Honolulu. She was the richest woman in the world; she took pride in being able to give away one-million dollars a year.

"It's a tough job," she said.

Doris and I would often go out on dates. She was a very generous person; she offered to buy me anything I wanted.

"Thanks, Doris, but I'm working."

She and I frequented the Copacabana and also John Perona's El Morocco. One night, we stopped by the Marcus place so they could accompany us. Mrs. Marcus opened large drawers that were filled with dazzling gems—one drawer alone was filled with diamond jewelry. She was dressed in gems from head to toe. Doris couldn't believe her eyes. "Who in the hell is that?" she mumbled.

* * * * *

Errol had his radio programs lined up. In those days, a star could make a lucrative income just by radio alone. He began with Kate Smith's program on October 10, 1941. Thereafter, he appeared on *Calvacade*, *The Eddie Cantor Show*, *Silver Theater*, and the *Phillip Morris* programs. I had a few lines to say in each show.

Errol starred in a radio version of *They Died With Their Boots On*. I excitedly held my script, waiting for my big line. As Custer arrives in Washington to see President Grant, I emoted with every ounce of drama I could muster: "I'm sorry Mr. Custer, but the president will not see you. . . . Wait! Where are you going? But you can't go in there!"

Apparently, my Southern twang had stuck out like a sore thumb. Later that evening, we were guests of John Perona at the El Morocco. John sat at our table, and a waiter appeared with an expensive ($36) bottle of Piper-Heidseck champagne. Perona then asked me: "How did a Southerner ever get in Grant's office?"

"Bad casting?"

"Buster, you would make a great character actor, but I sat up straight when I heard your voice in Yankee Washington."

Perona asked why I didn't become an actor, rather than a stuntman.

"John," I joked, "I just can't overtax my mentality with

burdensome dialogue."

"What are you, a half-wit?" retorted Perona.

"Well, that's better than none."

Each time I would enter the El Morocco, John Perona would see me and call out in a mock Southern accent; "You cain't come in here."

Many people have asked my why I never pursued my once-cherished acting dream. I could have been a character actor, especially in Westerns. I was indeed a member of the Screen Actors Guild (card 1738) and even had speaking lines in several films. The truth was I felt I could earn more as a stuntman. I would certainly work more often. And besides, I was always a leading man off-camera.

With all the parties and bar-hopping, Flynn and I tried to keep in shape by boxing at the Racquet Club. Whenever things got dull, I tried to liven up the situation. One afternoon, the phone rang in our suite. It was a reporter.

"Errol's not here now," I told him.

"It's you I want to talk to," he responded.

Was I ever surprised! The reporter was from a magazine called *Candide,* and he wanted to interview a real Hollywood stuntman. I was honored and decided to give him a good story. Before he arrived, I opened the window of our thirty-second-floor suite. There was a ledge and cornice where I could step out and cling to the building. When the reporter entered our suite, I asked him: "Say, do you mind if I step outside for a breath of fresh air?"

"Oh, no, let's go downstairs." He turned toward the door.

"That's too far," I said. I opened the window, and the guy's eyes stared in disbelief as I clung to the side of the building. Flashbulbs popped. The entire interview was conducted with me straddling eternity. As I spoke to him, the wind whipped my hat off. It floated to the pavement far below. Later, we went over to 47th Street, where I did a trick of having a taxi "hit" me, then rolled off the hood. I sensed that the reporter thought I was really nuts.

Flynn had slept during my interview and was disappointed that he hadn't witnessed my antics. But Errol managed to play a prank that remained one of his most famous. While in New York, he was to receive a movie recognition award. Before the ceremony, a press conference was arranged. Flynn had mischief in mind.

"What can we do to upset them?" he asked.

I had a great idea, which I explained to Flynn. He loved it. We had made friends with two fun-loving cigarette girls who worked at the El Morocco nightclub. I spoke with them, and they readily agreed to play key roles in our charade. In the midst of our large living-room suite, Flynn gave a cough. At this signal, the luscious girls emerged from our respective bedrooms at opposite ends of the living room. One was clad in my pajama tops, and the other the bottoms. That was all. You could have heard a pin drop. The newsmen practically broke their necks trying to get a better view. The girls were wonderful, acting natural, as if nothing was out of the ordinary. Flynn was great, too, playing the scene with a straight face.

"Gentlemen, don't you have any more questions?" he asked.

The two girls whispered to one another, then strolled off.

One evening when we were at a nightclub in New York, the waiter handed me a note: "Aren't you going to say hello, handsome? Dinah." I looked around, and there was lovely Dinah Shore. Flynn and I had met her in Boston. She was making quite a name for herself on *The Eddie Cantor Show;* she had a unique voice. She and I got to chatting and each discovered that the other was from Tennessee. We hit it off. Everybody seems to get older, but not Dinah. She is still beautiful.

We were having a great time in New York. One evening, when I was getting ready for a night on the town, Flynn saw me make a withdrawal from our bank account.

"Say, Buster, aren't you dipping into the box a little too often?"

"Well, that was our agreement, wasn't it? Everybody knows you, Errol. I've got to get acquainted."

"*Acquainted?* Every bar I enter, the bartender asks when is Buster Wiles coming back?"

"Well, I'm making friends. It's working. 'Night, Errol."

Harry Warner, Jack's elder brother, let us use his private box at the racetrack. There was a horse running called "Marriage." I got a strange hunch this baby was going to win. "This is our winner, Flynn."

"Which one?"

"Marriage."

The name was enough to set him off. After Lili, he was

convinced that matrimony was not for him. Said Errol: "I wouldn't bet on that nag if its nose was a half-inch from the finish line!"

I placed two ten-dollar bets. Returning to our box, I found a ticket someone had dropped. My hunch paid off, and Marriage won the race. Flynn just stared, with his mouth wide open, as I gleefully counted my winnings. Only one guy loved to win at the track more than Errol Flynn, and that was Buster Wiles.

Flynn and I got bored one night. I had been telling him about my days in New York, when I had to hustle newspapers to stay alive.

"Hey, let's do that!" said Errol excitedly.

We dressed as poor folks. To avoid being recognized, Flynn wore his fake mustache and sideburns. Our goal was to earn enough money to buy a meal. "Paper!" we shouted.

We earned a little money, but not as much as we had expected. We then walked in a restaurant and begged a meal. The manager told us to keep walking. We retreated to the restroom to wash the fake soot from our faces. A black attendant was offering gentlemen a fresh towel and cologne. We told him of our plight. "I'm starving," I said.

He took pity on us.

"Well, I get a little something from here, and I also bring a lunch sack from home. Here . . . ." He offered me a paper sack with food in it.

"Thanks," we told him.

We began freshening up. Flynn removed his fake mustache and sideburns, then peeled off a twenty and handed it to the attendant.

"What's you name?" he asked.

"Flynn."

We thanked him again, then entered the lounge for a drink. Word spread through the bar that Flynn the actor had arrived. The manager came over and offered us a drink.

"Get lost," I said. "You had your chance to feed us."

"Oh, it was you two!" he said, rather confused.

Flynn identified with down-and-out characters. He had been adrift during his youth and knew what it was like to be broke. He could be generous to someone who was really in need, but he was no sucker for a hard-luck story; he investigated things. If he knew a person really needed money, he gave it freely, and he tried to help a lot of guys. Unfortunately, many of them took advantage of him.

When news spread that Flynn was staying at the Ritz, baskets of letters arrived, including many requests for money. Errol asked a hotel official to sort out which were the truly needy cases and which were phoney pleas. Quite a sum of money, about five-thousand dollars, was given by Flynn to charitable organizations and destitute families.

Before we left New York, I met a fellow in a typical Buster Wiles situation. I was on my way to a debutante party for Leonore Lummons. As I approached the building, I saw two thugs beating on a guy who had just emerged from a taxi. Unfair odds. I rushed in and drove the two away. The dapper fellow brushed himself off.

"I'm Spencer Martin. Can I buy you a drink?"

I explained that I was on my way to a party. It turned out he was headed to the same event. He and I entered the festivities together, and he introduced me to his high-society friends. Each guest was given a bottle of champagne, courtesy of millionaire playboy, Tommy Manville, a man famous for his many wives and his lavish way of spending money. It was a magnificent party, a wonderful finale to my fun-filled months in New York. On my way home from the gala event, I happened to pass the spot in front of Loew's Theater where I had hustled papers years before. Now I had just completed a fabulous trip, courtesy of Errol Flynn.

Just as Flynn had promised, we spent the thousands that came from the radio shows and had a million dollars worth of laughs.

On his return to Hollywood, Errol was lionized as a conquering hero. His bout with isolationist Jimmie Fidler had raised his stature in the eyes of his peers. At a party given by Ben and Bebe Lyon, he was the center of congratulations. Photos showed him being hailed by Louella Parsons, Virginia Zanuck, George Burns, Edward G. Robinson, and others. Just a few days later, the isolationist movement came to a sudden, unexpected end.

In Los Angeles, Errol had his fifth and final radio show at the NBC studios on the corner of Sunset and Vine. It was December 7, 1941, and we were in the midst of a rehearsal with Ralph Bellamy, when an excited engineer shouted from the control room: "The Japs have bombed Pearl Harbor!"

We rushed to the teletype room and stared incredulously at the white sheet that poured out the horrible news. Surprisingly, the show went on the air. But the lives of Americans had changed overnight. We were now in the war.

The end of 1941 was momentous in a personal way too. My marriage ended. Dolly had been a patient wife, but Buster just wasn't able to settle down. Once, I went out to buy Dolly her favorite ice cream. On the way home, I saw a buddy of mine whose car was stalled. I helped him get his car running, then he invited me to Palm Springs for a day of fun. I came home ten days later, but I had the ice cream.

"It's the wrong flavor," fumed Dolly.

"Honey, let me go and exchange it."

"Don't you dare!"

I took it for granted that I could do as I pleased. I was wrong. Dolly told the judge that I used our home just to change clothes. Though we divorced, there was never any deep animosity between us. We managed to stay good friends.

Unfortunately, when Errol and Lili split up, there was a lot of bitterness, which increased over the years. Newspapers reported that Lili received custody of Sean, $18,000 a year alimony, and a share of community property estimated to be worth $150,000. But Flynn was relieved that the tempestuous marriage had ended. He had a new love—Mulholland Farm. Before our New York trip, Errol had driven me up Laurel Canyon to Mulholland Drive. We snaked our way along the highway, then Flynn turned onto a steep, dusty road. He said that this was all his property. He pointed out where he planned to have a home constructed. Now, after two months in New York, work had progressed. The home was situated high in the mountains, with a sweeping view of the San Fernando Valley far below.

We strolled through the partially-completed house, with Errol pointing out the living room and so on. Since I was now single, Errol kindly invited me to live at Mulholland Farm. Until it was thoroughly finished, we lived at Bruce Cabot's residence. I liked Bruce, as Flynn did. When Bruce was short of money, which was often, Errol provided a loan. Then Flynn would find him roles in films, just so Bruce could pay back what was owed.

Along with his new home, Flynn had another expensive item awaiting him after returning from New York—a custom-made Darrin convertible. As we tested it with a cruise down Sunset,

Flynn asked how I liked the car.

"There's just one thing wrong," I said.

"What's that?"

"It's too slow."

I stripped my hot rod of its dual carburetors and mounted them on the convertible. Now it had speed. It had something special, too. There was a lever so the front passenger seat reclined. Flynn let me use the sleek convertible as if it were my own. When word of the sensational seat got around everyone at Warners would hover about the car to take a look. Of course, Flynn's devilish reputation grew. It was nice living it up but after Pearl Harbor I thought for certain it was just a matter of time before I was drafted.

On February 2, 1942, Flynn and I were scheduled to take our physical exams for the Selective Service Board. I stood in line behind Errol as an Army clerk questioned him. The clerk didn't bother to look up but merely barked out questions.

"Name?"

"Errol Flynn."

"Profession?"

"Actor."

"Weekly income?"

"$6000."

The clerk looked up with an unbelieving expression on his face.

"What did you say?" When I met Errol afterwards he quietly said: "Heart murmur and tuberculosis." Errol had known about his heart condition but diagnosis of tuberculosis came as a surprise. But, as serious as the disease was, he didn't go to pieces. It was not an advanced case but Errol did begin resting more. The news came in the middle of *Desperate Journey,* a war film about an RAF bomber crew which crashes in Germany. The script called for a lot of action sequences after dark. Errol didn't want to work at night due to the damp air. Warner Bothers felt he was malingering but only a few people were ever informed of his tuberculosis. For a while he would sleep twelve to fourteen hours a night.

The studio released the information that Flynn was disqualified from military service due to a heart murmur. This was something that puzzled the public, since Errol looked healthy, and during the war years, he would star in heroic action pictures that required energy and stamina. But the physicians made the rules.

Just a few months earlier, while we were in New York, Errol confided to me that he was in touch with British Intelligence. I had accompanied Flynn to the office of British Security Coordination, where William Stephenson directed secret warfare against the Nazis. Flynn went up to their headquarters on the thirty-fifth floor of the International Building in Rockefeller Center, while I waited in the lobby. I'm not certain when his relationship with British Intelligence began, but it is possible that it dated back to his South American goodwill tour, in the summer of 1940. It was actually a Warner's publicity tour, but it became a rousing political event, as Errol made speeches promoting democracy and denouncing the Nazis.

The conflict in Europe worsened for Britain in April 1940, when the German armies marched into Denmark and Norway, and the next month into Holland, Belgium, and Luxembourg. In June came the heroic evacuation of the British fleet from Dunkirk. At that time, America was officially neutral, but British agents were doing everything possible to sway American opinion to assist Britain as it fought the Nazis alone.

Both the United States and Britain were worried about the inroads the Nazis were making in South America. In June, Flynn flew to Brazil, Argentina, Chile, and Mexico, where he came to Britain's defense in speeches and public appearances. In Santiago, he was the featured guest of Sir Charles Bentinck, British Ambassador to Chile, at a Red Cross banquet. *La Defensa* newspaper published on its front page a note, written in Flynn's own hand:

> With every hope for your success which, from your anti-Nazi policy, should be of great importance to every lover of liberty.
> Errol Flynn
>
> June 25, 1940

Errol met numerous government officials throughout South America, exchanging conversations and opinions. On his return, he told reporters of the growing tide of Nazi infiltration in South America. Said Flynn: "The United States is still in a dream and has not awakened to the grave dangers organized minorities are precipitating. I made it my business to investigate fifth-column activities. The danger for America is very near."

In later years, it was revealed that such celebrities as Leslie Howard, Greta Garbo, and Noel Coward had functioned as British agents. In September, Errol confronted Jimmie Fidler, the very prominent figure who had testified in Washington about "Pro-British propaganda." Looking back, this seems to have been a calculated gesture.

While we were in New York, Errol explained that he had a plan for us to travel to Europe as tourists. On our return, we would report to British Intelligence what we had observed. Everything looked fine. I was ready to telephone columnist Sheila Graham about Errol's overseas vacation, when Flynn said the trip was off.

Why the journey never took place I'm not certain; possibly, it was due to Errol's citizenship status. He had applied for U.S. citizenship, but had not yet been naturalized. While safe in neutral countries, he would have been in jeopardy in occupied Europe, since he was internationally know as a British hero, especially after his anti-Nazi statements in South America.

Flynn's high esteem in the eyes of the U.S. government was verified when he was contacted by William J. Donovan, founder of the OSS, for a special assignment relayed through the Hollywood Victory Committee. On January 24, 1941, I accompanied Errol to a recording studio on Vermont. From here, he made a special patriotic broadcast that was beamed to Australia.

Due to his heart murmur, Errol's contribution to the war effort would be his patriotic films, which greatly bolstered public morale. In addition, there would be USO and bond tours.

Ironically, years later, a worthless biography would claim that Flynn was a Nazi spy. The book is utter trash. I knew Errol Flynn for twenty-four years. Needless to say, I got to know him very well, almost as if we were brothers. Never did I hear him say the least sympathetic comment toward Hilter, Nazism, or Fascism. His opinion of the Nazis was one of detestation. He was a fervent admirer of President Roosevelt and democracy.

According to the appallingly incorrect biography, Flynn was also a Jew hater and racist. Lies. Flynn had no animosity against any creed or race. He simply accepted or rejected people for what they were. The vicious book about Flynn is filled with so many lies and inaccuracies, it's amazing it was ever published. Believe me, I knew Errol Flynn *very well.*

The Manpower Commission in Washington ruled that the motion-picture studios were invaluable in the war effort. Therefore, our occupations were judged as highly essential, and deferments were given to a vast array of jobs, ranging from animators to cameramen, writers, editors, and technicians. The studio asked me to join a special film unit to produce military training films, covering every aspect of a serviceman's life.

I spent countless hours before the camera, working for free. Warners supplied a great deal of combat footage, and I was constantly being blown out of foxholes, tanks, and trucks, along with my colleagues, Harvey Perry, Duke Green, Alan Pomeroy, and Jack Woody.

Flynn was so eager to reside at Mulholland Farm that we left Cabot's comfortable home on Kings Road rather prematurely. When I walked inside Mulholland House, I stopped dead in my tracks. It was empty, except for two pieces of furniture—a large, custom-made chair and a long sofa.

"Where are the beds?" I asked.

"I don't know," responded Errol, rather perplexed. "They were supposed to be here today."

For a few nights, we flipped a coin to see who got the sofa. I usually won and awoke feeling refreshed, while Flynn awoke groaning.

Mulholland Farm was to be my home until March 1944. Flynn delighted in telling everyone that he had invited me for breakfast, and I stayed three-and-a-half years. The days spent at Mulholland were some of the happiest of my life. My bedroom was at the top of the stairs. Flynn's master bedroom was just down the hall from me. He often slept in the den just below, which was his favorite room, where he enjoyed writing stories and novels seated at his desk, overlooking the oval swimming pool. On the wall was a portrait of his idol, John Barrymore.

In the den, we would work on his scripts, with me feeding him lines. In later years, he added another huge wing that was entered through the den. In this wing was the famous bedroom with the secret mirror, which, to my knowledge, was only used a couple of times. Once while Australian playboy Freddy McEvoy was in bed with a girlfriend, and another time while Bruce Cabot was making love.

When Flynn and his stand-in, Jim Fleming, admitted that they had peeked, Cabot was furious. I thought Flynn and Bruce would come to blows, but after tempers flared, they backed off, and a fight was avoided. News of the secret mirror spread so fast that it was an open joke among Flynn's friends. It became a prop that was not meant to be actually used, but only to shock.

Freddy McEvoy was a good pal, whom Errol liked. He was an easygoing guy, and his first wife was Beatrice Cartwright, an older woman and heiress to the Standard Oil fortune. His second wife was Irene Wrightsman, another wealthy woman. Freddy claimed to be a sports promoter, but I seldom saw him working. He would accompany Flynn and me on fishing trips, and he brought us one of the original hydraulic spear guns that we used while snorkeling.

Jim Fleming had started with Flynn as butler. He was a curious man—whenever he was around, I would count the silverware. I thought he had light fingers. Jim placed me in an awkward situation once, and I never forgot the incident. Flynn had a cellar where he stored expensive champagne, wine, and liquor. Fleming walked off with a case of Scotch. I saw him leaving with it. A while later, Errol noticed it was missing. Since I lived there, he looked at me as if I were the culprit. "Ask around, someone else took it," I said.

About a week later, Flynn was still angry because none of his friends had owned up to taking the booze. That afternoon, a driver brought Flynn home from the studio, and next to him was Jim Fleming. I was seething. I walked up to the car and hissed: "Step out of that car, Fleming. I'm gonna take your head off your shoulders." He just sat there, but Flynn knew who had stolen his booze.

Another time, at the Burbank Airport, Freddy McEvoy said something I didn't like. I told him to step out of the car. I ended up chasing him around and around the car until he apologized. When it came to anybody—friend or foe—I never backed down from a fight. But usually we all got along pretty well at Mulholland.

All of Errol's friends had a common trait—holding a cocktail glass, day or night, and I was no exception. Flynn had his vodka. He had a fabulous bar, with a bullfight mural behind it. The painting was by Australian artist Henry Clive. Flynn loved fine art. Nothing was more precious to him than his Gauguin, entitled "Au Bord du Mer." It depicted a Tahitian native, holding the hand of a small boy. He also owned original paintings by Van Gogh and Manet. These had been acquired through his talented artist friend John Decker.

Flynn was always eager to have a good time, and the estate was designed for his athletic activities, with a pool and a riding stable. But the most fun Errol had was on his tennis court. He loved to play. On the sidelines, making bets, would be John Decker, Norman Kerry, John Barrymore, W.C. Fields, Mickey Rooney, and Raoul Walsh. These were familiar faces, but anyone famous could be at Errol's on a Sunday afternoon. And, of course, there were always women around. I would be on the sidelines, cheering the player I had money on, when some sweet young thing would float by.

"Do you play, Buster?"

"No, honey, it's a racket. Let's go for a swim."

Beautiful women came to Mulholland like bees to honey. There was never a dull moment. If things got slow, we always thought of a way to liven things up. One of my favorite gags was the time I invited eleven British flyers to Mulholland for cocktails and dinner. Unfortunately, Errol was in Mexico and missed this wonderful scene. I welcomed the boys into the house and showed them around. At the bar, I lined up the bottles.

"Help yourselves, gentlemen. My secretary should be here to fix your drinks, but she's late."

I ushered the group into the dining room, where we sat comfortably at a long Chippendale table, waiting for the lavish meal to begin. I rang the service bell. Through the doorway, there was a spiral staircase, and one by one, heads turned in that direction—gazing at a pair of slim legs descending the stairs. An absolutely naked girl breezed into the dining room.

"Buster, I'm sorry I'm late. I was delayed in traffic."

I acted, as she did, as if nothing were out of the ordinary. Man, the look on those bewildered faces was priceless. They didn't know what to think.

But gags like this had to be carefully planned. Flynn had a French cook name Marie, who would raise hell at such shenanigans. She was quite religious and would threaten to quit whenever a guy would knock on her door during a rowdy party or a lady would flit about the house in some stage of undress. Flynn had mirrors carefully arranged in the house so that, at night, there was a stunning effect whereby moonlight would filter from room to room. I recall one summer night, at the height of a wild party, when folks began tossing their clothes to the wind. Soon, everyone was in the buff, diving and splashing in the pool. That was stunning too! We had a few parties so wild an animal trainer couldn't handle them.

Flynn didn't like to pay for romance. Why should he? He couldn't walk down the street without women mobbing him. They would rip a tie right from his neck or wrap their arms around his leg and wouldn't let go. I would often have to pry the girls off of him. Mulholland Farm was besieged by women, day and night. They would climb the fence or sneak inside somehow.

One night, two attractive women knocked on the door uninvited. They were looking for Flynn, of course. He came to the door, liked what he saw, and invited them inside for a cocktail. The four of us were listening to music and having a ball, when I happened to leave the living room for a moment. As I passed through another room, I saw a guy's face at the window. Man, he looked mad. I put two and two together right away. I went and got a Luger and stuck it in my pocket. I swung open the front door and said loudly: "Can I help you, buddy?"

He stepped out of the bushes. "I'm looking for my wife."

I had to think fast. "Well she's inside. Come on in and have a drink."

He still looked mad as he nosed around. I didn't know if he meant trouble or not. I gave him a drink.

"The ladies are getting Flynn's autograph. Let me go and get them."

They came running.

I got a friend of mine, an Armenian known as "Mr. George," to be the caretaker of the estate. He lived in a small house near the entrance. He was always complaining that there was too much to do around the estate. At Errol's request, Mr. George kept the grounds carefully trimmed and neat. Errol had bougainvillea planted around the house, because the colorful shrub reminded him of the exotic plants of his native Australia. Mr. George was usually seen clipping the flowers or chasing the numerous pets that roamed the grounds.

Flynn built a stable to house his favorite stallion, Onyx. There were also goats, chickens, swans, dogs, and cats. But my favorite creature in the menagerie was Chico, a sprightly monkey, who delighted guests every Sunday afternoon. Errol often had Chico dressed in a morning coat, purple vest, and tophat. He was a wonderful entertainer, able to perform a high-wire act along a telephone line. Cars would come to a halt along Mulholland Drive as Chico performed his tricks on the nearby line.

Chico was very possessive of Errol's Siamese cat. He would rock the cat in his arms, like a baby. Then, one of the dogs would lunge with a bark, and Chico and the cat would take off. Mr. George would grumble that he was more of a zookeeper than a caretaker.

The butler who ran the house was Alex Pavlenko, a Russian Errol had inherited from Freddy McEvoy. Flynn liked Alex. He was a good butler, but a desperate gambler, and he wouldn't pay off on bets he lost. I would walk in the kitchen to see Alex, hunched over the radio, listening to a fight or a horse race. If he lost, he would start yelling in Russian, then grab the nearest plate and smash it on his head.

"Gee, Alex," I would say, "I hope that's not the good china."

Except for his nervous frenzy over a gambling loss, he was able to maintain a dignified demeanor while guests were around. Another Russian (or so he claimed) who was often a guest was "Prince" Mike Romanoff. Mike was quite a character. He insisted on telling the world that he was really a Russian prince, and he kept up the charade for some time. He opened a restaurant at 140 South Rodeo Drive, which became the trendy place to dine. I enjoyed sitting in a booth in his elegant dining room. I would wait until Mike sauntered by, with his gold cigarette holder dangling from his lips; then I would boom out, "Say, Mike, how are things back in Memphis?" He would freeze and hiss, "Shhh, old boy!"

If Alex wasn't around Mulholland House, I would answer the phone in my female voice, if I wanted a laugh. Often, it was a girl looking for Flynn. He would signal to me if he didn't want to be disturbed.

"Honey," I would coo sweetly, "Mr. Flynn is out. This is his secretary."

Before long, we would be engaged in "girl talk." I would ask the most intimate questions: "Dearie, just between us girls, what kind of lover is Mr. Flynn? Oh, you don't say?" They would tell me everything. Flynn would burst with laughter at my antics on the telephone.

I loved to use my trick voice to confuse people. Flynn would be sipping champagne by candlelight with a beautiful woman, when I would enter, wearing a servant's jacket. I would pour champagne, then secretly emit a muffled female voice: "Help me! I'm trapped in the closet! He won't let me out!"

Flynn and I would exchange concerned glances. The woman's eyes would grow wide. I would turn to go, take a few paces, then another plea: "Help me!"

I would suddenly halt and slowly turn to Flynn with an ominous stare. He would lower his eyes. I would casually walk to the closet, pretend to unlock it, and say in a stage whisper: "Be quiet! Mr. Flynn has a date."

"Oh, let me out!" replied the female voice.

"Nothing doing! Now shut up!"

I would slam the door, relock it, then cast a dark look over my shoulder.

Flynn would rise and graciously take the lady's hand. "My dear, why don't you and I move into the study."

"W-w-where?" she would stammer.

It was a great scene, and it always got a hearty laugh, especially from the lovely victim. Flynn liked women with a sense of humor.

I played a great prank on Flynn one memorable morning, when we were downtown together. I was driving, and I rolled to a stop on a steep hill, while Errol went inside an office building for a business appointment. A few moments later, an automobile pulled up behind me, and a guy jumped out, leaving an elderly woman in the passenger seat. Suddenly, that car started rolling backwards.

I bolted like a streak of lightning and stopped the old woman's vehicle. She thanked me profusely, as a group of passers-by who had witnessed the incident ran up. I then telephoned Harrison Carroll of the *Herald-Express* and reported Flynn's heroic act in saving the woman. When we returned home, late in the afternoon, the telephone was ringing off the hook with congratulations on his brave deed. Errol ran for a newspaper. He read the story, and a genuinely puzzled look swept his face. "When in the hell did I do this?"

Wherever there was a party, Flynn was a welcome guest. Occasionally, we would be cruising through a neighborhood and see a line of cars along the street. If there was a party in full swing, in we would go. At any social gathering, Flynn would be surrounded by beautiful admirers.

I liked to give Flynn one of my standard lines: "It's getting late, Errol. You've got to look handsome in the morning. If you don't look handsome and swashbuckling, I don't work. I'll say good night to the ladies."

Sometimes, a sweet young thing would ask if I worked in pictures. "Sure, I do all the exciting stuff in Errol's films. Then he does my close-ups."

Flynn would agree: "That's right. I would be nothing without Buster."

Many a beautiful, famous actress came to Mulholland House for romance. They were never disappointed. My motto has always been: "Lots of fun with no harm done."

I tried to steer clear of married women. Unfortunately, there were times when a lady would inform me at the last moment that there was another man in her life and that sound I heard was his footsteps coming toward the bedroom. One time, I thought I was done for. I had been dating a girl in Lake Arrowhead, and we had arranged a romantic liaison at an inn. I had just folded my clothes and was ready to jump between the covers, when a heavy knock sounded at the door. The girl I was with turned white as the sheet around her.

"My boyfriend's found me!" she whispered excitedly.

"Stay calm, honey. You just go to the door, and I'll slip in the closet. Try to get him downstairs." I grabbed my clothes and hid, barely having sufficient time to slip on my drawers and hat! I sat in the closet, with the door cracked about an inch, so I could look through. The guy was built like a gorilla. He looked around suspiciously. She said something about going downstairs for a minute.

Her boyfriend sat in a chair. His narrow eyes came to rest on the crack in the closet. He stood up and came right in my direction.

Oh, oh . . . . He veered to the side. I could hear him opening drawers in the kitchen. He's looking for a knife, I thought. He sat down again with a glass of water in his hand, but his eyes kept coming back to the closet. Suddenly, he put the glass down, rushed to the door, pulled the light string, and saw Buster sitting in his underwear.

"Does the Sunset bus stop here?" I asked.

His foot shot out in the direction of my head. I pulled to the side, and he missed me. "Just calm down, buddy. You can't do that to Buster."

He stepped back and stared at me. "You wait here," he said, "I'm going down to my car and get something."

He disappeared. I dressed like a fireman. I was certain he didn't go for a bus schedule, so I picked up a chair and waited for him to come back. He never did. The girl was probably halfway to Los Angeles by then.

Another time, I was lying in a lady's arms in the wee hours, when I was roused from a blissful sleep by a distant sound. I rolled over, dimly conscious of the lady next to me rising in bed. Then the darkness was pierced by the unmistakable creaking of footsteps on the stairs.

"My husband!" said my companion, in a terrified voice.

"Your *what?*" replied Buster.

We were on the second floor—there was no place to escape but out the window. Still half-groggy, I sailed through the air in my underwear, tearing through the bushes below. I huddled in the shadows, wondering what to do. Just before dawn, I realized from the grayness of the light that I would have to act soon. Suddenly, the milkman drove up and began unloading bottles onto the sidewalk. I scurried from the bushes, feeling like Adam at the dawn of creation.

"Say, partner," I half whispered.

He looked me over with utter nonchalance.

"Do you think you could give me a lift?"

"Hop in," he said. "You're the second guy I picked up this week."

I tried to be careful when it came to women, and I usually stayed out of trouble. But there was great temptation on the Warner lot, which was always brimming with feminine loveliness.

But showing romantic interest in an actress or starlet was hazardous. Many actresses had their "protectors" in the upper echelon of the Warner hierarchy—a producer, director, writer, or star who was helping them up the ladder of success. Openly courting a beauty could result in jealous boyfriends leaving you without a job.

Errol had a nice bungalow in the Stars Building, near the tennis courts. He often entertained there. I also had a key to use when a young lady and I wanted to play gin rummy. But on the Warner lot, one had to be very discreet. Blaney Matthews, the head of security, had eyes and ears everywhere. Hanky-panky could ruin a career.

There was an up-and-coming actor who appeared in several films, including some with Ronald Reagan, and was on his way to becoming a big star, but he was caught coming out of a bedroom window after a torrid affair with the wife of a Warner executive. His career was finished at Warner Brothers, and it took him years to regain the momentum he had lost.

Flynn and I became closer while I was living at Mulholland Farm. Once, while he was vacationing in Mexico, I discovered something that surprised me. While searching in a dresser drawer, I came across an unknown document. Not realizing what it was at first, I read to my surprise that it was Flynn's will, and I was to receive fifty percent of his estate. I was very moved by this kind gesture.

When it came to money, Flynn was quite shrewd. He didn't care to give away something for free, if he could garner a profit. This was especially true when it came to interviews. If the studio arranged an important interview, he readily complied, or if he liked a particular writer he was glad to speak; but otherwise, he played hard to get. As a writer himself, Flynn penned numerous articles that were printed in newspapers, including several about his life in New Guinea. If a fan-magazine writer got pushy about an interview, Flynn gave me the go-ahead. "Tell the guy I'm not talking now, but with a good deal of persuasion on your part, you can get me, and it will cost two-thousand dollars."

I would pass the word along, the writer would inform his publisher; then, if they wanted to speak with Flynn, the money would come through. We then gleefully split it. There were variations on this routine, especially when his contract was expiring with a theatrical agent. Flynn would be upstairs, while I chatted in the living room with the agent.

"Gee, I guess you heard Errol's going to sign with so and so," I lamented, mentioning the name of another agent.

"He is?" came the startled reply.

"Oh, you didn't know? Well, I think you've done a great job for him. I think he's making a big mistake . . . . Maybe I can talk him into remaining with your company. If I succeed, perhaps a fee would be a way of saying thanks."

Once again, Flynn and I would split the profit.

He would hide large sums of cash in safe-deposit boxes in various banks. One weekend, we drove to San Francisco to pick up a bundle of cash Flynn had stashed away. In the bank vault, Flynn withdrew stacks of greenbacks.

"There should be eighty-six-thousand dollars here, Buster."

We started counting it. After awhile, I was counting by myself. The sum totaled two-thousand dollars more than Flynn thought.

"There's eighty-eight-thousand here, Flynn."

"Can't be," he responded.

I counted the pile of money again. The exact amount was $88,000 for certain. We stuffed the cash inside an old burlap bag.

"I've got to take care of some business," said Flynn. "I'll meet you later."

An hour afterward, I was sitting at the counter of a greasy-spoon hamburger joint. On the counter was the $88,000 in the burlap bag. Here comes Flynn.

"Say, Errol, did it ever cross your mind that I might not be here when you arrived?"

He just smiled.

Flynn told me of various hiding places where he salted away cash and gold bars. He may have tapped these secret hiding places when he left Hollywood for Europe, during the early Fifties. Then again, he may have left the money there for a rainy day.

On May 20, 1942, we began work on *Gentleman Jim*. Of all the films Flynn starred in throughout his career, this one was his favorite. It's strange to say, but Flynn didn't really enjoy seeing himself on the screen. We would go to see one of his pictures, and in ten minutes he would be ready to leave. He was a damn good actor, but he didn't revel in seeing his own image.

For *Gentleman Jim*, we both got in great shape physically. He and I would put on the gloves for sparring. I wore my boxing gloves so much that I began extending my hand and saying, "Please to mitt you." Newspaper columnist Phillip K. Scheuer came on the set to cover the production. He put me in his column, since my line was so bad it was good. Flynn and I were both boxing enthusiasts, so the picture was fun to make. Raoul Walsh put professional wrestlers in the film to portray boxers, since they looked exceedingly gruesome. Such stalwarts as Mike Mazurki and Ed "Strangler" Lewis were hired. Boxer Frank Muskie, from Gene Tunney's camp, was in the film. Former middleweight champ Freddie Steele doubled for Flynn in the barge fight scene. My main method of staying in shape was running seven miles a day, and I picked up good pointers about boxing by just watching the pros.

A few weeks before the picture began, Errol's close friend John Barrymore had collapsed: it was apparent he wouldn't be leaving the hospital alive. Flynn idolized the witty Barrymore, who often came to Mulholland to have a cup of cheer with Errol.

Once when Barrymore was in a restaurant, he was in dire need of a restroom, due to the huge quantity of liquor he had imbibed. He wandered about the restaurant, holding his manhood to prevent an accident. In desperation, he entered the women's restroom. A startled oriental attendant looked at him.

"Meesta Barrymore, thees is for ladies!"

"So is *this*, but I'm in a hurry."

For years, Hollywood gossip related how Raoul Walsh had taken the body of John Barrymore from Pierce Brothers Funeral Home on Washington Boulevard, after he had died on May 29, 1942, and propped it up in Flynn's home. The corpse was supposedly seated in the living room when Flynn walked inside. Seeing John, he is reputed to have screamed and run into the bushes. Flynn printed the story in his autobiography, and Raoul Walsh did the same.

The story is simply not true. Flynn wouldn't have run if there had been forty stiffs sitting there. It was Buster who was the initial source of the Barrymore story. Flynn and I had worked on *Gentleman Jim* that Friday. In the evening, we were having dinner at the home of George Burns and Gracie Allen. Present were Raoul Walsh and Jack Benny and his wife.

The phone rang. George Burns returned, saying sadly that John Barrymore had passed away. I suggested we all go out on the terrace and have a final toast to Barrymore. While we were out there, I said, "Wouldn't John really like it if we would steal him and take him to Ciro's nightclub. We could sit him at a table, drink, and have some fun."

"Yeah, let's do that!" they began saying.

They sounded serious! I mentioned that, if word leaked to the press that they had done something like steal a corpse, the churches would be in an uproar. Warner Brothers films would be banned. Besides, at this stage, *rigor mortis* would have made it impossible to seat someone in a chair. If poor Barrymore's body *had* been stolen, we would still be in jail. But the story got out from different sources that Raoul Walsh had stolen the body.

A few days after his death, we went to Calvary Mausoleum for the funeral and interment. Among the mourners was Clark Gable. He was making his first public appearance since his wife, Carole Lombard, had died in a plane crash. Amoung the pallbearers were Gene Fowler, John Decker, Herbert Marshall, David O. Selznick and W.C. Fields. John was gone, but the theft tale wasn't. The story has been told and retold—another fabulous Hollywood legend that is just legend.

The *Sirocco* moored off the coast of Mexico for a fishing expedition. Note shark's fin in water. (Photo: Jerry Hill Collection)

With Flynn in the Los Angeles courtroom, just moments after the jury began deliberating his guilt or innocence on charges of rape. (Courtesy of Robert Matzen, John Metzger and August Color Lab.)

NINE

Sad Days for Flynn

*"One of the striking differences between a cat
and a lie is that a cat has only nine lives."*

When I began living at Mulholland Farm, Errol was on top of the world. He was one of the biggest box-office stars in motion pictures. But bad times lay ahead. One day stands out in my mind as being a turning point in his life. A telephone call from Flynn relayed the information that someone was trying to extort money from him. I told him not to pay one dime.

The event that would change his life began to unravel on August 1, 1941. We drove down to San Pedro, to set sail aboard the *Sirocco*. Besides the crew, Flynn and I had two women along for a photo layout that would be shot by Peter Stackpole, of *Life* magazine. Stackpole wanted some spearfishing photos, and the women were there to enhance the atmosphere.

Elaine Patterson was the girlfriend of a buddy of mine. She was a waitress, quite attractive. When I met her, she told me, "I've never been on a yacht." I said that the next time there was room on the *Sirocco*, she would be a guest. Jim Fleming had arranged for the other girl to come along. She was Peggy Satterlee, a curvaceous brunette, who had met Flynn through her sister, Mickey June Satterlee. Both sisters were trying to break into pictures. No hanky-panky was ever intended for the sea cruise, and none occurred.

Errol had long suffered from intense sinus trouble. Many a time I had seen him hit his head against a wall in anguish, due to this painful condition. He was in agony during the entire weekend at Catalina. We anchored in the waters off Fourth of July Cove. Errol was photographed at the wheel of the *Sirocco* and spearfishing. He smiled for the camera but I knew he felt ill. Each girl had a private cabin; Flynn and I shared another one. It was quite clear to me that romance was not on his mind—Flynn was so miserable with his sinus trouble that he checked into Good Samaritan Hospital, almost as soon as we docked.

I was at Mulholland House when he telephoned from the hospital. He had spoken with Peggy Satterlee: her father was putting the squeeze on him for five-thousand dollars, instructing him to bring the money to the New Rosslyn Hotel in downtown Los Angeles, or else he would lie to the police that his underage daughter had sexual relations with Flynn.

"What should I do, Buster?"

"Don't pay one dime, Flynn, or they'll bleed you dry."

Despite subsequent threats, Flynn refused to pay extortion money. He knew, as well as I did, that he was innocent. On October 22, 1942, Errol was in court, charged with statutory rape. He supposedly had relations with two minors—Peggy Satterlee and Betty Hansen. Flynn was stunned by the accusations. He pleaded not guilty and was confident of exoneration.

Betty Hansen was a young woman who had attended a party at the home of Freddy McEvoy, on September 23, 1942. She claimed that Flynn had relations with her in an upstairs bedroom. I arrived at 321 St. Pierre Road while the party was in full-swing. Freddy was the host of the party at the Spanish-style home, and Errol enjoyed himself by playing a round of tennis with his pal, Bill Tilden. I left the party early, since I had a date arranged with Doris Duke. Flynn denied he had sexual relations with Betty Hansen at this party.

The day after the charges were made public, he and I were sitting around the pool. "Don't you notice something?" I said.

"What?"

"The phone has stopped ringing."

"You're right, Buster."

From being the most sought-after star in Hollywood, he was

now someone to avoid. His close friends stuck by him—Ida Lupino, Bruce Cabot, Ann Sheridan, and Freddy McEvoy all remained loyal. Flynn certainly didn't have to attack any dames— it was usually the other way around. Numerous times, I would see women throw themselves at him. Errol had his own style. He appeared a bit bashful, then he would turn on the charm, and the girls just melted.

Flynn's attorney, Robert E. Ford, suggested that we call one of the nation's top defense attorneys—Jerry Giesler. Bob Ford was a damned good lawyer himself. Flynn had been involved in a legal matter where Ford had represented the adversary. At one point during the proceedings, Bob Ford spoke up quite emphatically, exclaiming, "In a pig's ass you will!" A few days later, Flynn was talking about the importance of getting a lawyer on retainer.

"Why not that kid Bob Ford?" I said.

I had been impressed by his forcefulness. That phrase, "in a pig's ass," had made a lasting impression with Buster. I liked the guts Bob displayed. He and Giesler began preparing research for Flynn's defense.

One Friday night, soon after the charges were made public, Errol and I went to the Hollywood Legion Stadium to watch the fights. As Flynn was recognized by the crowd, spontaneous applause broke out. Later, I went to Barney's Beanery for a bite to eat. From across the restaurant, a familiar voice called out, "Hey, Buster!" I caught the smiling face of Jack Oakie. Jack had a bowl of Barney's famous onion soup before him. When I sat down, he looked at me with awe on his face.

"Buster, I was at the Stadium when you and Flynn walked in. That Flynn's got guts to appear in public, when so many people think he's guilty."

"He's not ashamed of anything, Jack, because he knows he's innocent."

Errol felt he was being dealt a very unjust situation that threatened not only his livelihood, but also his very freedom. If given the maximum sentence, he faced over a hundred years in prison. He was bitter. In October, he seemed to have been vindicated when a grand jury had failed to return an indictment against him concerning the accusations of Betty Hansen. Yet, the District Attorney's office proceeded to charge him with statutory rape. Flynn always suspected that he was a pawn in a shadowy political game involving Warner Brothers and its contributions to city officials, and he maintained his innocence, both publicly and privately.

We were in the midst of shooting *Edge Of Darkness* when the charges were filed. Both Flynn and I had confidence that Giesler and Ford would prove to the jury that he was innocent. Giesler had represented such notables as Clarence Darrow and Alexander Pantages, and due process of law had found them innocent. We tried to concentrate on the film. I know it was hard for Errol.

Part of the film was shot in Monterey. Special permission had to be granted to director Lewis Milestone to use the Monterey Pier to stage a realistic Nazi invasion. While we were staying at the Del Monte Hotel, a lot of gambling took place. We were shooting dice between takes on the set, too. One night at the hotel, I won $250 from some G.I.s. On my way back to Los Angeles, I put all my cash in my glove compartment. I picked up two soldiers, hitchhiking along the highway. They were headed for Fort Ord. We began talking, and the subject of gambling soon arose. These guys said that there was always a craps game taking place around the Fort. I asked one of them to hand me something from the glove compartment. He opened it, saw all that cash, and extended an invitation to Buster to join the wonderful sport of craps.

Buster gratefully obliged. I won $2,500 bucks in a marathon gambling session with a group of soldiers and bought my hitchhikers juicy steaks. Ann Sheridan said I was the greatest craps shooter ever.

During the making of *Edge of Darkness*, I injured my knees badly. We were working on a scene being shot at the Warner Ranch, in Calabasas. The sun was setting, and our light was diminishing rapidly. The crew rushed to complete a crucial scene, before wrapping for the day. Everyone was tired and in a hurry. The scene depicted the Norwegian partisans, pushing a wagon into a Nazi-held hotel. I was to lob a grenade into the hotel to demolish the Nazis. I threw the grenade, but lost my balance, due to fatigue. My knees struck concrete, and I burst the cartilage in both. The pain was excruciating. However, it was merely a day's work for a stuntman.

On January 7, 1943, I was with Flynn on Sound-stage 11, where we shot his scene for *Thank Your Lucky Stars.* Flynn sang a rousing "That's What You Jolly Well Get," and I played one of the guys drinking in the pub. Perfect casting, again. I doubled Flynn in the scene and was hurled through a window. Errol worked for free, along with Bogart, Bette Davis, and other stars, with the stipulation that Warner Brothers donate $50,000 to the Hollywood Canteen, a servicemen's club.

A few days after Errol appeared in *Thank Your Lucky Stars,* his trial commenced at the Hall of Justice in downtown Los Angeles. The case would be headlined in newspapers throughout the world. By the time the trial was underway, I had supplied Giesler with a great deal of shocking information about the two girls: what would eventually be revealed in court was just the tip of the iceberg. There was even a photo of one of the girls, stark naked.

As we were building Flynn's defense, I was incensed to hear that Johnny Meyer refused to help Errol. Meyer had started working for Flynn by walking the dogs. Then Flynn got him a job at Warner's, as a press agent. He was sharp when it came to handling money and a good public relations man. Flynn was very kind to Johnny. He even gave money to Meyer so he could support his parents. Flynn was innocent, but was facing years in prison if the jury found otherwise. Meyer had dated one of the girls who had brought charges against Flynn. It was very clear that the girls had "been around."

I located Meyer one evening at the Trocadero nightclub. I tried to convince him to testify on Flynn's behalf, reminding him of all that Errol had done for him and his family.

"I can't testify," he whined.

I was furious. I calmly walked out to the sidewalk near the entrance. I was seething with anger. When Meyer stepped outside— bam—my Memphis soupbone smashed into his face. Every time he poked his head out the door, I went for him.

But Meyer wouldn't testify. I did some searching and found some other guys who were willing to talk. Giesler had them ready to go, if necessary.

Flynn and Meyer ceased to be friends. The trash biography of Flynn quotes Meyer's statement that he had arranged a meeting between Flynn and Howard Hughes, for a homosexual liaison. The story is absolute nonsense. As I said previously, I knew Flynn very well. He had few secrets from me. As his friend, he told me a lot, and I saw a lot. Mulholland House was the scene of many romantic encounters, but none of them ever involved homosexuality, which was alien to Errol Flynn. I have absolutely nothing against gays. My belief has always been: live and let live. What angers me is that allegations of homosexuality were advanced merely to sensationalize even further a rotten book.

It was Errol who had introduced Johnny Meyer to Howard Hughes. Howard occasionally dined at Mulholland House. Meyer is quoted as saying that Hughes didn't like women! It was well-known, even back then, that Hughes had women stashed around Los Angeles, in homes he paid for. They were everywhere.

During the trial, I accompanied Flynn to the courthouse every day. Crowds of curious onlookers mobbed him as he arrived and left. I was a potential witness myself. From the outset, I expected to receive a subpoena any moment. I was eager to testify. Flynn's bunk had been right next to mine on the *Sirocco,* and he never left our cabin during the night. Giesler advised me not to listen to the courtroom testimony, since it was almost certain I would be called to the witness stand, so I roamed the corridors of the Hall of Justice or waited in the lobby to kill time until the day's hearing ended. In the lobby, at a cigar stand, I struck up a conversation with a lovely redhead who worked behind the counter. Her name was Nora Eddington, and she would eventually become Flynn's second wife.

As the trial progressed, Giesler brought out the truth: the girls had invented the stories of Flynn having sexual relations with them. The last week of testimony arrived, and Giesler asked me if I could disappear. I was surprised by his request. I wanted to testify, but Giesler was in command. Things were going so well that I presume he wanted no unforeseen possibilities. Perhaps he thought that Deputy D.A. Thomas Cochran would squeeze harmful information out of Buster. Flynn and I had few secrets. I knew who the ladies were who visited Mulholland House, unknowns and famous alike.

So Giesler put it to me straight: "Buster, can you disappear?"

"Jerry," I said, "I can make Houdini look like a man with paralysis."

I was in the Polo Lounge of the Beverly Hills Hotel, having a conversation with columnist Sheila Graham, when actor John Loder walked over.

"Buster, they've been searching everywhere for you at the studio."

"Shhh, if they want me, they can find me."

The day that the jury was to render its verdict, I was positive that Flynn would be fully exonerated. I was so confident that I arranged a victory celebration. Even though the jury was still out, I began herding the reporters to the party, which took place in the ninth-floor press room of the Hall of Justice. Warner Brothers provided a service crew, and a throng of journalists began sipping cocktails. I was handing out drinks, when I looked up to see District Attorney John Hopkins standing before me. Julian Hartt, covering the case for the International News Service, asked the prosecutor: "Will they find Flynn guilty?"

"No," he responded, "they'll find him innocent." He pointed at me, and said bitterly, "We prosecuted the wrong guy. There's the one we should have gone after."

I almost dropped my drink! Maybe he was just blowing off steam, angry at my victory party, but it was certainly a vicious remark. In that instant, I knew what Flynn, as an innocent man, must have felt like as the legal weight of the prosecutors tried to smash him into a jail cell. I was furious over the comment. Elaine Patterson had testified that she had been treated wonderfully on the cruise. If Peggy Satterlee had told the truth—that Flynn never had relations with her—a great deal of personal anguish for everyone could have been avoided. Hopkin's bitterness toward me was unwarranted. During the trial, he had called me Flynn's "bird dog." Another lie.

"This case should never have come to court," I shot back, "and the jury will prove it too." It was clear to me that the prosecutors were out to gain political mileage from the sensational trial. Just as I had predicted, Flynn was found innocent of all charges, on February 6, 1943. Judge Still told the jurors, "I think you arrived at the proper verdict."

I rushed inside the crowded courtroom, now in pandemonious fever, and elbowed my way to the defense table. I congratulated Flynn and his brilliant attorney. As I pumped Giesler's hand, he modestly told me: "You're the one who did all the work."

Flynn thanked Judge Still and the jurors. The jury foreman, Ruby Anderson, told reporters, "We felt there had been other men in the girl's life . . . . Frankly, all the cards were on the table, and we just couldn't believe the two girls' stories."

Other men, I'll say!

Each juror echoed strong sentiments, expressing belief in Flynn's innocence. Said Homer Jacobsmeyer, "I believe we arrived at the correct verdict." And Nellie Minear, "I have two boys, and I would hate to have had them face trial on such unsupported charges."

Errol tried to light a cigarette, but he was shaking so much I had to light it for him.

In the press room, the journalists fired questions at Flynn. I told Florabel Muir, of the *Daily News,* "I kept telling the kid he couldn't lose, but the last few hours he got to chewing his nails."

The reporters agreed that Flynn had been the victim, rather than the perpetrator of foul deeds. If they only knew what I had uncovered, they would have been outraged that a trial had even occurred. Errol later wrote in his autobiography that he had a plane waiting in Burbank, to fly him out of the country if he were found guilty. Like many tales in *My Wicked Wicked Ways,* he was merely dramatizing the action.

The postscript to Errol's trial was a fun-filled farewell party, tossed for him by the numerous reporters who had covered the event. It was the idea of Agnes Underwood, city editor of the *Los Angeles Herald-Express.* Agnes threw the party at her own home, after spending two days cooking a special dinner. Flynn and I appeared with wine and bottles of booze. It was a memorable evening. Reporter Florabel Muir wrote of the party in her memoirs, *Headline Happy:*

> Aggie's living room was decorated with gag pictures of the trial and a miniature model of the luxury yacht, *Sirocco,* where Peggy told the jurors she had lost her maidenly virtue. A bedroom window was turned into a ship's porthole. One of the photographers, masquerading as Peggy, kept staring through this porthole and begging Flynn to come and woo her. It was a burlesque on the Satterlee girl's story that she had been watching the

moon shining on the ocean waves through a porthole in the ship's saloon when Errol persuaded her to go to his cabin where she could get a better view of the lunar spectacle.

A kangaroo court was set up at the party, and Flynn became the defendant in a mock trial. Julian Hartt played the role of Jerry Giesler, and Buster Wiles did the prosecuting. Walter Ames, of the *Los Angeles Times*, was the judge. Robert Ford, Flynn's regular attorney, who assisted Giesler during the trial, was at the party but declined to enter into the tomfoolery. He was a little against the whole thing but was overwhelmed by the power of the press.

We all sang "Shine on, Harvest Moon" as the jury found the actor guilty and sentenced him to a life's sentence on his yacht in the custody of twelve beautiful eighteen-year-old girls to be designated by Judge Ames.

A tragic but revealing footnote in the case was the subsequent prosecution of William C. Satterlee, Peggy's father, the man who had tried to extort money from Flynn. Fourteen months after Flynn's acquittal, I picked up a newspaper and read: "Police seek W.C. Satterlee . . . , charging three counts of morals offenses against six- and seven-year-old girls." In October of 1944, he pleaded guilty to being a child molester.

The ordeal of the rape trial forged a further bond between us. Once again, the telephone began to ring at Mulholland House, but it took awhile before Errol was on the "A-list" of Hollywood parties. After Flynn was acquitted, Jack Warner summoned him to his elegant and foreboding office. Those arriving for an appointment had to walk down a flight of steps and halt at a gate, which only a secretary could buzz open. On occasion, Warner made visitors hover at the gate, just to flash his power.

In the inner sanctum, Warner lectured Errol in a fatherly fashion. He spoke of Flynn's personal life, the necessity of avoiding negative publicity, and so on. In summing up his words of wisdom, he exclaimed: "And another thing, your friend Buster Wiles has to go!"

"Well," replied Errol, "if he goes I go."

Jack Warner looked at the door. "There it is," said the studio boss.

"Goodbye, Jack," said Errol.

I was waiting downstairs and saw Flynn approach the staircase. Errol was halfway down the stairs when Warner's executive secretary, William Schaefer, suddenly appeared at the top of the staircase.

"Mr. Flynn . . . ."

Errol turned.

"Eh . . . , he doesn't have to leave right away."

Errol looked relieved. I know I was relieved when I heard the full story. Was Flynn a loyal friend? You'd better believe it.

One Sunday afternoon, Flynn and I were lounging about Mulholland House. "It's sure dull around here," he said.

I suggested that we invite some girls up, so we could have some fun. "Say, I know a really sweet girl you would like. Remember Nora? She's the one I met during the trial; she worked at the cigar stand. I just happened to meet her in a restaurant last week." Flynn's face brightened.

"Well, call her, and I'll give her a chance."

She was Nora Eddington, the lovely redhead. The following Sunday, she and a friend came up and met Flynn. Nora became Errol's secretary and later his second wife. According to Flynn's autobiography, I was sent out by Flynn to get him a date with Nora. Flynn never asked me to get him a date with Nora or anyone else. He was good enough at attracting women himself. In fact, I usually had to step in to keep women off of him or away from the house, so he could have a little peace and quiet.

But after the devastating notoriety of the rape trial, it took Flynn awhile to be accepted socially. He gave a party at Mulholland, and it was a dismal flop. Guests stayed away, still leery of Errol's reputation. I had been out with Nora. I knew she was a fine girl from a good family: her father was an assistant to Los Angeles County Sheriff, Eugene Biscailuz. On that fateful Sunday afternoon, when Flynn made the comment about boredom, Nora just happened to come to mind.

Errol invited Nora to Warner's to watch the production of *Northern Pursuit*. In this action film, Flynn portrayed a member of the Royal Canadian Mounted Police, who "always get their man."

In the film, Errol tracks Nazi saboteurs and, true to the Mountie motto, captures them.

We went on location to film outdoor sequences at Sun Valley, in Idaho. The interior footage was shot on sound-stages at Warner Brothers. To produce the effect of snow in the Canadian wilds, a flaky white substitute known as gypsum was used. When huge fans were turned on to create the impression of a blizzard, the gypsum was bothersome indeed. It caused all kinds of allergy and sinus problems for the cast and crew. Everyone began wearing surgical masks on the set. The sled dogs in the film were confused by the snow-like gypsum and tried to lap it up!

While at Sun Valley, Raoul Walsh had arranged for certain huskies to be used in the film. The publicity department at Warner Brothers promoted the fact that the lead dog, Yukon, had been born on Admiral Richard E. Byrd's exploration of Antarctica. The dogs were kept in air-conditioned kennels and treated like major stars.

As Flynn's stunt double, I had some rugged action shots in the film, including a twenty-foot leap onto a Nazi saboteur.

Flynn, Nora, and I went skiing at Big Bear one winter and had a wonderful time. Shortly before this outing, Errol had told me he couldn't ski. Neither could I, so we thought it was time to learn. In the midst of our instructions, I turned around to see the great swashbuckler going down the ski slope—*backwards.* I yelled to him, "Hey, Flynn, know why those skis are so long? So they can find you when you're buried in the snow!"

On the trip to Reno, we had stopped to see our pal Bud Ernst. He was stationed near Lancaster as an instructor, teaching pilots how to dive-bomb. Flynn and I drove to an abandoned airfield near the base. Bud soon touched down in his divebomber, and Flynn got inside for a spin. Bud took the plane high in the air, then suddenly nosedived. As the aircraft plummeted toward the earth, Bud sailed skyward again. My turn was next—Bud and Flynn intended to scare the you-know-what out of Buster.

As I climbed into the two-seater, Flynn grinned. We shot off the runway and climbed thousands of feet, then Bud put the plane into a sharp dive. I saw Bud's head snap down—he blacked out for a few seconds! Thank goodness he came around. When we landed, Bud shook his head, "You can't scare this old buzzard," referring to me. I always wondered what would have happened if Bud had been unconscious more than a few seconds.

As close as Flynn and I were, there was one area of his life that I hesitated to share: that was his use of drugs. When I became aware that he was experimenting with cocaine, I was alarmed. I had seen guys get hooked on dope. In the back of my mind was the example of Wallace Reid, a silent-film star who had become an addict.

"Errol, you can't beat it. It's been tried and tried. You have no chance," I pleaded.

"Oh, it's nothing," he scoffed. "When I want to quit, it will be easy."

It's hard to imagine someone as smart as Flynn getting involved with drugs, but it happens to a lot of celebrities. With all the adulation, fortune, and success, a star may really feel immune to bad luck. They think that their magic touch will last forever. Flynn never bragged about his drug-use or flaunted it. In fact, I never even saw him indulge. But sometimes, usually late at night, he would be high, in an eerie way—there, but not there. In the morning he would be himself, without any recollection of the previous evening.

It was around this time that John Decker painted a portrait of Flynn, which was rather somber. It was reproduced in *Esquire* magazine as, "Errol Flynn . . . A troubled and ennuied soul . . . ." Perhaps Flynn was getting rather bored. As for myself, I was too busy making a living to contemplate boredom. Although I shared Flynn's home and tried to help him whenever I could, I was never on his payroll, as many assumed. My living was as a stuntman.

A studio telephone call would convey the message: "Report to Stage 14 at 8:00 a.m. tomorrow morning." Stunts came and went so fast: *Passage To Marseilles*, doubling Bogart in action scenes on the deck of a ship; *The Desert Song*, doubling Dennis Morgan, diving from a rooftop onto a rider and falling off a train over a dozen times; *Adventures in Iraq*, doubling John Loder in fight scenes; *The Great Dictator*, playing a fighting storm-trooper in Chaplin's lampoon of Adolph Hitler; *North Star*, nervously rolling along in an army truck, pulling a set of pre-wired switches to set the rig ablaze.

Howard Hill was a great source of work. Whenever he would

get a job, I came along as the human target. While working in *Buffalo Bill,* I played a prank on Howard. The director, William Wellman, explained how he wanted a take of a rider getting knocked off by an arrow. Howard was a quiet, conscientious fellow, with nerves of steel. I've always had a mischievous streak, which resulted in my enjoyment in ruffling the feathers of the seemingly imperturbable.

I mounted my horse and began riding through a stream. The faint trace of a chalked "X" was barely visible on my chest. Underneath my shirt, I wore a metal protector, covered by a layer of cork. Off to the side, Howard stood on a high parallel with a raised bow. One mistake and I would be in the happy hunting ground.

The arrow suddenly thudded into my chest, and I toppled into the water, motionless. Wellman yelled, "Cut," but I lay still, with my head barely bobbing the surface. Howard excitedly yelled my name. No response. He yelled again.

"Buster, are you all right?"

No answer. Howard ran into the water, shouting. He splashed behind me and grabbed my shoulder. I opened my eyes.

"I'm fine, Howard, but I need a Seagram's 7 and 7."

He gave me a drink all right. He shoved me under the water and darn near drowned me.

Errol Flynn and USO troupe arriving in Adak, Alaska
December 6, 1943. *(U.S. Navy. Courtesy of the Academy of
Motion Picture Arts and Sciences.)*

Leaving the courtroom after Flynn's acquittal on all charges.
Attorney Jerry Giesler, Flynn and I are all smiles. *(Photo:
UPI/Bettmann Archives)*

TEN

American Hero: Captain Dudley "Mush" Morton and the War Effort

"The land of the free and the home of the brave."

In the middle of 1943, Americans were fighting and dying around the world. Brave men and women risked their lives in defense of American values and a love of freedom. Captain Dudley Morton was one of the thousands of heroes who kept America free. He was the most courageous man I have ever known. As skipper of the submarine *Wahoo,* he directed the sinking of numerous Japanese vessels. The *Wahoo's* victories inspired all Americans to admire this brave man and his crew.

Captain Morton was affectionately known as "Mush." This nickname was short for "Mushmouth." Being from Owensboro, Kentucky, he had a strong southern accent, as well as a great deal of courage. In 1943, Mush Morton made headlines with his submarine exploits. For his bravery, he had won three Navy Crosses and an Army Distinguished Service Cross. The *Wahoo,* named for a Florida fish, had received a citation from President

Roosevelt. This was, in effect, awarding a medal to a ship. The determination and bravery of the *Wahoo's* crew led to incredible military successes.

On one patrol, the submarine entered uncharted Wewak Harbor, in New Guinea. This feat was accomplished with the help of an Australian geography book that a crew member just happened to have aboard. Inside the harbor, the *Wahoo* began stalking a Japanese destroyer. The first torpedo was fired, but it missed. The destroyer was now alerted and came toward the sub for an attack. The *Wahoo's* other torpedoes also missed. There was one remaining torpedo left in the forward compartments. The *Wahoo* blasted the *Harusame* with a "down the throat" shot.

On the same mission, the sub sank four ships in a convoy. When the torpedoes were all gone, Mush attacked another enemy ship, with only the deck-gun firing. By the autumn of 1943, the *Wahoo* topped the record for enemy tonnage destroyed.

I met Mush Morton when he visited Warner Brothers Studio. He and his wife were living in Los Angeles, and Mush and I became friends. One night, we went to the Hollywood Legion Stadium to see the fights, and I had the announcer acknowledge the *Wahoo's* skipper. The Stadium exploded with applause. Mush Morton was the man of the hour.

Flynn and I went to Mare Island Naval Yard, near San Francisco, and I arranged a party for some of the crew members. We boarded the *Wahoo* and made two practice submersions aboard the submarine. When the diving horn blasted, my heart started to pound. Down below, I dipped a brush into a bucket of white paint. On one of the torpedoes I wrote: "Up your butt, Tojo!"

Flynn and I planned to stay on the *Wahoo* for its upcoming mission. Errol intended to write an article about how he and I had been "stowaways" on the submarine, but it would really be a serious piece about life and combat aboard the sub. Mush had originally planned to take us along, but he changed his mind. In his quarters, he told me that our unauthorized presence just wouldn't be right. He asked me if I could take a letter to his wife, Harriet, who lived on Highland in Los Angeles. I gladly did this for him.

On September 13, the ship left Midway Island for a combat mission. It never came back. On December 3, 1943, the Navy issued a statement that it was "overdue and must be presumed lost." I couldn't believe it. I felt that somehow Mush Morton and the *Wahoo* were invincible.

The sub had sailed into the Sea of Japan through the La Perouse Strait. After the war, it was determined that four Japanese ships had been sunk in this area. A Japanese report of October 1943 mentions an attack on a submarine in the La Perouse Strait. The eighty men of the *Wahoo* are Americans we should never forget. Captain Dudley Morton was thirty-six years old.

Hollywood was doing its part to raise funds through war-bond sales. Many performers embarked on tours to entertain the fighting G.I.s; Errol had been asked to take part in a USO tour to the Aleutian Islands. He had previously declined such tours, since he couldn't sing or dance, but at the request of the Hollywood Victory Committee, he went along, not quite knowing what he would do.

But Flynn ad-libbed with great style and flair. In Alaska, he told the audience of soldiers, "There were thousands of people waiting to see me off at the airport—all of them lawyers." The servicemen laughed, as Flynn poked fun at himself. He toured from November 24 to December 18, 1943, bringing cheer to obscure outposts in Attu, Amchitka, and Adak. I had intended on joining Errol on this trip, but unfortunately, when I returned from out of town, it was too late to arrange the necessary inoculations.

After this inspiring tour, Flynn immediately set off on another patriotic venture: he joined a contingent of Hollywood celebrities participating in the Treasury Department's Fourth War Loan Drive. On the eve of the month-long campaign, President Roosevelt told the nation: "All of us will have an opportunity to do our share in shortening the war and causing the unconditional surrender of the enemy. Every dollar invested in war bonds is an addition to our offensive power, a contribution to our future happiness and security. Let's all back the attack."

Errol was assigned the state of Louisiana for bond sales, and I was invited to accompany him. As soon as our Delta aircraft touched down at New Orleans Airport, an exciting two weeks in Louisiana began. As we descended the ramp, a throng of city dignitaries, reporters, and fans anxiously waited on the tarmac.

They pressed around Flynn, and our official host, K. Kirby Newburger, chairman of the Orleans Parish finance committee, gave him a warm welcome.

Reporters then crowded around Flynn, who spoke of his recent trip to the Aleutians. Quipped Errol: "I didn't see a woman on the whole damned trip and for once in my life came back without a summons."

Errol was scheduled to headline the evening session of the Four Freedoms War Bond Show, but he graciously agreed to make a brief appearance at the Municipal Auditorium, where the afternoon event was already under way. We were shown to a waiting car, and our chauffeur, a pretty girl in a Red Cross uniform, sped us to the nearby auditorium. Huge posters proclaimed the show's theme:

Freedom of Speech
Freedom of Worship
Freedom From Want
Freedom From Fear

Flynn stepped on the stage, and thunderous applause broke out from the thousands of spectators. His remarks were about the soldiers in the Aleutians. Said Errol: "They've got a gag in Attu that you can find a girl behind every tree. Only there are no trees in the whole place. Martha Driscoll was with our show, and when she had finished singing they yelled for more. So I told them, 'Fellows, she doesn't know any more songs.' And they said, 'Well then just bring her out and let us look at her.' Miss Driscoll was wonderful, undergoing hardships of life in the Aleutians without a single complaint. She never let out one squawk, and this business of getting herself out of long flannel drawers into an evening dress in the back of an Army truck was no small job. You have to be a contortionist."

He continued in a more serious vein. "I was up there seven weeks, and when I got back to Hollywood again, back to a real fire and real eggs instead of powdered eggs, I could hardly believe it. Sitting in front of my fire at home, I thought back to Christmas Day in the Aleutians and a young soldier without a leg, who was very happy just because for the first time in a year the sun was shining. Well, I've felt pretty cheap in my life at times, but I never felt as cheap as I did then. Here I was by a fire, with all the good food I wanted and a check from the Treasury Department for interest on war bonds in my hand and my two legs to go around with anywhere I pleased. And I made up my mind then and there that I would take another troupe overseas, maybe to New Guinea. Attu is such a horror, it's hard to understand how the fellows stand it. No trees, the wind howling all night and all day. And air raids! They had one while I was there. I was taking a shower and so I said, 'What do I wear for a raid? My double-breasted suit?' Seriously though, when the fellows applaud you up there, it's wonderful to feel you are doing something. It gives you a lift for days."

After his speech, Errol went to a booth where he purchased a war bond. Frenzied fans closed in on him, and I had to gently keep them from mobbing him. Errol told the press: "Now I know what Frank Sinatra feels like."

Our host, Mr. Newburger, accompanied us to the Roosevelt Hotel, where we were given Huey Long's former suite—elegant rooms, with a sweeping view of the city below. Kirby Newburger was a wonderful guy, who couldn't do enough for us. He was a prominent cotton man, and a wealthy one too. It was a coincidence that I knew his uncle, who lived in Memphis. After dinner at Antoine's, we stopped at Count Arnold's, a well-known watering hole. I started to pay for the first round, but Mr. Newburger spoke up: "Oh, no, let me pay. That's why I'm here. I'll take care of everything."

"The entire tab?" I asked.

"Certainly."

He pulled a thick wad of bills from his pocket.

"All right!" I said. "Okay, bartender, give all the help a drink too!"

The evening bond show opened with patriotic music by the forty-five-piece WAC orchestra from Fort Des Moines, Iowa; then *Army Flash,* an Army demonstration of an Air Raid Warning Center, with a simulated attack of an enemy raid over New Orleans, dramatically presented with music and sound effects; afterwards, a government film, *Baptism of Fire,* showing soldiers and airmen in combat. A change of pace was *Women Of Two*

Wars, an exhibit featuring thirty-five models wearing uniforms of women in the last two wars.

At 8:00 p.m., Victor Mature, Chief Boatswain's Mate in the U.S. Coast Guard, just returned from fifteen months service, introduced various singers and film comedian Billy De Wolfe. But the centerpiece of the program was Errol Flynn. At 9:00 p.m., he strode onstage and again related his experience of entertaining the troops in the Aleutians. He told the audience he was restricted in describing places he visited and in discussing various phases of military life, but he assured the spectators, "Equipment provided is the best. It meets the boys' approval, and that's where the money you put into bonds goes."

In discussing his tour of the Aleutians, Errol recounted the air raid attack he had been in: "I slung something around me—they caught me in the middle of a shower—and jumped into the nearest foxhole, which was half filled with mud and snow. Then I realized that entertaining the boys here was really doing something, and I felt I had found a place—after being turned down by the Army and Navy." He closed with a dramatic appeal for more and more bond purchases.

Following Errol was Major Allen Martini, a heroic bomber pilot with three-hundred combat hours over Germany. He had commanded four Flying Fortresses, each named "the Dry Martini." The first three aircraft had been shot up from nose to tail-turret. No longer flyable, they were turned into "hanger queens" and stripped for parts needed by other Fortresses. He was touring the country, asking fellow citizens to buy more bonds. He poignantly told the audience, "I'm representing the kids who were knocked off." Martini was only twenty-three himself. Like the spectators, Flynn and I were quite moved by Major Martini's words and deeds.

The bond show continued another two days, with Errol's appearance attracting thousands daily. After the hectic day, we would unwind with a tour of the local nightspots, celebrating with the people of New Orleans until the wee hours.

Late one evening, Mr. Newburger came up to me, shaking his head wearily. He pulled a gigantic roll of bills from his pocket. "Buster, take this. I'm not used to this living. You guys are going to kill me. When the money runs out, call me and I'll bring some more."

Mr. Newburger went home.

I helped Errol with his busy schedule, coordinating personal appearances, arranging interviews and photographs. Newspapers hailed Errol's presence at the bond programs, printing his dynamic speeches and never failing to note that he was constantly "pursued by admiring women begging for his autograph." On numerous sound-stages, I had seen Flynn deliver lines in memorable scenes that touched audiences the world over. Now, before thousands of spectators, he had sparked the same enthusiasm with his rousing speeches. In print, his words pale, yet my memory of his ability to stir an audience remains strong.

One afternoon he brought cheers with the following words, later published in the *Times-Picayune:* "It's sound economy to buy war bonds. No one is going to make you buy them. No one is going to hold a pistol over your head. Thank God we live in America. But if you don't buy them, there may be someone holding a pistol to your head if we lose this war, and it'll be loaded, too."

After a week in New Orleans, Flynn and I flew from town to town in a plane furnished by the Air Transport Command. People flocked into factories and auditoriums, listening to Flynn's plea to buy war bonds. Sales, prompted by Flynn, brought in millions of dollars, to our great satisfaction. Errol was heartened by the huge turnout in each little town and felt he was doing all he could to aid the war effort.

Our pilot was a wonderful guy named Colonel Bickerstaff. He was the Air Command's chief pilot, whose main responsibility was ferrying government and military dignitaries. He saved our lives one night as we were trying to land in fog-shrouded New Orleans. We had been cleared to land, but we suddenly found ourselves in an unexpected fog-bank. I felt the landing gear go down, then the aircraft suddenly nosed skyward. The colonel later told me it had been a split-second decision not to risk such a dangerous landing. We were on our way to Mobile, Alabama, when the tower informed us that we could return, since the fog had dispersed.

During our two-week stay, the people of Louisiana were very generous in their warm hospitality. Errol and I crisscrossed the state, and Louisiana reached its quota of war-bond sales—the first state in the nation to do so.

Colonel Bickerstaff flew us to St. Louis, where Flynn was to appear in another bond show, along with Gene Tierney and Anthony Quinn. Flynn was scheduled to do a Red Cross radio broadcast in the Chase Hotel, and we schemed an elaborate gag, with Tony Quinn as the victim. We had sent a script to Tony and asked if he would kindly participate in the show.

The radio personnel were all in on the joke, playing it straight as Flynn and Tony began rehearsing their material. The director gave notice that the live broadcast was about to begin. Once underway, Flynn suddenly blurted out some very foul language, then in a shocked voice, he exclaimed, "Why, Tony! Why did you say that?"

Tony turned white and tried to continue. More foul language from Flynn. The director stormed from the control booth, indignantly yelling at Quinn.

Errol, in a shocked tone, said, "Tony, you shouldn't talk like that."

"But . . . , but I didn't," responded poor Tony.

"Yes, you did!" shot back the director, "I heard you!"

Flynn just shook his head: "Shame on you, Tony."

Another guy ran up, saying, "We're getting telephone calls from around the country, wanting to know why Anthony Quinn cursed on the radio!"

"I'm ruined," said a distraught Quinn. "I won't even be able to do a B-picture now . . . ."

When Flynn told him it was only a joke, Quinn didn't believe it was only a prank. Tony was a great sport. He really loved Errol, and Flynn wouldn't have played the joke on him if he wasn't a good friend. All three of us laughed and laughed.

Late that night I was handed a message from Colonel Bickerstaff, stating that he had immediate orders to fly off, despite the fact that he was supposed to take us to another bond show in Springfield, Missouri, the following day. In the morning, I handed the note to Flynn.

"What are we going to do now, sharpie?"

"I'll get us a plane," I said.

"How? Steal one?"

"Just wait."

The old hustler in Buster Wiles went to work. I telephoned the commanding general at Cook Field, in East St. Louis, and explained the situation. The general had his driver at the Chase Hotel within the hour. I glanced at Flynn. "And what were you saying about stealing a plane?"

Errol was genuinely impressed by my fast-talking.

When we landed in Springfield, there was a military honor guard waiting for the general's airplane. When we exited there was a surprised look, but they presented arms and flashed them about. We were shown to a car, with a colonel as an escort. Due to the manpower shortage, I had been informed that I was likely to be drafted. I told the colonel that I was entering the service soon.

"Oh yeah?" he said. "Well, Wiles, what kind of job do you want?"

"Yours. I'd like to be a colonel too."

He laughed.

For our bond tour, the U.S. Treasury Department gave us special certificates expressing gratitude for our hard work.

Back in Hollywood, things seemed dull. I drove up to Mulholland late one afternoon, in a big Duesenberg.

"Where'd you steal that?" asked Errol.

"It's Gary Cooper's."

I had a hot date, and I certainly couldn't have shown up in a bigger automobile. I had become friends with Gary in *Saratoga Trunk,* when I doubled him in the action shots. I had the opportunity to gaze at Ingrid Bergman, but, just as exciting, I would discuss automobiles with Gary Cooper. We spent all of our spare time talking about cars. I drove my hot-rod to the studio one day, and he practically turned a flip. In 1939, I had set a speed record with my car, using an engine I had designed myself. *Popular Mechanics* ran an article about my motor. High-compression engines were blowing gaskets, so I chiseled indentations in the motor to create a vacuum for better cooling. I loved to take my hot-rod out to the Mojave Desert and open her up to 130 miles per hour. This was incredibly fast in those days. Gary fell in love with my hot-rod and had to take her out on the road.

"Well, why don't we just trade for a few days?" I asked.

So we did, to our mutual joy. Anytime Gary worked at

Warner's, the Duesenberg was at my disposal. It made a great impression, but it was like a tortoise compared to my hot-rod. My speed was always—fast, fast, fast!

I never needed to sleep that much. When I lived at Mulholland with Flynn, we would straggle in about three in the morning. He would say, "Well, good night," and I would say, "I gotta run out for a little while." He would shake his head and say, "I don't know how you do it." At 3:00 a.m., I was up and moving into the night, and within half an hour, I was in a lady's arms.

Buster never stopped moving, but sometimes he got caught. Barbara Gillis was a young girl who became my second wife. We were married barely long enough for the preacher to open and close the book. She and I were just wrong for each other, but from our marriage came a beautiful baby we named Susan. After our divorce, Susan lived with her mother. I resumed my carefree living.

Soon I saw a golden opportunity. I saw a financial chance of a lifetime, ready and waiting for the lucky investors. I had gone to Vegas and met a man named Wilbur Clark. He was seeking investors for his planned Desert Inn. When it came to investment percentages, I knew the odds were always in favor of the house, so I asked Flynn and Bogart to invest $100,000 each. Both declined. Bogart said, "I don't want to invest in a craps game."

Flynn and I later went to the Desert Inn when it was in full-swing. We went down in the money room and watched them counting the day's take. Money was stacked everywhere— hundreds of thousands in profit. Flynn would have been a billionaire.

May 1, 1944, was a red-letter day for me. It marked the beginning of a grueling four months spent filming *Objective Burma*. The boldness of the British military strike against the Japanese, deep in the Burmese jungles, had inspired Warner's to cast Flynn as a major in charge of a similar mission. Raoul Walsh wanted a truly realistic war story, not another phony-looking combat film made entirely on a studio sound-stage. Walsh carefully chose locations that resembled the harsh jungles of Burma.

A great deal of the jungle footage was shot at Whittier Park. While on location, Flynn and I stayed at a classy place called

Eaton, located at the corner of Foothill and Rosemead. We had a plush bungalow near the pool. Our sleeping quarters were comfortable, thank heavens, for our days were miserable.

I started the picture doubling Flynn and the other principals as they waded through swamps. I would rise at dawn and arrive as Raoul Walsh and his camera crew were lining up shots. According to the script, the commandos parachute into the jungle to destroy a radar post. After completing their mission, they become stranded, with Japanese soldiers in deadly pursuit.

The script was still being written as the production began, a situation Errol hated. He dutifully studied his lines at night, but disliked being handed rewrites at the last moment or having scenes suddenly changed. He often gave the public the image of a star who wasn't serious about his acting career, but I know otherwise.

At night, while we rehearsed lines together, Flynn would come up with ideas regarding how the scene should be played. He often made suggestions that were utilized by his directors.

The picture started rough, and it stayed that way. In the cool morning air, I donned my tattered uniform, lifted my Tommy gun and machete, and marched into the group of technicians huddled about the camera.

"In you go," said Walsh.

I sunk in the brackish water, chest deep, making certain that the stream had no hidden sinkholes or submerged objects that could injure a performer. The camera crew would follow me, carefully rehearsing how the scene would be shot. When it was apparent that the watery course was safe, I splashed onto the bank.

"Your turn, Flynn."

The tropical clothing was little protection against the early morning chill. I would shiver on the bank, waiting for Walsh to film the key scene and close-ups. Then, for long shots and over-the-shoulder takes, I was back in the swamp, hacking and slashing my way through a mass of green foliage. By day's end, my hands were torn and blistered, muscles ached, and my feet were swollen from the constant immersion in water. Once, a snake slithered right past me and disappeared in the dense undergrowth.

When we finished for the day, I would practically collapse from the tortuous work. Ripped and ragged in my damp clothing, I would report to Frank Mattison, our unit manager, and quote my fee for the day's exertions. I was on salary as a paratrooper, earning a hundred bucks a week, but for strenuous work like this, my salary skyrocketed. Mattison was usually grateful for my painful efforts and nodded in agreement when I stated my daily fee for my back-breaking eight hours in the swamp.

At the end of a particularly rough day, I trudged wearily up to Mattison, who had just arrived on the set from Warner Brothers. "You're going to be surprised by how much you owe me."

"Oh?"

"Three-hundred and fifty dollars."

"I won't pay it."

"Wait a minute, Frank. You weren't even here today. You don't know what I did. Listen . . . ."

"I'm not going to pay it!" he said, quite emphatically. He walked away.

I was stunned and angry. After wrapping for the day, we usually had a cocktail before dragging our whipped bodies back to our bungalow.

"What'll you have, Buster?"

"Nothing."

When Buster refused a cool drink, Flynn knew immediately that something was wrong. "What's the matter?"

"Flynn, how much do you think the studio should pay me for today's work?"

"All you can get," he shot back.

"Well, Mattison doesn't agree. He refused to pay me three-hundred and fifty dollars. I know I'm worth that much."

"Hell, yes," said Errol, "I'm getting sick. Let's go home."

Flynn hated to see the studio take advantage of anyone, especially old Buster. We drove to Mulholland, glad to escape the Burma jungle.

The next morning, Flynn reported that he was ill. Daily calls were met with the same answer. The studio was frantic; there was a big crew out on location, a company without a star. After three days, our absence from the production prompted Frank Mattison to figure out what was happening. Early one morning, while we were having breakfast in the dining room, the phone rang. It was

Mattison. Alex said he wanted to speak to me.

"Buster, do you think Flynn might get well if we pay you the three-hundred and fifty dollars?"

"You want to pay me my three-fifty?"

Flynn's eyes lit up. As Mattison squawked about how much money was being lost due to Flynn's absence, I was being given advice.

"Well, you know, Frank, that day is going to cost you, oh, let's say . . . five-hundred."

"All right," he fumed.

"Besides, I've missed two other days of work."

"So?"

"It's going to cost you the same for those days. You owe me fifteen-hundred dollars."

Mattison just about exploded, but he agreed to pay me. I flashed Errol the thumbs-up signal.

"So you think he's going to get well *soon?*"

"Why, Frank, Errol was just telling me this morning how he feels so much better. Why he might even be at work today. Watch out, he might run you down, he's so eager to work."

Errol Flynn was a friend I could count on. After our little tiff, Frank Mattison was more appreciative of my strenuous exertions.

The story was shot out of sequence, a truly bothersome technique as far as Flynn was concerned. But the studio called the shots their way, to Errol's profound displeasure. At the beginning of June, we were on Stage 14, preparing to film the interior of the transport plane that drops the parachutists over Burma. This was my BIG ACTING ASSIGNMENT. I had lines, as the airplane crew chief. The night before I pored over the script, memorizing my dialogue.

After a restless night, I arrived at Warner Brothers, quietly mumbling what I was to say. I walked onto the set with my heart thumping. When the great moment arrived, I stepped between the rows of parachutists, perspiring heavily under the hot lights. Walsh came over and explained how I was to play the scene. I began clowning and turned up the bill of my cap, giving me a jaunty air. "That'll work," laughed Raoul. I was always making Walsh laugh, that's how I got the role which required a light, humorous touch. Walsh pointed to the marker where I was to turn toward the camera, then he disappeared in the darkness.

"Action," he said quietly.

"With my back to the camera, I secured the plane door, while a soldier talked to me about his girl back home.

"Yeah, I know what you mean," I responded. Then I strode down the center of the airplane. "Boys, after this war's over, I might even make a jump. If this trip gets a little rough for you, there's a bucket back there—and use it!

I tripped over a guy's foot, the paratroopers laughed, then I disappeared into the cockpit.

"Print!" said Walsh.

I walked over to where he sat. "How was it? Did it sound like I was selling cantaloupes and watermelons?"

From the shadows came Flynn's voice: "Gable couldn't have done it any better."

For a month, we filmed at the Lucky Baldwin Estate in Santa Anita, where a Burmese village had been erected. The story had the commandos discovering their slaughtered friends, then being attacked by the enemy. Flynn had a moving scene with William Prince, a young lieutenant whom the Japanese have butchered. He begs for Flynn to kill him. The audience never sees the mutilated American but reads the horror on Flynn's face, as he recoils at the terrible sight. In the battle scene, I played soldiers on both sides. The weather was steaming, with the sun blazing overhead, and I fell in the dust over and over, as the commandos blasted the Japanese to pieces.

After a few days, I was doubling Flynn again, this time in scenes of the commandos fleeing in the jungle. Between takes, the cast would collapse in the shade, remove the hot metal helmets, and dream of ice-cold cocktails. Then, just as our sweat-soaked bodies relaxed, we would hear the assistant director's loud voice: "Places!"

We would struggle to our feet, throw on our packs, and grab dummy rifles, which were stacked nearby. By the weekend, Flynn and I were drained. Errol usually returned to Mulholland Farm, but I remained in our bungalow.

I recall a Saturday morning when we were beat and trying to sleep late. From outside, loud voices broke my blissful slumber. I sleepily peered through the blinds to see a well-dressed group of hotel guests "oohing" and "aahing" around the swimming pool. My heavy eyelids opened wider to see where the women were. Then it struck me that the noisy group was admiring the flowers! By now, Flynn was awake and grumbling about going home. Our much-needed sleep had been cruelly interrupted.

"I'll make 'em pay," said an angry Buster Wiles. I put on my outfit, then let fly a series of blood-curdling screams. At Bungalow Number 6, the door burst open, and out I came in a cowboy hat, raincoat, and Army combat boots. The startled flower-lovers backed away as I lifted my coat to display my knobby knees. I ran to the diving board and began clowning, springing high in the air, bouncing on my bottom. Flinging away the raincoat, I completed my little show with a handstand and did a cannonball in the pool, splashing water in every direction. From the doorway of Bungalow Number 6 came hearty applause and a "Well done, Buster!"

One morning, I arrived with my mother and son. Mama had a picnic basket filled with fried chicken. Little Don had begged to come, just to see what I did for a living. Walsh was now filming the destruction of the radar center. I was again a soldier of the Rising Sun. I calmly waited inside a hut while the powdermen set up their explosives. My son had wanted to see me get blown out of the place, but I had second thoughts. He was still a kid, and I didn't want to scare him; there was always the chance that something might go wrong and I might be injured.

As the countdown started, I crouched in the stifling heat, listening attentively to the voice outside counting, "three..., two..., one." I sprang up and leaped for the door. A second later, the concussion from the powerful *boom* hurled me through the air, and I crashed in the dust, head splitting and ears ringing. Splintered bamboo floated over me. Fortunately, we did it in one take.

I staggered to my feet, stripped off my shirt, and walked away in a daze, moving slowly through the woods to where my mother and son waited. When Don saw me, he ran toward me and leaped in my arms, elated that I had emerged—seemingly unscathed—from where all the noise was coming. But I was still stunned by the fierce explosion. A few moments later, a pal snapped a photo of Don and me coming down the path, hand in hand. I felt like hell, and the strain is evident on my face.

Ironically, when I saw the stunt on film, I was disappointed.

The camera had captured me from quite a distance, in an extreme long shot. It was over the shoulders of a machine-gun crew, whose chattering weapon was mowing down enemy soldiers. I came sailing out of a door through a puff of smoke. I'll never know why actual explosives were used. I could have simply dived out of the building.

I had such a bad headache I sprawled on a blanket without touching Mama's delicious chicken.

"Buster," said Mama, "you must feel bad."

My mother was living in a twenty-six-unit motel I had built on Garvey Boulevard in El Monte. Every time I would save a sum of money, I would give it to Mama and let her build another unit at the motel. She was the manager of the place. Close by, there was a bar and restaurant called Cocaninos, and Mama and I frequented the place to have drinks and a bit of fun.

One Sunday night, Mama came up to Mulholland to have dinner with Errol and me. She told us how she had walked into Cocaninos the other day and called for a round for everyone. A new waitress happened to be working. The new girl said in a loud voice, "Who *is* that lady buying drinks?"

Someone replied, "That's Buster Wiles' mother."

"Well, *who* is Buster Wiles?"

"Don't you know? He's a friend of Errol Flynn."

"Well, *that lady* certainly doesn't know anybody who knows Errol Flynn."

Mama told us this and laughed about it.

The next day, we were shooting out at Whittier Park and had to pass Cocaninos on the way to Arcadia. I decided to show that waitress that my mother did know Mr. Errol Flynn. "Hold it right here," I told the driver.

We walked in, and I saw a waitress I didn't know. I asked to be seated in her section.

Flynn and I had a seat. Then I was surprised to see Mama come inside. She had no idea we were going to be there, and we didn't expect to see her that afternoon. No sooner had we sat at our table when Mama passed through the door and said, "Give everybody in here a drink."

I stood up and waved.

Seeing us, she said, "And give my two babies a drink too!"

Mama came over and joined us. I could see the new waitress slowly making her way toward us.

"You're new here, aren't you?" I asked.

"Yes."

I asked her name, and she told me.

"I would like to introduce you to a couple of friends of mine. This is my mother, Mrs. Wiles."

I turned to the man sitting beside me. "And what the hell's your name, buddy?"

"Flynn."

"Oh, yes. Errol's your first name, isn't it?"

He nodded.

The waitress stammered, "I . . . I . . . I've seen him before."

"Well, he's a friend of my mother."

Sun and sweat, dust and heat, day after day—it was utterly draining. Before long, the exhausting production began to wear down everyone's spirits. At the Warner Ranch in Calabasas, the heat was more oppressive than in the city. We were in Calabasas to complete the long shots of the assault on the radar station. Tempers were short-fused. The dust had plagued Flynn's sinus condition, and he was eager for the behind-schedule film to end.

The story's dramatic climax was a fierce enemy night assault against a handful of American survivors, who were dug in atop a mountain. By now, the production had dragged on into a sweltering August. At the Providencia Ranch, we spent more hours in the broiling sun. My metal helmet was like an oven, leaving me soaked with perspiration, constantly blinded by stinging, salty rivulets that rolled from my forehead. It seemed like the film would never end. Once again, Frank Mattison began haggling over my salary, and a simmering dispute threatened another walkout.

Late one afternoon, Flynn and I straggled down from the mountain after a hard day's shoot to discover that his dressing room—a raggedy tent—had vanished, along with his clothes. He searched the area, finding his pants along the side of the road, but sixty dollars was missing. Hot words were exchanged between Flynn and Frank Mattison. I threw in my two cents, and Mattison reported to the studio that he had "a mutiny" on his hands.

Flynn penned a letter to Tenny Wright, studio production chief, complaining of the dismal situation:

August 12, 1944

Mr. T.C. Wright
Production
Studio

Dear Mr. Wright:

For the last four months our company has been on a number of different locations and I wish to acquaint you with a few facts concerning the dressing rooms. As you know, locations are never comfortable particularly the sort we have had on "Objective Burma."

My dressing room, as we laughingly call it, had certain novel features. I counted as many as ten holes in the canvas sides through which I found some children examining me in the act of robing and disrobing. One other quite noticeable feature was the floor. At Whittier, for instance, it consisted of a thin strip of moth-eaten matting, much torn and ratted. It only covered a minute portion of the dressing room, the rest was solid cow-dung. This undoubtedly explains the fascination the room held for ten million assorted insects. There was no privacy of any kind, and perhaps you are not aware that not one of these dressing rooms had a latch unless you can call one of my shoes jammed in the opening that.

I cannot adequately describe the general filth. But the topper came when I discovered one day that my dressing room had been changed overnight and that I was now dressing in one that I had myself used the previous day as a toilet (in company with two or three hundred gentlemen). The only marked change between the toilet and the dressing room was that it now had a broken down chair instead of the usual receptical. I am enclosing a picture by way of illustration.

Conditions such as these are pretty bad but I might never have gotten around to complaining had it not been for the day before yesterday. When I came down from the top of the mountain, where I am currently working, my dressing room had completely disappeared! At present I am not familiar of its whereabouts (unless Eddie Blatt is using it for a set). A hue and cry was raised to find my clothes. Several gentlemen at last located them by the side of the road beneath one of the curious delapadated matted things we refer to as mattresses. I dressed by the open roadside—fortunately no Tanner Busses passed by. Upon plugging my hand into my pocket I discovered that I had been ratted for all the money that was in my pockets. No, pardon me, the sum of 78 cents was left. But the $62.00 green was on its way to Glendale or elsewhere. Your Unit Manager is to blame for the loss for ordering my room struck while my clothes were in it.

Frankly, Mr. Wright, everyone is familiar with your noted objection to actors being comfortable on locations. So actually you might just as well dispense with dressing rooms all together.

I certainly never pause one second more than is vital in these unsanitary precincts. One can stand anything for a few days but we have been on this picture four months with everyday outside.

By contrast I would refer you to the trailer dressing rooms both Fox and M.G.M. use on locations.

Yours sincerely,
Errol Flynn

EF:b
cc:Mr. J.L. Warner
   Mr. Steve Trilling

P.S.

Without wishing to draw envious comparisons between my own plight and that of others consider Miss Bette Davis. When Miss Davis goes on location, even for a day, her dressing room is loaded on a truck and sent along with her. Miss Davis is thus accorded a double-edged advantage, for Nature is on her side too. If, reluctant to enter the nauseating precincts of the canvas structure marked 'WOMEN,' she seeks fragrant solace of the Californian shrubbery, there is little chance of her acquiring a dose of Poison Oak upon those hanging appendages with which Nature has endowed the male of the species.

Errol included a photo of himself posed before his canvas dressing room. Clearly visible on the tent was MEN. He made his point and the studio improved his dressing facility.

When the dressing-room matter was smoothed over, the studio pushed to complete the picture as soon as possible. Rather than waste valuable time on distant location sites, Raoul Walsh cleverly shot a few scenes on the hillside just behind the Burbank studio. The crew set up around a lone tree; directly below us was a stream of traffic on Olive Avenue.

Flynn and Henry Hull, who was playing an elderly news correspondent, lean against this tree together, discussing their bleak prospects of being rescued. On another occasion, I doubled Flynn in a sunrise scene, standing alone on a ridge above Mulholland Drive. When I saw *Objective Burma,* the scenes all melded beautifully, and the film got fine reviews as a gripping, realistic war drama. However, Flynn was disheartened when an international incident arose on its release in England. The British felt that they had been overlooked in the film. Warner Brothers pulled the film from release. Unexpectedly, it was Errol who received the brunt of criticism, as if he had written the script.

Despite the unfavorable response in England, Flynn always felt that *Objective Burma* was one of his best efforts. Without doubt, it was one of the most physically exhausting productions I ever worked on.

Our next picture was *San Antonio,* a Western, with Errol as a gunslinger out to nab cattle rustler, Paul Kelly. In doubling Flynn, I had a very close call. He and Kelly were staging a pistol fight in the Alamo. Kelly creeps around back of me, grabs a horse, then tries to gallop away. The cameras rolled, I made a leap to stop Kelly, but was a little early. The horse trampled me. After being knocked to the ground, I was run over by the horse. Blood oozed down my legs, but luckily, no bones were broken.

Escape Me Never was a different sort of Flynn picture. Errol was featured as a composer in Venice who writes a ballet. The dancer who captures the composer's masterpiece was the great George Zoritch, a charming man who captivated audiences around the world. I spent most of the picture falling out of gondolas. It was a special pleasure working with Ida Lupino, who co-starred as Flynn's wife. Ida had a wonderful sense of humor. One morning, I stopped by her home on North Beverly Drive to give her a lift to the studio. Along the way, I picked up a young kid who was hitchhiking out to the Valley. I thought I would have a laugh. I told the young guy I had to stop for someone. We went inside Ida's living room and waited. She breezed down the stairs with a cheery, "Good morning." Her four-footed pet, Duchess, tagged behind her.

Seeing lovely Ida, the kid's jaw dropped six inches. I winked at Ida, then turned to the hitchhiker. "What's wrong?" I asked, "haven't you ever seen a police dog before?"

When we left the kid on Ventura Boulevard, his jaw was still around his knees.

On the set one afternoon, Flynn and Ida had a dramatic scene where she cried. Errol was supposed to wipe a tear away. Between takes, I told Flynn, "Don't brush the tear away—kiss it away."

"Yeah, that's a good idea," agreed Errol.

When he suggested the touch to the director, Peter Godfrey, there was additional enthusiasm.

"Yes! Let's try it!"

Maybe I should have been a director. I had a chance. One time, Raoul Walsh telephoned me and asked it I wanted to become a second-unit director on a picture at MGM. I turned it down. I was happy as a stuntman.

My suggestion to Flynn would be my last piece of movie work

for a while. Opening my mail one afternoon, I unfolded a greeting from Uncle Sam. I was in the Army. Before my departure, I enjoyed a little farewell party at the Trocadero nightclub. Harry Hays Morgan, Jr., and I became "blood brothers." We drank heap big firewater. It was a fitting farewell to Hollywood.

I was sent to basic training in Texas. Among the mementos of my military service is a jumbo postcard issued by the U.S. Army. It boldly states, "The Home of the Tank Destroyers—Camp Hood, Texas." The symbol of the tank destroyers was a menacing panther devouring a tank, and the motto of our unit was printed around the panther: "Seek, Strike, Destroy." Near this it reads:

> The ENEMY is listening—Don't SAY it!
> The ENEMY can read—Don't WRITE it!

Well, I got the message. But, printed clearly on the jumbo postcard was interesting military information: "Here, in a reservation containing 170,000 acres and approximately 80,000 men—one of the largest in the United States—is the Army's newest offensive weapon—the tank destroyers!" There was a photo of the new weapon too. I wonder if any of the enemy saw the postcard?

During our indoctrination period, we were led into a theater to watch training films. When the lights dimmed, I was surprised.

"Hey, that's me in that tank!" I said proudly. The guys around me looked at me like I was nuts.

"Yeah, that's me too!"

"Aw, come on, Wiles," they muttered. "Who you trying to kid?"

I had the hardest time convincing my fellow soldiers that I was a Hollywood stuntman. The old hustler in me surfaced. I had a plan for some profitable wagering.

Newspapers were speculating as to whether or not Flynn had married Nora Eddington. I wrote him, inquiring if the rumors were true. Errol sent me a letter confirming that he and Nora were man and wife, and that he would soon tell the press. I circulated through the barracks, making bets regarding Flynn's marital status. Needless to say, when the truth was revealed, I cleaned up.

I did my best to join the paratroopers for the final attack on Germany, but unfortunately, I was considered too old at age thirty-five. Instead, I became a driver for General Alexander O. Gorder. The first day I was driving, I asked the general how fast I was to go.

"I'll leave that decision to you," he said.

When the jeep hit ninety miles per hour, the general spoke up. "That's fast enough!"

One day, I felt horrible and couldn't get out of bed. The sergeant thought I was malingering, and he pestered me to get up. I yelled at him. Privates seldom yell at sergeants. He must have been convinced I was ill, since he disappeared. Eventually, someone drove me to the infirmary, and I walked inside by myself. I watched as two men were worked on by an emergency team. They had been shot with their own weapons when their jeep overturned. A doctor came over, and I explained my symptoms.

"Don't move!" he told me.

After a thorough exam, I was informed by the physician that I was lucky to be alive—my appendix had burst. It was extremely rare. The area had sealed itself off, preventing peritonitis from setting in. I asked the doctor where he had received his medical training.

"The University of Tennessee Medical School in Memphis."

"Who trained you?"

He mentioned some of his professors. They had been my teammates on the UT Docs football team. One of his medical professors had been Dr. Sam Sanders. I knew I was in competent hands. When my pal Sam learned of my predicament, he offered to fly to Camp Hood himself to operate. The Army doctor couldn't understand why I wasn't dead.

During my military service, I managed to escape death again. I had hitched a ride with some Navy flyers to Memphis: the pilots were delivering twelve Lockheed Lodestars. I stayed in Memphis for a few days rest, visiting relatives. The day I was to leave, I didn't make the airplane, since my buddies kept me drinking in a bar. The plane going to Los Angeles crashed near Salt Lake City, killing most of the passengers.

When the war ended, I once again returned to Warner Brothers to resume my career. Many good men never came home. It was also a tragedy that President Roosevelt didn't live to witness the victory. I've always considered him to be one of our greatest presidents.

Back in Los Angeles, Errol graciously invited me to return to my old room at Mulholland House, but I declined. He and Nora were married, with a child, and I felt that I would be intruding. It was characteristic of Errol to help his friends.

A few years later, in early 1949, Howard Hill asked Flynn's assistance. Though a skilled archer, with incredible patience and determination, he was having little success in raising money for his cherished dream of producing a full-length adventure film in Africa. Howard had gone from studio to studio trying to generate interest in his African safari. Despite his reputation as a fabulous archer, the studios turned him down.

As a last resort, he went to Flynn, his former partner, with whom he had made numerous short-subject archery films. Howard was a very independent person. He disliked borrowing money from his friends and would never have asked, except for the fact that the African safari was a childhood dream, one he had to seize before it was too late.

He had mortgaged his home and sunk his life savings into the film project, but it wasn't enough.

"How much do you need?" asked Errol.

"I've raised one-hundred-thousand dollars from my own assets. I need one-hundred fifty thousand."

"Hmmm, that's quite a lot. Let me ask my business manager how things stand."

Flynn discussed the matter with Al Blum, who forcefully advised him:

"You'd be crazy to give him the money! What if he's trampled by an elephant and dies? What then? You would have no picture and no money."

"Well, I'm going to give it to him."

"What?"

"It's my money. I'll take the risk."

Errol wrote Howard a check for $150,000.

For nine months, Howard traveled through Kenya, Tanganyika, and Uganda, filming *Tembo*. He was filmed bringing down a wild rogue elephant that had been menacing a Swahili village. He felled the enormous beast with a bow and arrow, the first white man on record to accomplish such a hunting feat.

Howard toured from city to city with the movie, guaranteeing packed theaters by performing with his bow before *Tembo* was shown. The picture was a remarkable success. When the profits had accumulated, he returned to Mulholland House, intending to write a check for the loan, interest, and sizable profit for Flynn. But Errol refused additional compensation.

"Howard, just write me a check for one-hundred and fifty thousand."

"I'd like for you to earn something, too."

"No, I never intended to make a profit off my friends. All I want is what I loaned you."

Ironically, Flynn's business manager, Al Blum, stole quite a sum of money from Errol. After Blum's death, a note was found informing his client of the theft. Flynn rushed to one of his safe-deposit boxes, and, as he told me, "It was empty. All I found were wrappers. The cash was gone."

Flynn and I drove to Balboa to see his new yacht, the *Zaca.* After the rape trial, he had rid himself of the *Sirocco,* which he felt was now jinxed. He had been so eager to sell the boat that he let it go for considerably less than it was worth. While in the Army, I had read of Errol and Professor Flynn leading a scientific cruise to remote islands off Mexico to collect marine life. I was disappointed that I had missed the cruise. Flynn was very proud of his enormous luxury yacht. It was white, two-masted, and expensive. When Flynn showed me around the boat, it was apparent that he loved every square inch of his new craft.

Back in civilian clothes, I resumed my career as a stuntman. In *Wild Harvest,* I had a chance to meet one of the nicest stars I've ever worked with—Alan Ladd. I had been assigned the fight scenes on the picture. The first day of work I drove to Paramount early in the morning. I was seated on the set, reading a newspaper, when I looked up to see Alan Ladd standing in front of me.

He politely introduced himself and said it was great having me working on his film. "My wife Sue and I were in San Francisco one weekend. We entered our hotel elevator, and on the next floor, you and Flynn got on. By the sixth floor, you two had everyone laughing."

I found Alan to be a very modest and down-to-earth gentleman.

After awhile, stunting became less and less interesting. I started a new job—jockey's agent. The racetrack had always been a wonderful place for me to have a great time. With my love for wagering, the track was paradise. After a day at the races, I would frequent the watering-holes near the track. My favorite hangout was The House That Jack Built, near Santa Anita Racetrack.

After a race one evening, I walked in Jack's to see a bartender arguing with a customer. The guy was complaining that there was no soda in his bourbon. The bartender insisted there was. I was a regular patron, so the bartender waved me over to settle the dispute.

"Buster, taste this, and see which one is with soda and which is with water."

I gulped one drink in a big swallow. "No, I'm sorry, that's bourbon and water. Let me check and see if this is the same." I downed the other drink. "Now *that* was the bourbon and soda!"

"I was right," said the customer. Then he stared at two empty glasses. "Say, where in the hell is my drink?"

One evening, a couple of jockeys I knew were lamenting that they had no horses to ride.

"I can find you a mule," I said.

"Hell, I'd ride it," said one.

"Not if I got there first," said the other.

When I realized that these guys were only half-kidding, that they were jobless, the inborn hustler in me emerged. "You guys will be riding next week," I told them.

"Oh, yeah?" they responded, with obvious disbelief.

"I'll find you guys something to ride, even if it's only a bicycle."

The following morning, I was at Santa Anita as trainers put their thoroughbreds through vigorous workouts.

"Say, partner, I've got a winning rider for you."

Just as I had proclaimed, the jockeys who had been crying in their beer all had work the following week. That's how I became a jockey's agent. It began as a part-time job, in 1947. Performing stunts was still my major way of making a living, but I found myself at home in the stables, and I loved to travel when my boys raced out of state.

In the summer of 1950, Errol was on his way to Europe to make *The Adventures of Captain Fabian* for his own company. He invited me along, but I declined.

"That's not like you, Buster. What's up?"

"I'm in love."

"Oh, I see. Well, you know, there's going to be lots of excitement and adventure in France."

"Flynn, I'm telling you, I have found her."

"The real thing?"

"Absolutely! She's the girl of my dreams, partner."

Flynn wished me the best, then told me of his deep attraction to Patrice Wymore, a lovely actress, whom he had just met while filming *Rocky Mountain*. We both remarried for the third time in 1950.

While racing in Vancouver, B.C., a friend had invited me to the MacPhail home for a party. I laid eyes on Donalda, and it was simply love at first sight. Her mother introduced us, and then I asked her for a dance. I made about two turns with this lovely girl, then told her, "I'm going to be spending a lot of time with you." We've now been married for almost forty years.

In San Francisco, we said our vows. On emerging from the judge's chambers, we saw that there was a parade passing down the street: "See, honey, you didn't know what an important man you were marrying." She laughed. We've been laughing ever since. We spent our honeymoon in San Francisco's Continental Hotel. This was my lucky hotel. While on the racing circuit, I used to invite friends over, and we would soon be having fun gambling.

After awhile, we were placing bets on the toot of the cable car. Was it going up or down the street? Buster asked the cable-car operator if he would kindly toot his horn three times if he was going up, four times if down. I cleaned up on my bets. Titanic Thompson had taught me a few lessons.

A few days after my bride and I arrived at the hotel, my funds were dwindling. Whenever this occurred in my life, I would find a streak of luck. I recall once when I was down to my last quarter on Hollywood Boulevard. After seeing a picture, I decided to spend my last coin on a beer. I walked in a place called Kelly's and saw a friend named Roy Gatewood. He made a suggestion. "Let's rent the Rose Bowl, Buster."

"Fine," I said. I thought Roy was talking through the bottom of his beer glass.

"I'm serious, Buster."

He loaned me a hundred dollars. He said he would meet me in the morning for details of our scheme. The next day, Roy explained that a driller's association would put up the funds to finance a "charity event." Roy and I would get a percentage of all tickets sold. Everybody likes to contribute to a worthy cause, and Buster's cause was worthy: I was broke. Roy and I made a killing on our tickets.

On our honeymoon, Donalda discovered that I had another romance going—a lifelong affair, too.

"Donalda, darling, I've got to go out for awhile."

"Where?"

"To the racetrack."

"Now?"

"Yes! One of my crazy lucky feelings has come over me." My friend Pete Pelleteri and I pooled our hunches, and we chose winner after winner. I returned to the hotel with eight-hundred dollars, presents, and champagne. As Donalda looked on with wonder, I popped the cork and proposed a toast.

"Here's to our life together," I said happily, "and here's to those thoroughbreds who made me a winner."

PART THREE

FROM STUDIOS TO STABLES

Wearing a fake beard at Warner-Bros. with my pal, jockey Maurice "Moose" Peters.

In the winner's circle, at far left, with my jockey Jay Fishburn, who has just ridden "Duke of Brujo" to victory. *(Photo: Courtesy of Jay Fishburn)*

ELEVEN

The King of Sports

"A woman and a horse should never be loaned."

My first pony, Captain Billy, had shown me what superb creatures horses can be. As a kid, I would climb a fence so I could mount him, and once astride, I felt like I was on top of the world. We would sail through the pastures and countryside, exploring the terrain. Riding at a full gallop was an exciting sensation that I never forgot, and the world of thoroughbred racing conveys the same feeling of adventure and excitement.

Working as a jockey's agent was a gamble in itself. Income was based on a percentage of the winnings—no wins, no income. I usually handled two contracted veteran riders and one apprentice. I have the greatest respect in the world for jockeys. There is a certain amount of danger atop a thousand-pound thoroughbred. Flying down the track at forty miles per hour, a horse's leg can snap like a toothpick. The result can be deadly. Since 1942, one-hundred jockeys have been killed.

Ironically, one of the most dangerous phases of racing is when the jockeys are atop their steeds in the starting gate, before the gates open. They have little control over a mount at that precise moment. A nervous horse can suddenly bolt and topple over, crushing a man's spine. The stakes are high indeed.

In 1952, Flynn again begged me to accompany him to Europe.

His tax situation was so heavy, he determined he should live and work abroad to maintain his elegant style of living.

"I'll make you a millionaire, Buster."

"Flynn, I've got enough trouble with English. How am I going to communicate in foreign languages? I've got a wife and a kid."

"Bring them along."

"No, Errol, I just can't. I'm just too American."

"Patrice and I are leaving."

"Best wishes to you."

I was happy that his marriage was working. A while later, he told me, "She's the one I really love."

In 1956, I did my last stunt work, in a Western called *The Brass Legend*. This film starred Raymond Burr and Hugh O'Brien. Tumbles from horses and strenuous fight scenes were getting to Buster, and the aches, pains, and broken ribs were taking longer to heal. Los Angeles had expanded tremendously in the postwar years. I wanted my family to live in a peaceful environment. We settled in Beaverton, Oregon, a small town, but one filled with natural beauty and fine people.

By now, Flynn was an international traveler, constantly moving around the world. This month in Jamaica, the next in England, then France. When he was in the States, we would speak on the phone; the rest of the time, I would receive a stream of postcards from abroad.

I was still traveling myself, up and down the Pacific Coast, with my riders. This week, we would be racing at Santa Anita, the next at Portland Meadows. Win or lose, there was never a dull moment. The life of the racetrack was just as fascinating as my previous work in pictures. Thoroughbred racing had once been the sport of kings, but for millions of fans like myself it is the king of sports.

Horse-racing is indeed big business. Investments in breeding farms, new tracks, equipment, and personnel amount to millions of dollars—if not billions. One horse alone can be worth a million bucks.

To be a racehorse, it is necessary to be a *thoroughbred*. The thoroughbred is the noblest of the horse family. To be eligible for registry in the stud book of the country where he originates, the horse must be traceable to three famous sires. In the unbroken male line, every thoroughbred in the world can be traced to Herod, Eclipse, or Matchem, grandsons and great-grandsons of three desert horses brought to Britain in the eighteenth century—the Beverly Turk, the Darley Arabian, and the Godolphin Arabian. Recorded racing in England goes back to Henry VIII. Racing in America was begun in 1745, and such notable founding fathers as George Washington and Thomas Jefferson were breeders of fine racing horses.

The term "thoroughbred" is not in the public domain but is registered in the United States Patent Office and in foreign countries. As long as the horse is eligible for the American Stud book, it can be called a thoroughbred. Selective breading has improved the aristocratic thoroughbred tremendously, and these horses are the handsomest and most valuable animals in the world. I've never ceased to be amazed by the ability of the day-old foal to run swiftly alongside its mother. It is a truly wondrous spectacle.

Time goes by so fast; we're not here very long. My philosophy of life has always been to be happy and laugh. We can't waste our time getting too serious. Race-courses are a wonderful way of enjoying an afternoon. At the track are interesting people, beautiful pageantry in pleasant surroundings, and the possibility of being a winner.

Not only does the king of sports provide recreation and excitement, but also substantial *revenue*. When a racetrack accepts a bettor's money for a wager, it merely functions as a broker for investment in a ticket. A commission, fixed by the state and shared by the state, is deducted, and the money from racing goes to the construction of public institutions, such as schools. The revenue also adds to old-age pensions and can be spent in numerous ways for the benefit of the community and state. One of the major benefits of racing is that it reduces the burden of local taxes.

There are still some who think that racing or gambling is wrong. I firmly disagree. I sincerely hate to see people lose more than they can afford. I hate to see people make any type of mistake that hurts their family. Betting should not be an obsession or a get-rich-quick scheme. I had a friend who made the most delicious pastries in Portland. She often stopped by my home to give

Donalda and me some exquisite goodies. She started asking for tips for the races. Fine. I gave her some good horses—four out of five won.

The next thing I knew, she was at my door. "Buster, my husband and I have fifteen-thousand dollars we'd like to invest . . . ."

"Stop right there. I know what you're going to say. Forget it!"

I wouldn't give her any more leads. When gambling becomes an obsession to risk everything, then it's time to stop. I should know—BELIEVE ME! I was a born gambler.

Sometimes, the financial situation around the Wiles home would be tough. Donalda and I were blessed with two lovely daughters, Laura and Carole Anne. Occasionally, my lucky streaks would vanish and the bills would mount. Even though there would be only a few dollars in the bank, there was never a word of complaint from Donalda. I've got the Man Upstairs to thank for her.

I once saw two elderly ladies studying a racing card. They were using a hat-pin to determine the victors. They picked eight winners in a row. I went over to them and asked, "Why not use a fork to pick win, place, and show?"

Everyone likes to win, and gambling has always intrigued me. I think I was a born gambler. I enjoy taking chances. Some people don't like to gamble, because they don't feel they can win. I recall a friend telling me about his first time at the tracks.

"When I was a boy, my father took me to the racetrack. Every horse my Dad placed money on lost. About one-hundred dollars was gone. We were sitting in the stands, watching, when one of the caretakers appeared. He began shoveling what the horses had left.

"My Dad turned to me, 'See that man, son? He's the smartest guy here.'

"'Why, Dad?'

"'Because when he leaves the racetrack, he *knows* he's going home with money in his pocket. He'll have his paycheck. The rest of us will be broke.' "

That's one way to look at gambling. Straight gambling is merely pure luck. I was walking down the street once when a pal ran up to me.

"Say, Buster, I heard you won thirty-six-thousand dollars in a craps game!"

"Well, Jim," I told him, "you know how talk distorts the truth. It was actually fifty-four-thousand."

Jim's eyes grew as large as half-dollars. That's the biggest win I've ever been blessed with. Several months later, it was gone. I had loaned, spent, gambled, or squandered it away. Excessive gambling is just like any other form of overindulgence. When it comes to gambling on horses though, I've always felt that there is a definite science that can be applied to improve your chances of winning.

Just like the jockeys who move down the course, trying to get an advantageous early position, a bettor can do the same. Horses can be studied just like books. Don't wait until your selection is in the home-stretch to wonder if he's going to win. Before you even go to the track, you should have an idea which thoroughbred looks like a good choice. In my years of being around the racetrack, I have developed ways to determine likely winners.

• Examining the thoroughbreds for the forthcoming race is very important. In the paddock, look for horses that are calm and not really sweaty. In general, the horses that sweat don't do very well. I look for a calm horse, but one who steps out very briskly, with good determination. I like a horse with a large chest. Those horses can run.
• If a horse is six-to-one or over, you should back your bet up. Bet win, place, and show. Under six-to-one, just bet win and place.
• Study the racing forms carefully. Learn about speed ratings, mud markings, performance charts, and past races. It is very important to examine dropping in class or moving up in class. The first month of the season is especially crucial, and many analysts suggest holding one's bet until the second month.
• Reading as much racing material as possible makes betting on horses a scientific guess.

Some publications to pick up:

• *Daily Racing Form* and *New York Morning Telegraph*. This is a daily publication, providing information about the past performances of the day's entries at the tracks.

• *Thoroughbred Record* and *Racing Calendar.* This is the nation's oldest racing and bloodstock journal, containing interesting articles on horses, jockeys and races.
• *American Racing Manual.* This annual volume is an excellent guide to the year's racing records. There are statistics on all aspects of racing—owners, trainers, jockeys, horses, and racetracks.

Any library should have a collection of racing books. The Thoroughbred Racing Association (or T.R.A.) furnishes a good pamphlet explaining the intricacies of racing. It is complimentary at most tracks.

I love the excitement of horseracing. People with a few dollars in their pockets often walk away richer. Sometimes, it's the opposite. I've experienced both situations. I was at Golden Gate Fields, in San Francisco, when I had a feeling—"Hope's High" was the horse to bet on. I placed a bet with a bookie for fifteen-to-one odds. At the track it was twenty-to-one. I stopped at the Ben Franklin Hotel in San Matteo for a little refreshment on my way to the track. I saw my pal Felix behind the bar. Felix was a Filipino who shared the thrill of horseracing, but not that day.

"Buster, I no bet no more. I break my money too much."

"I'll place a ten-dollar bet for you, Felix."

Sure enough, Hope's High came in first.

I jetted to my bookie to pick up my winnings. It amounted to $18,000. He placed it in a high stack. I grabbed the stack and cut it like a deck of cards. One-half went in my left pocket, one-half went in my right. The bookie stared at me.

"Aren't you even going to count it?"

"Hell, I only had five dollars on me when I came in here. I'm happy to get anything."

I stopped at the Ben Franklin and gave Felix his share. He didn't want to accept it. "But, Buster, I don't even know the horse's name."

"Hope's High."

Felix looked at his winnings. He grinned. "When is he racing again?" Felix was back in the sport of thoroughbred racing.

I was once at Del Mar with my buddy, actor J. Carrol Naish. We were having a great time deciding which horses to bet on. J. Carrol pulled out his wallet—it was stuffed with thousands of dollars in cash. He always carried big money with him. I had a good hunch about the horses in the next race, and J. Carrol went to place the bet. He kindly handed me four fifty-dollar tickets. I presumed he had his own tickets too.

Well, the regular announcer was sick, and the substitute got the horses all mixed up. J. Carrol couldn't figure out who was in the lead. But old Buster knew, since his eyes were glued on his baby. There was no mistake. After the confusion subsided, our horse won. It paid what I like to call "a clear vision": $20/20. I had won two-hundred dollars.

"Go and get your tickets cashed, J. Carrol." He should have won $2,200. He lowered his eyes.

"Buster, while I was in line, I saw someone I knew. He gave me another horse . . . . I bet on the one that came in last!"

I offered to split my winnings, but he wouldn't hear of it. When Buster gets a hunch, it's usually the right one.

As an agent, I found mounts for such greats as Ismael "Milo" Valenzuala, John Ishihara, Basil James, and Ray York. The finest jockey I ever booked was, without a doubt, the king—Johnny Longden. Johnny was born in Wakefield, England, and raised on a farm in Taber, Alberta. He rode his first winner in 1927. When he rode "Arrogate" to victory in the Del Mar Handicap in 1956, he became "the winningest jockey" in racing history, having won 4,871 in his career. In 1943, he won the Triple Crown of racing on Mrs. John Hertz's "Count Fleet." From 1927 to 1964, Johnny rode 31,490 horses; he had 5,913 wins. In 1964, I booked Johnny aboard "Viking Spirit," and he won the Longacres Mile. Johnny is a racing legend.

He rode until he was sixty and won his last race. His fabulous career record of 6,093 victories was broken in 1970, by the equally terrific Willie Shoemaker. The four-foot, eleven-inch Shoemaker is a towering champ, with 8,443 wins and $100,000,000 in purses. For thirty-six years he has been booked by only one agent, Harry Silbert. The association is also a record in racing annals. Johnny Longden and Willie Shoemaker are not only the greatest riders ever, but champion human beings as well.

My riders usually managed to earn winnings in six figures. The biggest win I ever booked was when jockey John Cavalli rode

"Miche," an Argentinian horse, to victory in the Santa Anita Handicap. Our trainer was Don Cameron. The prize money was $140,000.

Being a jockey's agent was a wonderful life. We had tons of fun. One season, I was booking horses for races at Golden Gate Fields in San Francisco, and I spread the word that I was organizing a frog race. I phoned the press that the Calaveras Classic would take place, in honor of Mark Twain's famous short story, "The Celebrated Jumping Frog of Calaveras County." I told the reporters that I was training my frog at the racetrack. The newspapermen came out to the track for a press conference.

"How's the training coming, Buster?"

"Just fine," I told them. "My frog is going to be a champion. His little legs are becoming so powerful that he's splitting stall doors."

"But can he jump, Buster?"

"Can he jump? Only yesterday I had to put a parachute on him."

"When are we going to see this phenomenon?"

"Oh, it's top-secret training, gentlemen. He might be ready for showing in a few months though."

The victims of my prank caught on fast. One reporter shouted at me, "You're lying, Wiles. You're broke, and you ate him!"

My daughter, Carole Anne, was born during the Western Handicap Race at Hollywood Park. The great Willie Shoemaker won. Along with Willie's wife, Jenny, we three rushed to the hospital with the blanket of roses given to the victor of the race. At the hospital's admittance desk, a nurse looked at Willie. "No minors allowed," she said. I started to say something, but Willie, being the gentleman he is, merely told her "That's all right."

When the nurse brought the baby to Donalda's room, she asked me if I was the grandfather! When the medical staff saw the blanket of roses, they figured I was in the racing business and began asking for tips. I gave the nurses three winners. The next time I visited the hospital, Donalda was perturbed.

"Please don't give out any more tips. I've been bombarded day and night with nurses asking for information."

The tips stopped, while the winners were ahead.

I was always lucky in picking winners for L.B. Mayer, head of MGM Studios. While I was a jockey's agent at Santa Anita, I got to know him. He would send his chauffeur to find me and then ask me for a tip. One day, I picked seven winners in a row for him—he must have thought I was part horse. The next time he came to the track, his chauffeur located me. I went up to Mayer's private box and offered my opinion. He gave me two-hundred dollars to bet for him. Sure enough, the horse won. When I went looking for Mayer, he was gone. Someone said he had traveled back east on business.

I had $550 of his money burning a hole in my right pocket. My left pocket was empty. I was tempted to borrow, but didn't. A few weeks later, Mayer's chauffeur approached me. I went up to Mayer's private box and pulled out the $550. He looked puzzled.

"What's this for?" he said.

I almost passed out. He had forgotten about the bet! Awhile later, L.B.Mayer heard that I was going to the Pacific Northwest to work. He was sad to hear the news. "Don't go, Buster. I've got something lined up for you."

Gee, what could it be, I wondered excitedly. Managing his horses? Assistant director at MGM? I waited and waited and waited. Finally, L.B.Mayer died. What he had in mind for me is one of the unsolved mysteries of my life.

Though the years were passing rather fast, I still saw no reason to abandon the pranks of my youth. At the Richland Golf Course in Oakland, I played a dramatic scene for my golfing partners. Two women were about to tee off, when I turned my back to them and began a conversation with a garbage can. There was a footlid on the big can, and when I stepped on this, the top flew open as if someone were trying to escape.

"Get back in there!" I said forcefully. Then, switching to my female voice, "Help me out of here!"

"Shut up, girl! You got yourself in there, now get yourself out!"

I angrily walked away, pretending not to notice the women behind me. From the bushes, we had a big laugh, watching those gals search through the garbage. Back in the clubhouse, as I was sipping a cocktail, I looked up to see one of the women glaring at me with a withering stare: "Mister, that wasn't very funny." If looks could kill, I would have been dead, dead, dead.

Another time, I did a pal a favor by stopping at a supermarket so he could pick up "a few items." I was in a hurry and urged my friend to speed up his shopping.

"Where's the fire, Buster?"

"I'm in a hurry, man. Come on, let's move it!"

The few items turned out to be a shopping cart filled with groceries.

"I'm going to leave you here . . . ."

"Where's the fire? Look, I'm finished."

My patience had worn thin by the time he moved through the checkout line. He stood there, with his sack of groceries in his hands, casually chatting with the cute girl behind the counter.

"I'm gonna be late," I hissed.

"Aw, where's the fire, Buster?"

I slipped a cigarette lighter from my pocket and flicked it beneath his sack. The burning bag went flying in the air, then landed on the floor, with spectators gaping at the strange sight. Through the glass window, I waved goodbye to my pal, who was chasing an apple across the floor.

My girls: Carole Anne, Donalda and Laura.

TWELVE

The Long Black Train

"Every light has its shadow."

Death has no favorites. Even film stars must follow when he beckons. Yet, actors and actresses of the silver screen have a way of achieving immortality. Stars will never be forgotten as long as their movies are shown. As for Flynn, *Captain Blood, The Adventures of Robin Hood, They Died With Their Boots On,* and other legendary films will keep his memory alive forever.

The last time I saw Errol was about a year before he died. One of my top jockeys, Jay Fishburn, was riding at Santa Anita Racetrack. I was walking through the crowded grandstand, when I heard a familiar voice: "Hey Buster!" Flynn was waving from a private box. He jumped over the rail, gave me a bear hug, and we swiftly made our way to the bar for a celebratory drink. Errol was in good spirits.

Over the years, I had often seen his name in the newspapers, usually an article related to a lawsuit. I had read that he and Patrice were now living part. Flynn kept company with a young actress named Beverly Aadland, a relationship that kept him very much in the public eye, undoubtedly Errol's intent all along.

Between races, we reminisced about old times. Then, he asked if I was happy being a jockey's agent.

"I wouldn't trade it for anything."

"Buster, if you had gone to Europe with me, you would be a millionaire."

"I am a millionaire, Errol."

His eyes lit up. "Yeah? How'd you do it."

"I've got a wife and two lovely daughters, and I wouldn't take a million for them."

Roy Rogers came over to say hello. He was decked out in cowboy regalia, and around his neck was a solid-silver, hand-crafted Western tie.

"What a nice tie," remarked Errol.

"You like it? Here, take it." Roy removed the tie and gave it to Flynn.

It was a very kind thing for Roy to do, a spontaneous gesture, which Errol appreciated. He positively beamed as he examined the tie. Besides the unexpected gift, Flynn had a great day choosing the winners. It was a wonderful last encounter.

The next time I saw him, I wish that I hadn't. He was dead.

On October 14, 1959, I was sitting in a bar in Beaverton. A guy walked inside and sat next to me. "Your buddy just dropped dead."

"Who?"

"Errol Flynn had a heart attack."

"Aw, don't kid me."

"No, really."

I telephoned Donalda and asked if she had heard anything. I left a number where I could be reached. Five minutes later, she called and verified Flynn's passing. The sad news was like a punch in my guts. After a few drinks, I contacted Patrice Wymore in Washington, D.C., to offer my condolences and assistance. Though she and Flynn were estranged, Patrice was still his wife and legally responsible for the funeral arrangements.

"Where do you want me to take the body?"

"Los Angeles," she said tearfully.

I never thought Errol would die at fifty. But looking back, I can see how we burned the candle at both ends, and in the middle too. While I had slowed down, Flynn kept on with his fast living. He was a man who wanted to experience everything, and somehow or another, I thought he would go on forever.

When Donalda and I arrived in Vancouver, the situation was dismal. Flynn's girlfriend, Beverly Aadland, was understandably upset and was insisting that Flynn's body be taken to Jamaica for cremation. Threats were being made that the body would be hijacked. After a flurry of phone calls to Patrice and her lawyer, I was given immediate permission to transfer Flynn's remains to another funeral home. My wife knew the proprietors of Herron Brothers Mortuary, so the body was secretly taken there, leaving swarms of reporters in the dark about Flynn's whereabouts.

In my suite at the Georgia Hotel, I did some investigating and learned that Flynn had come to Vancouver to negotiate a lease agreement for the *Zaca*. George Caldough, a businessman, had planned to use the yacht to entertain clients. But Flynn never intended to sell the *Zaca,* as most news stories reported. He loved that boat more than any woman and would never have parted with it.

On his arrival in Vancouver, Flynn had told the press: "My future is dedicated to two things—women and litigation."

How prophetic, I thought, when legal papers were made out, authorizing me to take Flynn across the border, thereby resolving the dispute between Patrice and Beverly over his final resting place.

The following day, I took a cab to Herron Brothers. In the somber hush of the director's office, I was handed a large envelope containing the items Flynn had on his person when he died. I was also given a death certificate, attesting that Flynn had died of natural causes. Then, I was asked to verify the remains before the coffin was sealed for the long journey to Los Angeles.

In a private room, Flynn's body lay on a table. The face was swollen, the handsome features that had dazzled women barely recognizable. I quickly turned away from the sad sight.

Outside the mortuary, my spirits lifted. By the time Donalda and I arrived at the railway station, I told myself that Flynn would prefer laughter to tears. When reporters flocked around me, asking for reminiscences of Flynn, I recalled him as I truly remembered him—as a great friend who enjoyed a prank and a pretty face. I displayed my legal documents, then told the newsmen: "Errol would have laughed and said, 'I can't even die without lawyers bothering me!'"

The train departed in the evening. In Portland, the wooden container was placed inside a railway baggage car belonging to the

Southern Pacific rail line. I said goodbye to Donalda, who had to return home to take care of our daughters.

All night I rode in the railway car, at Flynn's side, reminiscing about the good times we had shared. The steward kept me supplied, very generously, with Seagram's whiskey. When I arrived at Los Angeles Union Station, my son Don and brother Vernice were there to greet me. I immediately went to see Patrice and offered my heartfelt sympathy to her and Flynn's son Sean, who was with her. I gave Sean his father's money clip.

Later, I hit the bars to drown my sorrow. I decided to visit every watering hole that Flynn and I had frequented. It was a long list. I started at the Cock and Bull on Sunset, the place where we had a late-night toast to John Barrymore when he passed away. Then it was on to Romanoff's in Beverly Hills, but it was closed. After several stops, I ended at Chasen's, for a final toast to Flynn's memory.

On Monday, October 19, the funeral was held at the Church of the Recessional at Forest Lawn Memorial Park. Reverend Kermit Castellanos conducted the ceremony. I stood next to Flynn's dear friend Ida Lupino, who was heartbroken by his death. Dennis Morgan sang the *Requiem,* and Jack Warner delivered the eulogy. Among the celebrities present were Mickey Rooney, Raoul Walsh, Jack Oakie, Alexis Smith, Craig Stevens, Mike Romanoff, Otto Reichow, Big Boy Williams, and Johnny Weissmuller. I'm certain Errol would have appreciated his friend's presence at the last farewell.

After the service, I emerged from the church to see Raoul Walsh, surrounded by reporters. He had loved Flynn like a son. "Hey, Buster!" He waved me over. "Do you remember the time we stole Barrymore's body?"

"Ummmm, that's quite a tale, Raoul."

He launched into the details of the theft that never took place. Not wishing to embarrass him before the press, I merely listened. Boy, he could tell a great story. When the reporters moved on to someone else, Raoul and I reminisced in a more realistic vein about Errol. After awhile, I quietly said: "Raoul, you know we didn't steal Barrymore's body."

"We did too," he said emphatically. He had told the damn thing so many times, I guess he really believed it.

So many stories have been told about Flynn. Some are true, and some are not. He was one of the cinema's most dashing and romantic stars. Even today his films are enjoyed by new audiences the world over. He was a legend, even in his lifetime.

In his eventful life, Flynn managed to do all of the things other guys merely dream about. He was wild; he was reckless; he was an original. I have the fondest recollections of Errol Flynn. He never let me down.

When Sean Flynn disappeared while working as a journalist in Cambodia, I was very saddened. Not long after his disappearance, I heard that his mother, Lili Damita, was coming to Portland, Oregon. I was ready to offer any help I could to locate Sean. Unfortunately, Lili never came, and I had no way of reaching her elsewhere. Why some lives are snuffed out at such an early age I don't know.

Luck is something that is unpredictable. I was very lucky in my career as a stuntman. I was never seriously injured. A lot of guys have lost limbs, and even their lives, performing daredevil feats. The only time I ever received a serious injury was the result of carelessness. I injured my neck, horsing around, and I wasn't even at the track. A group of racing friends had gathered at a famous restaurant called Uncle Tom's Cabin. The party was in full-swing when my pals asked me to do my famous "dive from a table." This feat was a trick I enjoyed doing. I would dive from a table as if I were plunging into a swimming pool.

Well, I neglected to secure the table properly. I jumped on the table, made a funny diving gesture, then sailed headfirst into the floor. The table slid, and I struck the hard floor with my neck in an awkward position. Later that night, my neck felt very sore. After three days, the pain was excruciating. I went to a chiropractor and explained my pain. He put his hands on my neck and started to twist. I suggested that he take X-rays first. When the chiropractor emerged with the X-ray negatives, he was visibly shaken. I had fractured the fifth vertebra.

"If I had snapped your neck, you could have been paralyzed or even died . . . ."

Bad luck often brings out the best, or the worst, in individuals. Life can put us behind the eight-ball before we know it, so it has always been my policy to help a friend in need. I've had friends help me, and it has been my belief that borrowed money should be repaid.

I had a friend who was a golf pro. His winning streak had disappeared. He was destitute. His family was suffering inside a cold apartment, in the middle of winter. He borrowed money from me so he could pay his heating bill and put food on the table. Several months later, I heard he was making big money on the golf circuit. I was now the guy in a tight spot, so I paid him a visit. As he shook my hand, he gave me a dozen golf balls. That was it. No money, and no mention of repayment was uttered.

I've always been a guy who kept a sharp eye open for financial opportunities. But I came to realize a long time ago that there is something more valuable than money, and that is friendship. When I was a jockey's agent at Portland Meadows, I was honored by a very kind act of friendship. In the midst of a hectic racing season, the racetrack found itself in a serious predicament. We immediately needed a celebrity to present the trophy to the winner of a major race—the Salem Handicap. After pondering the situation, I suggested a friend who was a superb actor. He had even attended school in Salem, Oregon.

"Who is it?" asked one of the track executives.

"Victor Jory."

I contacted his agent. He informed me that Victor was in Hong Kong. I phoned him at the Carlton Hotel.

"Buster, I don't know if I'm free that date, but if I can possibly make it, I'll be there. By the way, how did you know where to find me?"

"I know everything. I even know where you're going when you hang up."

"Where's that?"

"Back to the bar."

He had a good laugh.

Victor did get to come for the race, and there was a police escort for him when he arrived.

After Victor had awarded the trophy, the executives asked him how much they owed him for his services.

"Nothing. I did it for Buster."

I later learned that he had canceled an appearance on *Rawhide* to be in Portland. He could have earned six-thousand dollars. He was a wonderful man and a superb actor. I thank you once again, Victor.

Buster as a placing judge at Longacres Race Track.

The saddest journey I ever made. Arriving at Union Station with Flynn's body. My brother, Vernice, and my son, Don, stand behind me. *(photo: UCLA Special Collections)*

A Service of Memory

for

Errol Flynn

at the

Church of the Recessional

Now abideth Faith, Hope, Love these three; and the greatest of these is Love.
—inspired by I Corinthians 13:13

In the belief that a heart filled with Love knows no separation from those who live on in memory, these words are inscribed above the chancel of The Church of the Recessional, a faithful re-creation within Forest Lawn Memorial-Park of the church at Rottingdean, England, where Rudyard Kipling worshipped and found inspiration for his immortal poem "The Recessional."

Born	June 20, 1909 Hobart, Tasmania
Passed away	October 14, 1959 Vancouver, B.C., Canada
Services held	October 19, 1959 10:00 a.m.
Services conducted by	The Reverend Kermit Castellanos All Saints Episcopal Church Beverly Hills, California
Eulogy Delivered by	Mr. Jack Warner
Soloist	Mr. Dennis Morgan *'Requiem'* - by Homer
Organist	Mr. C. Harold Dick *'Ah, Sweet Mystery of Life'* *'I Believe'* *'Yours Is My Heart Alone'* *'Ich Liebe Dich' (I Love You)*
Funeral Director	Forest Lawn Mortuary
Interment	Forest Lawn Memorial-Park Glendale, California

With the Queen of England.
(Photo: UPI/Bettmann Archives)

Dr. Hermann F. Erben at his residence in Vienna. (Photo: William (Donati)

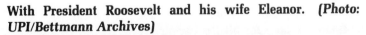

With President Roosevelt and his wife Eleanor. (Photo: UPI/Bettmann Archives)

Two of the best jockeys in the history of racing — Willie Shoemaker, left and Johnny Longden. Great jockeys and great guys.

What the hell is it?

With my friend Mickey Rooney. We can never thank Mickey for all the happiness he's brought us. Lindy Aliment stands nearby.

My boys—The Tennessee Docs, reunited in Memphis.
Seated: Leggett, Gullet, Munn and Palermo. Second row:
Weinel, Underwood, Beck, McCarthy, Little Sullivan,
Sam Sanders, Charlie Campbell. Behind: Jake Plesofsky,
Sam Raines. Back row: Sullivan, McLaughlin, Holt, Ford,
Payne, Williams, King, White and mascot Buster Wiles.

With my idol Yakima Canutt,
the legendary stuntman. *(Photo:
William Donati)*

At the ceremony for my induction into the Hollywood
Stuntman's Hall of Fame. With Dave Cross, my son Don
and Mort Lickter. *(Photo: William Donati)*

The view from Errol's upstairs bedroom.
(Photo: William Donati)

The dining room. I can still see the astonished faces of the British airmen, staring at my naked secretary. (Photo: William Donati)

Revisiting Mulholland Farm. It was later torn down. (Photo: William Donati)

THIRTEEN

Longacres

"To a friend's house, the road is never long."

Eleven miles south of Seattle is my second home—Longacres Racetrack. From April to October, you'll find me at Longacres, working as a placing judge. All of the people who work there are like a second family to me. When I traveled the track circuit of the Pacific Northwest as a jockey's agent, Longacres was a favorite stop. After awhile, I realized I didn't want to travel any further.

For twenty years I've had a ball, working with my friends, at the most beautiful racetrack in the Northwest. I could have earned a lot more money at the tracks in California, but Seattle is good country, and the nicest people in racing live here. I would say wholeheartedly that this region is the mother lode of fine people.

For fifty years running, Longacres has delighted hundreds of thousands of patrons with its exciting racing atmosphere. I had the pleasure of working with the track's founder, Joseph Gottstein. He opened the one-mile, river-loam track in 1933. Initially, I ran the cupola atop the Turf Club. Distinguished visitors would often watch the races from here and receive the track's special hospitality. John Wayne was an honored guest many times. The first time he came to the track, he was accompanied by Bruce Cabot. In his inimitable voice, he said, "Well, I've heard a lot about you, Buster."

"Gee, I've heard a lot about you, too."

Recently, one of my Hollywood friends was in the Seattle area—Mickey Rooney. I've known Mickey for over forty years, but even if you've only known him for a few hours, he makes you feel like a long-lost pal. While in Seattle, Mickey came out to the track for an afternoon of fun. I decided to play one of my favorite pranks.

There was a gathering of people in the Turf Club to see our distinguished guest. I walked over to a small cabinet along one wall of the room, bent down, and—with my back to the gathering—opened the cabinet doors.

A falsetto voice, apparently coming from within the cabinet, inquired, "Is Mr. Rooney there?"

"Just a minute. I'll get him," I replied and beckoned for Mickey to come over. Mickey walked over to the cabinet, got down on his hands and knees, and said, "Hello?" In the long silence that followed, it dawned on Mickey that he'd been had. When the truth hit home, he collapsed in a fit of laughter.

Mickey wasn't my first victim. I pulled the same gag on Senator Warren Magnusson, as well as many financiers and noted visitors who found themselves on their hands and knees, staring inside an empty cabinet. Mickey was a good sport. He has always given me many hours of enjoyment watching the classic films he has appeared in over the years. While he was performing in *Sugar Babies* on Broadway, I sent him a letter. I just wanted to thank him for all the happiness he has brought audiences. Mickey's greatest gift is the ability to make people laugh. When we laugh, we forget our problems and life looks better.

Other routines among my endless supply depend on the illusion of self-destruction. Thanks to years of perilous falls in movies, I've developed sight-gags of unnerving violence. I'll walk into a door with a shattering crash that sends alarmed spectators rushing to help. Or else, I'll be sitting on a bar-stool and suddenly go over backwards. Veteran bartenders come to my aid as I moan and groan and even spit out a few fake teeth.

"Are you all right, buddy?"

"I just need another drink," I moan.

"You've had enough already," they admonish.

I spring up miraculously.

"All right, then," I say, bouncing out the door. "So long."

I also have a gag phone I use to amuse my friends. I'll be strolling down a busy thoroughfare and stop at a corner. I press the buzzer in my pocket that sounds just like a telephone bell. I then pull a phone receiver from my vest pocket. The people standing around always stare.

"Yes sir, Mr. President. What corner is this? Let me see."

I ask the person next to me for the location.

"This is Second and Main. Why yes, I'll be there right away, Mr. President."

I stroll on.

Who in the hell is *that?* they wonder.

In addition to my track duties, I'm active in many community projects. I'm often called on to host charity events. As master of ceremonies, I enjoy being center-stage with my jokes. Sports editor Glenn Drosendahl of *the Journal-American* calls me "A one-man act that refused to die with vaudeville."

If you see me coming, *watch out.* You're bound to hear the following:

"I was born in Caruthersville, Missouri. We were country folks, so poor that, on Christmas Eve, Dad would go out in the backyard and fire a shotgun and come in and tell us Santa Claus had committed suicide. On Easter, Dad would hide doornobs instead of eggs because we didn't have a hen. But we had only one door. And that one had a crescent moon on it.

"We were poor, but Mama loved our family dog so much that she always managed to save some scraps. And in the evening, when it got dark, she'd go out on the back porch and throw the scraps out to the dog. He would catch 'em in the dark and eat 'em. And us kids, well, we got smart, and we started hiding out in the dark, too, so we could catch the scraps. Like I said, we was poor. It worked swell for a while, but then the dog got smart and started signaling for a fair catch.

"I was not only poor but ugly as well. Mama had to tie a pork chop around my neck so the dog would play with me. Oh, they were crazy about me. In fact, they loved me so much that, one night, they sent me out to chop some stove wood in the backyard, and while I was out there chopping, they moved. That's when it dawned on me why they'd always wrapped my school lunch in a road map.

"I spent three years in the third grade. If they had promoted me to the fourth grade, I'd have to sit with my father.

I've always loved an audience, and the racetrack is the ideal place for me. Jeff King of *the News-Journal* wrote, "At Longacres, Wiles is part of the show. A member of the cast."

Racing is indeed a big show. The track is the greatest life there is for me. Every Saturday morning, Longacres has a workout program designed to entertain the entire family. Guess who is the emcee? I introduce visitors to the jockeys and trainers, and they can see the splendid thoroughbreds up close, watching them run in workout sessions.

We get all kinds of wonderful kids on Saturday mornings—they even laugh at my jokes. One little boy made a lasting impression on me. Little Jack Belvins was suffering from leukemia. He and I became friends, and he sent me a card showing potatoes with huge pop-eyes. It read: "We see eye-to-eye on so many things." His mother later wrote me that Jack had passed away. I keep the card in my room at Longacres. What better sentiment expresses the essence of friendship—*We see eye-to-eye on so many things.*

FOURTEEN

Buster Wiles: Senior Citizen

"Success makes a fool seem wise."

Gee, it is hard to imagine myself as a senior citizen. At heart, I'm still eighteen years old. But we all know that every race with Father Time has but one winner. Not long ago, I was rummaging through my garage for some photographs. I happened to discover an old address book filled with phone numbers. I casually thumbed through it and was saddened to notice the many friends who have passed on—Errol Flynn, Alan Hale, Victor Jory, Bruce Cabot, J.Carrol Naish, Howard Hill, as well as dozens of non-celebrity friends.

Not long ago, I was in Los Angeles visiting my son, and I decided to make a sentimental journey to Mulholland Farm. I had read in the paper that the estate was on the market for a million dollars. I recalled when Mickey Rooney had offered to buy Mulholland for $125,000, but that had been decades earlier. Flynn lost his beloved home to Lili, in lieu of back alimony.

As I drove along Mulholland Drive, I noticed an enormous hawk circling above. As I turned onto the steep road leading up to the house, I noticed the changes. The gate was gone, and the caretakers home had been replaced by a modern structure. The new owner was having the place remodeled, and a handful of workmen were about. The foreman welcomed me inside, and . . .

there was Mulholland House.

The garage where Flynn had kept his expensive sportscars was filled with rubble. On top of the pile was a bidet. I peeped in the wine cellar, only to see an old tire.

Seeing the pool brought a rush of memories, and I half-expected to hear Flynn's voice—"Hi, Buster. What's your pleasure?" But there was no Alex with a tray of cocktails. Outside, the house hadn't changed a bit. Once inside though, I was taken aback. The place was only a shell. The flooring and walls had all been torn out. I wandered downstairs, recalling where the Gauguin had hung and where the furniture had been placed. Upstairs, I looked at the space that had been my bedroom and walked down to the far end where Flynn had his master bedroom. I glanced out the window to the pool below. From here, Flynn had viewed the world. And the world had viewed Flynn. Returning, I paused at the top of the spiral staircase and thought, "Man, the tail that has passed this way." Later, I was saddened to learn that Mulholland House had been torn down. A lot of memories vanished with the home.

One of my friends recently remarked, "Buster, you're the last of Flynn's cronies. You outlived everyone."

"Let's keep it that way," I said.

Yes indeed!

Fortunately, longevity seems to be inherent in the Wiles family. My dad and mother were both in years when they passed away. Mollie went out as she had lived—having a ball! One day, she decided she was moving to Las Vegas. She liked the excitement of the casinos. At her funeral, the mortuary was filled with flowers from her many friends who worked along the Strip. Everybody loved Mollie. She knew how to enjoy herself. I'm going to follow Mama's example: I'm going to be eighteen forever!

We all hate to age. Wrinkles appear from nowhere, hair vanishes (I was unkindly scalped by Father Time years ago), arthritis and other ailments besiege us. What do I do? Complain? Yell? Raise hell? No. I just splash a little horse lineament on me and KEEP MOVING!

I stay busy. There is so much that one can do, especially in the way of assisting less fortunate people. Churches and civic groups are always seeking volunteers to aid the handicapped or bedridden fellow citizens. I'm very lucky when it comes to being active. My wife Donalda positively insists that I keep working and stay active. Donalda has done the most to keep the old horse in the race. I often find little notes and messages from my girl—"Thank you for the lovely anniversary. I love you with all my heart —your angel."

Don't you know that makes me feel good? You'd better believe it. I keep an essay my daughter Laura wrote while a youngster. It has always given me a sense of pride as a parent;

> I admire my dad for everything he does. He is always willing to help anyone in trouble and expects no favor in return. He makes me feel happy all the time by telling jokes and just the funny things he says. He has done so many things in his life and succeeded in all of them. When you've done something wrong, he first hollers at you, but then when he knows you've learned your lesson, he's back to cheering you up again. He trusts me completely and never even thinks that I would sneak or tell a lie. He gives me his complete confidence too. He thinks I can do anything if I put my mind to it. He's never a phony and says exactly what he means, unless it would hurt someone's feelings. My dad is all of these things and many more, and I just hope I will be able to bring as much happiness to everyone, or at least someone, as my dad has.

The essay would make any father feel proud. But I have my shortcomings. Life presents difficult decisions. No matter how hard parents try, mistakes are made, especially when a divorce breaks a family apart. Yet, time has a way of healing what has been torn asunder.

One weekend, I was in Los Angeles visiting my son Don. I called my wife on a Sunday morning to see if everything was all right. Donalda mentioned that I had received a letter from my daughter Susan. Although I had spoken with her over the years, I had not seen her since she was a child. Her mother had remarried, and Susan had grown up with her. She had decided to write to me after one of her friends had seen me on television in Seattle.

I phoned Susan, and we made arrangements to meet that Sunday afternoon in a restaurant in Hermosa Beach. I anxiously watched as each young woman passed through the door. Finally, a slim, brown-haired Susan appeared. It was a true father-and-daughter reunion. She had shown a good deal of courage in meeting me after the many years of separation. My son Don was with me, and he was just as overwhelmed emotionally as I was.

I was amazed that her personality was typically Wiles. She was full of energy and not the least bit shy. She had just raced her Porsche and emerged the victor. Susan told me of her recent trip to Europe and the adventures she had experienced. In the course of our long conversation, it was apparent that she had the most Wilesian trait of all—a wonderful sense of humor.

We later went to Susan's beach home, and she decided to telephone her grandmother, who was nicknamed "Beano." My former mother-in-law had been nice to me. I came to the phone, and we had a lovely talk about old times. When Susan finished speaking, I asked her about my former sister-in-law. Susan suggested that we speak with her. We called, and she was surprised to hear from me. There was just one more person to call. I hesitated. Why not? Susan dialed the number of her mother.

"Hello, Barbara, this is Buster. . . . I want to thank you for raising such a beautiful young lady."

My other two daughters have Donalda's beauty and their father's love of adventure. They both fell in love with Hawaii and moved there. Laura teaches children, and Carol travels the world, searching for unique items to sell in her gift shops. My son Don has his own firm in Los Angeles selling business machines. All of my children have given me so much happiness.

In the spring of 1984, I was inducted into the Hollywood Stuntmen's Hall of Fame. I flew down for the ceremony. The president of the association, John Hagner, placed my foot in cement. The biggest thrill of the day came when I embraced my idol—the legendary Yakima Canutt. I hadn't seen Yak in a good while, but he looked great. Even at the age of eighty-nine, he looked like he could have gone before the camera and performed one of his famous stunts. I thought back to when I had met him on the set of *The Last Days of Pompeii.*

Years earlier, Yak had paid me a great compliment. We were racing in San Francisco, when I read in the newspaper that he would be honored at a rodeo at the Cow Palace. He introduced me to his son, Joe, as "the best stuntman around." I was genuinely moved by the sentiment, but quickly responded, "No, I'm not. You were always the best, Yakima." No doubt about it.

A special message from the White House was sent to the Stuntmen's Hall of Fame. It read:

> John G. Hagner
> President
> Hollywood Stuntmen's Hall of Fame
>
> It is a very special pleasure for Nancy and me to send our warmest greetings to those who gather for this induction ceremony for some of Hollywood's greatest stars.
>
> The men and women associated with the Hollywood Stuntmen's Hall of Fame are to be commended for their efforts to recognize the contributions of stuntmen in all facets of the entertainment industry. The skills and expertise of stuntmen have thrilled audiences since the earliest days of the motion picture business.
>
> I am pleased to join you in paying tribute to these outstanding actors, and I wish you the very best for an enjoyable and memorable event.
>
> Ronald Reagan

Another honor came my way when Bear Hudkins, nephew of my old friend Ace Hudkins, presented me with a unique plaque at a gala tribute. It was inscribed:

> We are proud to bestow on you an honorary membership in the Stuntmens Association of Motion Pictures in deep appreciation of your unselfish contributions and the great friendship between you and stuntmen.

My profound admiration goes to today's daredevils who make their living by stunt-work. There are about a thousand stuntmen and two-hundred stuntwomen who belong to the Screen Actors Guild. It's a tough life; jobs are sporadic. Today, stuntpersons earn the basic SAG rate of $379 a day. In my heyday of the forties, the minimum was $35! Of course, just like I did, they get more for each "gag" performed. Driving a car can bring in $1,000; flipping it over, as much as $5,000. About a hundred stuntpersons earn the big money—$250,000 to $300,000 a year.

Hey, Bear, can I make a comeback?

One of the reasons I decided to write my autobiography was to set the record straight about my dear friend, Errol Flynn. I've seen so much misinformation presented about Flynn that I felt it was my duty to give a true portrait.

During the writing of this book, CBS Television released the motion picture, *My Wicked Wicked Ways*. The film was publicized as a "dramatization of the star's autobiography," but it should have been labeled a "fictionalization." The movie is full of inventions and fabrications. The characterization of Errol was a pale imitation of the man himself.

What offended me most was the movie's deviation from the known facts of Flynn's life, which anyone could have verified with research. The entire situation regarding how Peggy Satterlee came to be aboard the *Sirocco* was incredibly erroneous. The film gave the impression that Flynn had romanced the young woman on the *Sirocco*. Nother could be further from the truth. During the trial, Peggy Satterlee had claimed that Flynn asked her to go below with him to a stateroom, because, "The moon looked more romantic through a porthole." Flynn denied this statement in court. In the picture, Flynn speaks the line about the porthole! And the film is supposedly based on Flynn's autobiography!

Not only was Flynn misrepresented in the motion picture, but I was also. The character in the film known as "Billy Welch" was obviously supposed to represent me. Even the initials "B.W." were suggestive of my name.

"Billy Welch" is Flynn's stunt double, closest friend, speaks with a Tennessee accent, always at Mulholland House and aboard the *Sirocco*, doubled Flynn in *The Charge of the Light Brigade*, etc. There is no doubt that the writers had me in mind. There is no one in Flynn's autobiography named "Billy Welch." Many of my friends throughout the country phoned me after the film was shown to ask me about the accuracy of the picture, especially the scene where Flynn and "Billy Welch" go to a Mexican bordello. I was *never* in a Mexican bordello with Flynn—or with him in any bordello, for that matter.

The writers had "Billy Welch" fall from a horse and die during the making of *They Died With Their Boots On*. Of course, the only person who died during the making of the film was Jack Budlong. The changing of my name and the death scene of "Billy Welch" was nothing more than a clever subterfuge on the part of CBS to avoid paying me for the use of my name, life, and professional work. And CBS had the audacity to give the impression to the viewing public that the film was from Flynn's own book. How shameful! I can only thank the good Lord that I am around to recount my life and set the record straight about Flynn.

Writing my memoirs has been a wonderful experience. I've had the opportunity to relive memories and remember friends who are no longer with us. At a party I met Nora Eddington with her daughters, Deidre and Rory. Nora, still a redhead, was just as vivacious as the day I met her in the courthouse years ago. She told her daughters: "If it wasn't for him, you two wouldn't be here."

By playing matchmaker I had indeed brought her and Flynn together. Nora and the other guests were introduced to my son Don. He's now over six feet tall. Just like his old man, he's bald, sports a dapper moustache and has a great sense of humor. "This is my baby boy," I proudly told everyone.

"Baby!" remarked one of the crowd.

"When he was a kid he used to have two heads but I tore one off because he ate too much."

Nora and I had many laughs going over "old times." As for Deidre and Rory, I had known them as children and they had grown to be charming women. Errol would be very proud of his daughters; both work in the motion picture business, Rory as an actress and Deidre as a script supervisor.

But Nora was the one who really floored me. I learned that she was a racing fan, just like me. The previous day, she had placed bets at her favorite track, Santa Anita. As I listened to her talk of the jockeys and horses I was really impressed. Her love for the great sport of thoroughbred racing equals mine. She should print a tip sheet.

I've also had the pleasure of making new friends. Jerry Hill is one of them. I was saddened to learn of the death of my great friend Howard Hill in 1975. But his nephew Jerry carries on the family tradition as a superb archer. The past and the present join hands. I like that idea.

It also thrills me to see friends like Mickey Rooney, Olivia de Havilland, and Anthony Quinn still entertaining audiences. Why retire? Not long ago, I had a wonderful conversation with Anthony Quinn. We were discussing the old days, recalling Flynn and the prank we pulled on him.

"Tony, I just want to congratulate you."

"For what?"

"For becoming a star. No one worked at it harder than you. You've come a long way since playing Crazy Horse in *They Died With Their Boots On.*"

"I guess you're right," he laughed.

Tony was on tour with *Zorba the Greek,* and lines were stretched around the block trying to get a ticket. Those who were lucky enough to see Tony as Zorba were inspired and uplifted by a simple man caught up in the joy of existence. What a wonderful story.

Friends ask: "Don't you ever get depressed, Buster?"

"Sure, sometimes, but I always try to laugh. It's good medicine."

Long ago, when my head was   smooth as a baby's bottom and I was still just a young pup, a guy snidely remarked: "so young, so bald."

"Yeah, you're right," I shot back, "but who needs hair? Look at all the money I've saved on shampoo, haircuts, hair oil, combs, and flea powder, like you need. So there!"

He shut up.

"And," I added, "the girls still love me."

I've had one of the greatest lives a guy could have. I was in a restaurant the other day, and the waitress asked me if I was finished.

"Gee, I hope not," I replied.

See ya', partner. Keep laughing.

APPENDIX

The Vejarano Statement

Federal Bureau of Investigation
United States Department of Justice
New York, New York

INFORMATION CONTAINED
HEREIN IS UNCLASSIFIED EXCEPT
WHERE SHOWN OTHERWISE

January 29, 194_

JLF:JSG
65-7124
Director, FBI

Re: CARLOS VEJARANO y CASSINA
ESPIONAGE - G;
REGISTRATION ACT

Dear Sir:

The above captioned subject who was sentenced on December 27, 1943 to a year and a day in violation of the Registration Act, recently advised this office of an incident that occurred to him in Berlin, Germany in 1937.

VEJARANO stated that in May and June of 1937 he was being treated at the La Scharite Hospital in Berlin, and occasionally paid visits to the Spanish Embassy there. He explained that one ANTONIO VARGAS, who was liaison man between Spanish military officials and German military officials in Berlin, was known to his family, and his father had particularly instructed him to call upon VARGAS in Berlin.

On one occasion he recalled that he had gone to the Embassy to pay his usual respects to VARGAS, and was introduced in VARGAS' office to a German, who according to VARGAS was from Los Angeles, California. VARGAS explained that this German had just completed a tour of the various Spanish fronts in company with ERROL FLYNN, the movie actor, and had taken numerous pictures of gun establishments and military objectives in "Red" Spain. These pictures lay in a huge pile on VARGAS' desk. When VARGAS stepped out of the room, this man stated he was a friend of ERROL FLYNN and FLYNN had decided to go to Spain during the Spanish Civil War to observe the fighting on the various fronts and that they had gone to London with the idea of getting permission from the Franco forces. France officials in London, however, had refused visas to FLYNN and the German, but they had been able to secure visas from the Spanish Republican officials there. The German had exhibited his Republican visa issued in London, and also his American passport, and had discussed various cities in the United States, particularly Los Angeles and Washington, D. C.

After this German left, ANTONIO VARGAS advised VEJARANO that

RECORDED & INDEXED
COPIES DESTROYED

this German was a member of Military Secret Service of Germany and had been working for Germany in the United States. One of the German Military officials had called the Embassy advising that they were sending this man over in order that members of the Spanish Embassy in Berlin who were at that time superiors of General Franco, could view the pictures that their agent had taken in Spain with a view that this might be some help to the Franco forces. VEJARANO advised that he had looked through these pictures and noticed several pictures of the German in company with ERROL FLYNN and the various military objectives which the German had photographed.

VEJARANO advised that his memory of the specific details of this incident had faded inasmuch as he had not thought a great deal about it at the time. He advised that he had heard in 1939 that VARGAS was sent to Buenos Aires, Argentina to work in the Spanish Embassy there. He had never heard of this German since then, but could recall only that VARGAS had introduced him with the title of "doctor".

According to VEJARANO a description of both VARGAS and this German as he was observed in 1937, were as follows:

VARGAS

Age	52
Height	5' 10"
Weight	165 lbs.
Race	Spanish
Build	Strong
Profile	High forehead

DR. ___

Age	45 to 50
Height	5' 10"
Weight	160 lbs.
Hair	Completely grey
Dress	Ruddy
Race	German

The Washington Field Division is requested to check the records of the State Department to ascertain if visas were granted to movie actor ERROL FLYNN in 1937 to visit Spain, and whether any notation appears as to his companion.

APPENDIX

THE FLYNN CONTROVERSY

The Flynn Controversy

One rainy afternoon, I sat in my bungalow at Longacres Racetrack, gloomily staring at a picture of Errol Flynn. I had seen thousands of photos of Flynn during the course of our long friendship. But this one was different. There was a Nazi swastika imprinted on his face. It was the cover of *Errol Flynn:The Untold Story*. As I read the text, I was shocked. Charles Higham wrote that my deceased friend was an admirer of Hitler, a Nazi agent, a homosexual, and a murderer—all lies.

I had provided information to Higham for the biography, but I was never informed of the Nazi angle. I felt as if I had been swindled. I spoke of Flynn as I had known him—a fine fellow who had always treated me like a brother. Flynn was certainly no saint. He had faults; yet to call him a Nazi was a vicious smear. Flynn would have been furious over such a rotten book.

When William Donati telephoned me to ask my opinion of the Higham biography, I was elated to comment: "It's a terrible lie. Believe me, I knew Flynn, and he certainly did not admire Nazis. You can get it from the horse's mouth, or you can get it from the other end." William Donati has taken the time to carefully examine *The Untold Story*. He shows quite clearly how the unsuspecting public was duped. Was Errol Flynn a Nazi? Of course not. The facts prove otherwise.

—Buster Wiles

APPENDIX

The Flynn Controversy

by
William Donati

"Biography: One of the new terrors of death."
—Arbuthnot

The Higham Book

Errol Flynn always managed to capture headlines during his career as one of the world's most colorful and popular film stars. Decades after his death, Flynn was once again the focus of media attention, due to the sensational accusations leveled at him by author Charles Higham. In *Errol Flynn: The Untold Story,* the late actor is charged with being a Nazi spy. According to Higham, the espionage activity of Errol Flynn was carried out in unison with Austrian-born Dr. Hermann F. Erben.

Previous to the book's release, news accounts stated that Charles Higham based his claims on material he had declassified under the Freedom of Information Act. The declassified government files supposedly gave "evidence" of the Nazi activities of Errol Flynn. On February 3, 1980, a lengthy article in the *Los Angeles Times* presented a story about the forthcoming book and how the author had come to acquire the documents that supposedly exposed the espionage efforts of Flynn and Erben.

The following weeks brought denials and denunciations in the *Los Angeles Times* from defenders of Flynn. An April 3, 1980, interview by Roderick Mann quotes Higham: "I don't mind people arguing with me. . . . But I do feel that they should at least take a look at some of the 5,000 documents I waded through before attacking me."

When the biography was finally published, after a barrage of publicity, the controversy became even more heated. *The Untold Story* portrayed Flynn as the devil incarnate. Critics judged the book to be a hardbound version of gossipy, outrageous material, usually printed in cheap tabloids.

Those who knew Flynn personally simply denounced the book as a sensationalistic smear. Said David Niven: "I knew him very well, both before and after the last world war, and I never heard him show Nazi sympathies" (*The London Times,* Jan. 6, 1980).

For the historian expecting a scholarly work detailing how Errol Flynn had procured secret material for Nazi Germany, the book fell flat. The most serious error, stylistically, was the appalling lack of documentation. The book lacked footnotes, as well as an appendix providing a page-by-page reference guide concerning where the author found pertinent facts.

The conventions of documentation are a basic means of letting the reader or scholar know where information originated so it can be analyzed for further research. Professional biographers and academics always utilize meticulous research notes, since such material provides concrete credibility for the author.

The hardbound version of *The Untold Story* merely had a list of titles regarding "declassified secret documents" at the end of the book. The reader is confronted with the perplexing situation of determining what each surveillance document fully contains. By the time the paperbound version appeared, someone apparently realized that source material would have to be presented. There appears at the end of the paperback book thirty-nine "documentary excerpts."

Consequently, the reader must be satisfied with the basic text of the book, along with the thirty-nine "documentary excerpts" proving, according to Higham, that "This man who personified patriotism on the screen was a spy for the Nazis . . . " Or else the reader can obtain the "5,000 documents" that Higham declassified and discover exactly what they state.

That is what I chose to do. A request was placed to every government agency that maintained files pertaining to Flynn and

Erben. Obtaining documents from various government agencies may take months or even years, due to the enormous backlog of Freedom of Information requests currently being processed.

As the declassified documents began to arrive, it became apparent that the true figure being investigated by U.S. agencies was Dr. Erben and not Flynn. The Federal Bureau of Investigation, State Department, Army Intelligence, and the Immigration and Naturalization Service maintain thick files on Dr. Erben. Flynn is mentioned in certain files as a friend of Erben and was questioned by the officials about Erben's activities.

Comparing the declassified documents to the narrative of *The Untold Story*, if becomes apparent how Higham crafted his text. Dry surveillance pages are transformed into a lush, detailed thriller that weaves a tale of exciting espionage exploits of Flynn and Erben. However, Flynn "the Nazi agent" does not exist in the government files.

Higham claims that the FBI was unable to apprehend Errol Flynn. Writes Higham: "Had British Intelligence been in charge of the Flynn matter, there is no question that they would have succeeded in arresting him." A person who certainly had supreme knowledge of the activities of British Intelligence was Sir William Stephenson. This superspy was Winston Churchill's secret envoy to President Roosevelt and was the legendary chief of British Security Coordination, the hub for all branches of British Intelligence. His comment:

> I am unaware of any connection Flynn had with any Nazi Dept., and doubtless the FBI would have had knowledge of it if he had. Appears nonsensical on face of it.
>
> Yours sincerely,
> William Stephenson
>
> (sent to Trudy McVicker May 5, 1980)

Indeed, the official position of the FBI is as follows:

> In response to the claim of author Charles Higham that Errol Flynn was a Nazi spy, any conclusions reached by

Mr. Higham were no doubt based on his review of records released to Mr. Higham by this Bureau as well as documents obtained from other Federal Government agencies. As you are aware, while Errol Flynn was either the victim or subject of several investigations conducted by the F.B.I. none were based on alleged espionage activities and no information was developed to indicate that he had been a Nazi agent . . . .

David G. Flanders, Chief
Freedom of Information Branch
Federal Bureau of Investigation
July 16, 1980

In an interview on *A.M. Los Angeles,* May 15, 1981, Higham claimed that the British government also maintained an espionage file on Flynn. Charles Higham: "I was horrified when the Ministry of Defence in London which handles all of the MI5 and MI6 files, that's British Intelligence as you know, confirmed that Errol Flynn from the very beginning, from early 1933, which was Hitler's first rise to power, was clearly marked as an espionage agent. Indeed, the two major files on Errol Flynn at the Ministry of Defence in London are stamped clearly 'Errol Flynn: Espionage, Germany.'"

The official British governmental response to Higham's charges is as follows:

We see so reason to question the reported statement of his friend and fellow actor David Niven that the suggestion that Errol Flynn was a spy was a 'lot of nonsense.'

Lt. Colonel D.A. Betley MBE RRF
Ministry of Defence
Whitehall, London May 6, 1981

The statements of the FBI and the British Ministry of Defence show quite clearly that Charles Higham concocted an espionage theory concerning Errol Flynn.

The actor is mentioned in various surveillance documents, due to his association with the individual being investigated—Dr. Hermann F. Erben.

Dr. Hermann Erben was born in Austria on November 15, 1897. In March of 1924, he arrived in New York on the *SS Esperanza* with his first wife, Countess Claire Gottschalk. He received his medical degree from the University of Vienna on July 23, 1926. For a year, Dr. Erben practiced medicine in Morristown, New Jersey, where he had won a Rockefeller Fellowship as a member of the Psychiatric Institute for Medical Research. He later worked in Washington and Louisiana.

He was naturalized on November 19, 1930. As early as 1928, he had served as a ship's surgeon in order to travel the world and develop his expertise as a tropical-disease specialist. His voyage out of the U.S. as a ship's surgeon before being naturalized would be of considerable importance when he eventually was forced to surrender his passport in 1938 for making fraudulent statements about his travels before becoming a U.S. citizen.

Dr. Erben met Errol Flynn in Salamaua, New Guinea, in 1933. They traveled together for several months and became friends before Flynn departed for Britain to pursue an acting career and Erben went to Vienna for medical research courses. Dr. Erben's life and medical career comprise a fascinating yet complex story, the most controversial aspect being his involvement with German Intelligence. Dr. Erben appears in Flynn's autobiography, *My Wicked Wicked Ways,* as the Dutch physician "Dr. Geritt H. Koets." Flynn describes him as being an eccentric adventurer, with a penchant for miserliness and trouble.

Charles Higham states: "I solved a mystery that has puzzled Flynn buffs for years," concerning the true identity of Koets. Actually Higham found this information in John Hammond Moore's well-researched book entitled, *The Young Errol: Flynn Before Hollywood* (Angus and Robertson, Australia 1975).

Why was Erben's real name not used by Flynn?

Earl Conrad, the writer who assisted Flynn with his autobiography, states that the reason was legal: "Flynn didn't change the name. That was done by someone at Putnam's. Nobody knew where Dr. Erben was located to obtain clearance for use of his name in the book. The publisher wanted to avoid the possibility of a lawsuit " (March 28, 1981).

The friendship of Flynn and Erben is verified in the auto-biography. Dr. Erben is described by Flynn as being apolitical: "He was detached about everything but medicine. He professed not to give a damn who killed whom. He could have been quite capable of taking a Nazi belt and bashing the brains of a Communist, and do the same thing to a Nazi with a Communist belt—just to study the reactions of each. Yet he wanted to get into medical work where he could be dedicated to saving life."

However, it wouldn't have been difficult for anyone to figure out Erben's identity. He was constantly mentioned in newspaper articles and fan magazines as a friend of Errol Flynn. In fact, Flynn himself wrote an article about his life in New Guinea (*Los Angeles Times*, Jan. 12, 1936), which stated: "I looked up in astonishment and saw for the first time Herman F. Erben, who was then an independent motion-picture producer and who, incidentally, was one of the strangest characters I have ever encountered." Erben was never a film producer, but he was, by all accounts, a mysterious and exceedingly bizarre person.

THE SURVEILLANCE FILES

Dr. Erben's activities were first seriously scrutinized by U.S. officials when he was placed on the international list of suspected narcotics smugglers on January 7, 1933. Although his name was eventually dropped, his movement throughout the world was watched very closely for many years. He also was involved in constant passport difficulties. By March of 1937, the Immigration and Naturalization Service had initiated a legal investigation of his passport use, due to "the discrepancies in this man's statements concerning alleged departures and reentries to the U.S., it is believed that this naturalization was secured through fraud and we are endeavoring to determine if he had the necessary legal entry and residence to justify his naturalization . . . . " (INS letter of Eugene Kessler, Mar. 24, 1937). In 1938, his naturalization certificate was confiscated. He managed to continue traveling and earning his living as a ship's surgeon by use of a seaman's protection certificate.

In the numerous surveillance documents pertaining to Dr.

Erben, there are attributed to him political statements of a conflicting nature. U.S. consular officials came to believe he was extremely pro-Nazi in his sentiments, yet Dr. Erben maintained his loyalty was to the United States. It is important to note the dual nature of comments attributed to Dr. Erben.

Dec. 6, 1935 statement of Dr. Erben to the Passport Division:

> I have never in my life at any time or place actively engaged in politics of any sort. I have never been a member of any political body, society, party at any time or place. I have never independently and on my own carried out any political propaganda neither in word nor in publications in this country or abroad . . . .

March 25, 1938 memo of C.E.Gauss, American Consul General, Shanghai, China:

> Erben appears to be an ardent "Nazi" and his usual greeting is the Fascist salute. He said he was a member of the Nazi party in Austria and Germany and showed his alleged membership card. He also stated he was affiliated with so-called Nazi organizations in the United States . . . .

March 20, 1940, Statement of Dr. Erben to the Passport Division:

> I remained only about 12 days in Spain . . . . I applied for permission to work as a surgeon, in Red Cross capacity, to use my skill as a surgeon, at a place where Red Cross help was badly needed. Not for adventure, not any political issues such as communism—fascism—nazism, no, for I am an American, but to help where I felt I could help . . . .

An FBI report of March 26, 1940, contains information that the doctor had appeared at the Washington Field FBI office to offer his assistance concerning any investigation of his activities:

Dr. Erben stated that he is a loyal American citizen, and has nothing to hide as far as his activities are concerned; that he is not now, and has never been before engaged in any espionage activities, and that his apparent German leanings were but a camouflage, with the aim in mind to maintain his good standing in the eyes of the German government in the interests of the safety and welfare of his mother who lives in Vienna, and of his two sons who are in Germany . . . .

Flynn and Erben went to Spain together in 1937. On March 13, 1980, ABC television aired a *20/20* segment that briefly discussed the controversy regarding the Higham accusations. Higham said that "Errol Flynn was an agent for the Gestapo . . . ," proclaiming that the two had gone to Spain to spy on the Loyalist soldiers fighting against Franco. In his autobiography, Flynn writes that his reason for going to Spain was boredom and marital unhappiness; "I had a lot of sympathy with the Republican Government, but I would have gone to either side just to get away."

Flynn's early ambition was to be a writer. His first articles appeared in Australian newspapers in 1931. Throughout his life, he wrote two novels and numerous magazine pieces. These were collected and published by Tony Thomas in *From A Life of Adventure: The Writings of Errol Flynn* (Citadel 1980). Flynn had an eye for color and an abundance of imagination. He entered Spain as a foreign correspondent with Dr. Erben as his photographer.

In *The Untold Story*, an FBI document is printed by Higham. It concerns information given by Carlos Vejarano y Cassina. According to the FBI dossier on Vejarano, this man was second cousin of the Duke of Alba, Spanish Ambassador in London. Vejarano furnished a signed statement that, during the latter part of July, 1940, he became acquainted with Captain Richard Weiss, who was in charge of the German occupation forces in Biarritz, France.

After meeting Captain Weiss on several occasions, Weiss told Vejarano that he was connected with the Military Intelligence of Germany. Weiss knew that Vejarano was coming to America to study shipping business operations as a representative of the Spanish Line. He would be of assistance to Germany if he would furnish information concerning the attitude of the people of the United States regarding the European war.

Vejarano was eventually charged with violation of the Registration Act. In the course of interviews, he gave the FBI information concerning an event he had experienced in 1937.

The report, as published by Higham, is an amazing distortion of the actual meaning of the document. It is supposedly "slightly condensed," yet on examining the original document, the fraudulent nature of Higham's version is blatantly apparent. This is the Higham version, with the pertinent distortion circled.

FEDERAL BUREAU OF INVESTIGATION
January 29, 1944

CARLOS VEJARANO Y CASSINA
ESPIONAGE-G2
REGISTRATION ACT

Dear Sir:

The above captioned subject who was sentenced on December 7, 1943, to a year and a day in violation of the Registration Act, recently advised this office of an incident that occurred to him in Berlin, Germany, in 1937.

[One paragraph cut].

On one occasion [May, 1937] he recalled that he had gone to the Spanish Embassy [Franco's] in Berlin, to pay his respects to _____ and was introduced in _____'s office to a German [Hermann Erben] who according to _____ was from Los Angeles, California. _____ explained that this German had just completed a tour of the various fronts in company with Errol Flynn and (they) had taken numerous pictures of gun establishments and military objectives in Loyalist Spain. These pictures lay in a huge pile on _____'s desk. When _____ stepped out of the room, [Erben] stated he was a friend of Errol Flynn and Flynn had decided to go to Spain during the

Spanish Civil War to observe the fighting . . . they had gone to London with the idea of getting permission from the Franco forces. Franco officials in London, however, refused visas to Flynn and the German, but they had been able to secure visas from the Loyalist Spanish officials there. The German had exhibited his Republican visa issued in London and also his American passport, and had discussed various cities in the United States, in particular Los Angeles and Washington, D.C. After this the German left, _____ said that this German was a member of the Military Secret Service of Germany and had been working for Germany in the United States. One of the German military officials had called the Embassy advising that they were sending this man over in order that members of the Spanish Embassy in Berlin who were at that time superiors of General Franco could view the pictures that their (agents) had taken in Spain with a view that this might be of some help to the Franco forces. _____ advised that he had looked through these pictures and noticed several pictures of the German in company with Errol Flynn and the various military objectives which (he) had photographed.

Very truly yours,
[Signed] E.E.Conroy

The report without it's distortion is printed below:

FEDERAL BUREAU OF INVESTIGATION
United States Department of Justice
New York, New York

Director, F.B.I.   January 29, 1944

RE: Carlos Vejarano y Cassina
     Espionage - G;
     Registration Act

Dear Sir:
    The above captioned subject who was sentenced on December 27, 1943 to a year and a day in violation of the

Registration Act, recently advised this office of an incident that occurred to him in Berlin, Germany in 1937.

VEJARANO stated that in May and June of 1937 he was being treated at the La Scharite Hospital in Berlin, and occasionally paid visits to the Spanish Embassy there. He explained that one ANTONIO VARGAS, who was liaison man between Spanish military officials and German military officials in Berlin, was known to his family, and his father had particularly instructed him to call upon VARGAS in Berlin.

On one occasion he recalled that he had gone to the Embassy to pay his usual respects to Vargas, and was introduced in VARGAS' office to a German, who according to VARGAS was from Los Angeles, California. VARGAS explained that this German had just completed a tour of the various Spanish fronts in company with ERROL FLYNN, the movie actor, _and had taken_ numerous pictures of gun establishments and military objectives in "Red" Spain. These pictures lay in a huge pile on VARGAS' desk.

When VARGAS stepped out of the room, this man stated he was a friend of ERROL FLYNN and FLYNN had decided to go to Spain during the Spanish Civil War to observe the fighting on the various fronts and that they had gone to London with the idea of getting permission from the Franco forces. Franco officials in London, however, had refused visas to FLYNN and the German, but they had been able to secure visas from the Spanish Republican officials there. The German had exhibited his Republican visa issued in London, and also his American passport, and had discussed various cities in the United States, particularly Los Angeles and Wash., D.C. After this German left, ANTONIO VARGAS advised VEJARANO that this German was a member of Military Secret Police of Germany and had been working for Germany in the United States. One of the German Military officials had called the Embassy advising that they were sending this man over in order that members of the Spanish Embassy in Berlin who were at that time superiors of General Franco, could view the pictures that their <u>agent</u> had taken in Spain with a view that this might be some help to the Franco forces. VEJARANO advised that he had looked through these pictures and noticed several pictures of the German in company with ERROL FLYNN and the various military objectives which <u>the German</u> had photographed.

VEJARANO advised that his memory of the specific details of this incident had faded inasmuch as he had not thought a great deal about it at the time. He advised that he had heard in 1939 that VARGAS was sent to Buenos Aires, Argentina to work in the Spanish Embassy there. He had never heard of this German since then, but could recall only that VARGAS had introduced him with the title of "doctor." According to VEJARANO a description of both VARGAS and this German as he observed in 1937, were as follows:

VARGAS		DR——	
Age	52	Age	40 to 50
Height	5'10"	Height	5'10"
Weight	165 lbs.	Weight	140 lbs.
Race	Spanish	Hair	completely gray
Build	Strong	Dress	Shabby
Profile	High forehead	Race	German

The Washington Field Division is requested to check the records of the State Department to ascertain if visas were granted to movie actor ERROL FLYNN in 1937 to visit Spain, and whether any notation appears as to his companion. The Los Angeles Field Division is requested to ascertain from its sources of information regarding ERROL FLYNN's visit to Spain in 1937 and the identity and present whereabouts of his companion at that time.

Very truly yours,
E.E.Conroy
SAC

Years later, Dr. Erben would deny the accuracy of the Vejarano statement. In a personal interview, he informed me that he was not a German agent in 1937. In 1946, he had testified at the China War Crimes Trials that he began working for German Intelligence *officially* in 1941. Yet, the Vejarano statement provides strong evidence that Dr. Erben was indeed affiliated, in some capacity, with German Intelligence in 1937. However, it is Dr. Erben's own espionage activities that form the nucleus of the controversy surrounding Errol Flynn.

That Charles Higham forced the spy charge on Flynn is apparent by analyzing how Higham rewrote the Vejarano statement. As printed by Higham: "*they* had taken numerous pictures of gun establishments . . . ." The grammatical logic of the actual sentence, and indeed the content itself, makes it clear that only Dr. Erben had taken the photographs. But Higham prints "*they.*" In addition, he twists another key phrase. The Higham version: "the pictures that their *agents* had taken in Spain . . . ." It is quite clearly Dr. Erben who is mentioned as being an "agent," and *not Errol Flynn.*

Had the internationally famous Flynn been an agent or subagent, the information would undoubtedly have surfaced in the conversation between Vargas and Vejarano. Surely: "this man and Flynn are working for Germany." The most obvious person is never identified as a spy. This is Higham's key piece of evidence and he had to rewrite it to make it fit his premise. Readers were given a false document-*their agents.* The fraud perpetrated by this deceitful misprint is indicative of *The Untold Story.* Actions attributed to Dr. Erben in various intelligence files become the actions of Flynn. In fact, the document shows that there was no "Mission to Spain." Flynn had apparently intended to cover the war from the Franco side.

Speculation can be made that Flynn had knowledge of Erben's spy activities but there is no proof. What would Flynn's motive be in spying? Money? Ideology? Had he been a secret Nazi activist, his value would have been in propaganda.

Higham claims that Esmond Romilly, Winston Churchill's nephew, had assisted Flynn in gaining information about the Spanish Medical Aid Committee. This unit was formed in England to assist the International Brigade, which fought in Spain. The accusation by Higham is that Flynn manipulated a position in the

Committee so that Erben could spy on German volunteers in the International Brigade. Jessica Mitford, Romilly's wife, informed me: "I don't think Esmond Romilly knew Errol Flynn; he never mentioned him to me. The dates are all wrong . . . ."(letter, August 17, 1981).

As for Flynn's trip to Spain, he later wrote an article that appeared in *Photoplay* (July 1937). It was an account of what he had seen and done in the war-torn country. Accompanying the text were photographs taken by Dr. Erben. Wrote Flynn: "Erben had brought along his camera to take some night shots . . . ." It was certainly no secret to Loyalist authorities that *Erben* was taking photos. If any were of value to military strategy remains unknown. However, what Erben did with photos *he* had taken—and *he* later took to Berlin—had nothing whatsoever to do with Flynn.

Spanish author, D. Pastor Petit, is a specialist in the area of international intelligence services. Among the seventeen books he has published are several dealing with international espionage. He has investigated extensively the involvement of foreign agents in Spain during the Spanish Civil War. His forthcoming book is entitled *Espionage in World War II*. It is eight-hundred pages in length and the result of fourteen years of research. His comments regarding Errol Flynn:

> I have spoken with many important ex-agents from America, the Soviet Union, France, Germany, Britain, etc., and not one of them had knowledge of Mr. Flynn being a spy . . . . I put this question to Dr. Gert Buchheit, a very important member of the Abwehr and later a historian with exhaustive works on the German spies. He said to me: "I'm sure that Errol Flynn has not worked for Germany in the Abwehr, Gestapo, SS, or Foreign Affairs. In all our archives there is not the name of this man. Not one of our historians or surviving agents knows of him as a secret informer." Neither is there any mention of Flynn's spying in *Die Nachhut*. This is a very informative publication issued from Munich by surviving members of Nazi Intelligence (letter, Feb. 1, 1984).

When Dr. Erben was facing his denaturalization hearing for supposedly making misstatements about leaving the U.S. prior to becoming a citizen, Errol Flynn solicited the assistance of Eleanor

Roosevelt. On March 20, 1940, Flynn addressed a telegram to Mrs. Roosevelt, stating that Dr. Erben was in danger of losing his citizenship because of a technicality: "A telephone call from you to Miss Perkins to see either him or his lawyer, Mr. Tramutolo, Mayflower Hotel, asking her to review his case, would probably solve his difficulties."

Writes Higham: "This telegram was a pure act of treason to Britain." This is an absurdly dramatic accusation. It is apparent from Flynn's comments to government officials that he did not believe Erben was a German agent. He termed Erben "a screwball." As Flynn told the FBI, "He is the type of person who would do everything in his power to make it appear that he was in fact an espionage agent." While in Buenos Aires, Flynn told Ambassador Norman Armour, "he felt an injustice had been done the man in believing him to be a German agent, but that no one was to blame but Dr. Erben himself" (June 21, 1940).

Charles Higham writes that "records show" Mrs. Roosevelt contacted "J. Edgar Hoover, the Attorney General, the Secretary of Labor and the Secretaries of the Navy and Army. In March 1940, the grueling investigation of Erben and Errol was suddenly suspended." Once again, Charles Higham misstates the facts.

The correspondence between Errol Flynn and Eleanor Roosevelt regarding Dr. Erben is present in the Roosevelt Library in Hyde Park. It is clear that the only person she contacted after Flynn's telegram was Frances Perkins, Secretary of Labor. Before she did anything, however, a letter arrived from Erben's attorney.

April 5, 1940
Mrs. Eleanor Roosevelt

President Hotel
Palo Alto, California

Re: United States of America, Petitioner, v.
Hermann Frederick Erben, Respondent

Dear Mrs. Roosevelt:

Due to my inability to see you while you were here in San Francisco your secretary told my office that I should write you about the above case.

The respondent Dr. Hermann Frederick Erben is a friend of Mr. Errol Flynn's and I believe Mr. Flynn spoke to you about this case recently while you were in Los Angeles. The action by the Government, instituted through the Department of Labor, involves the cancellation of Dr. Erben's citizenship papers, which the Government alleges he obtained illegally. The complaint charges that Dr. Erben, a native of Austria, did on August 1, 1930, file a petition for citizenship in the United States District Court at San Francisco, California, and thereafter on November 10, 1930, obtained a decree of court admitting him to citizenship. The Government contends that Dr. Erben wilfully and falsely represented that immediately preceding the date of his application for citizenship he had resided continuously in the United States for five years and that this representation, namely that he had resided in the United States continuously for five years immediately preceding the application for citizenship, is untrue and that he had in fact been out of the United States on several occasions previous to filing papers for citizenship.

The trend of the Government's case seems to be that while out of the United States Dr. Erben served on vessels of foreign registry and that such service, while out of the United States and on foreign registered boats, made him ineligible for citizenship. This, briefly, is the Government's position and I am of the opinion that the court will order a cancellation of Dr. Erben's citizenship papers unless through your intercession Mrs. Perkins will have the complaint withdrawn.

Dr. Erben is unquestionably a man of ability for he served as Junior Medical Officer of the Manhattan State Hospital, New York, and also as Senior Assistant Physician at the Eastern State Hospital, located I believe in Jackson, Louisiana. In 1927 Dr. Erben was assigned by Dr. Stutht, Public Health Director of the State of Washington, to treat malaria cases at the various Washington state hospitals, in which treatment he was a specialist.

The hearing of this case is set for Monday, May 6, here in San Francisco, so whatever you have in mind doing must be done as quickly as possible. I would have preferred, had your time permitted, to talk this case over with you in person but in the absence of this I have related the foregoing facts in the hope that they will be sufficient for you to take whatever action you contemplate.

Anticipating your courtesy, with kind regards, I am

Very truly yours,
Chauncey Tramutolo

Mrs. Roosevelt penned a brief note on the upper portion of Chauncey Tramutolo's letter:

April 19, 1940

Dear Frances,

Errol Flynn tells me this man was a ship's doctor and he had no idea that he endangered his citizenship. If there is no reason to suspect him could he be told what to do to get his status regained? E.R.

The response soon followed:

April 24, 1940

My dear Mrs. Roosevelt:

I am returning the letter addressed to you by Chauncey Tramutolo, which you sent with your note of April 19th, together with a report on the case which I have received from the Immigration and Naturalization Service.

Sincerely Yours
Frances Perkins

Eleanor Roosevelt then sent out the following letters on May 6, 1940:

My dear Mr. Tramutolo:

I am enclosing the report which I have received from the Secretary of Labor concerning Dr. Hermann Frederick Erben. The case apparently seems hopeless and I am sorry that there is nothing I can do about it.

Very sincerely yours,

My dear Mr. Flynn:

I asked Secretary Perkins about Dr. Hermann Frederick Erben, whose case you spoke to me about, and she had the matter carefully gone over. The report she sent to me I have forwarded to Dr. Erben's lawyer, Mr. Chauncey Tramutolo. I am sorry but the case apparently seems hopeless.

Very sincerely yours,

"Hopeless" stated Mrs. Roosevelt; yet Charles Higham claimed that Flynn and Erben were never apprehended because "Mrs. Roosevelt's umbrella of protection held good" and "Erben was exhilarated by the protection of Mrs. Roosevelt." There was no "protection" at all. The Immigration and Naturalization file of Dr. Erben makes it clear that Erben's trial did not take place in May, since it was transferred from Judge Louderback to Judge Welsh. It was further delayed due to court congestion.

In the fall of 1940, the trial for the cancellation of Dr. Erben's naturalization was held in San Francisco. For two days in September, Judge Welsh listened to the evidence, then announced he was recessing the case for thirty days to take a deposition. In the interim, Erben tried to find work aboard various ships. On October 8, 1940, he appeared at the San Francisco FBI office, quite perturbed because he felt the FBI was questioning his employers, which discouraged anyone from hiring him.

The previous September, he had been sent by the Sailor's Union of the Pacific to work aboard the *S.S. Garfield,* but he had been removed from the vessel after agents began asking questions about him. On September 27, Erben shipped as a sailor aboard the *Admiral Nulton.* Again, an FBI agent inquired about him, and, according to the FBI file, "the captain persuaded Erben to quit at Seattle."

On October 8, Erben complained to San Francisco FBI agents about the incident. He informed the agents that he intended to depart on another ship the following Friday and would return in sixty days. On this voyage, Erben was given his pay and asked to leave the ship. He then complained to the U.S. District Attorney's office and was advised that it was necessary for him to be in San Francisco on November 12, 1940, for his continued court case. On October 23, a subpoena was issued. Higham writes that "a federal warrant was put out for Erben's arrest." This is erroneous. The subpoena was merely a writ commanding Erben's presence in court under penalty. In fact, the subpoena was never served on Dr. Erben, because he had gone to Los Angeles.

On January 29, 1941, Dr. Erben's citizenship was officially revoked. By then, he was no longer in America. He had gone to Mexico, as he would later claim, on his attorney's advice, since it was obvious that he would lose the case and be subject to immediate deportation to wherever U.S. authorities chose to send him. Charles Higham claims that Flynn helped Erben to escape from America, either by "hiding him on the *Sirocco*" or "driving him to the border." According to Higham, "whichever these versions is true, Errol committed an act of treason."

Despite the author's claim, the truth of the matter is quite different. Josef Fegerl's *Errol Flynn-Dr. Hermann F. Erben* (Vienna 1985) presents excerpts from Erben's diary of 1940. It is crystal clear that Flynn wasn't hiding Erben from anyone. The entries between October 26 and November 15 show that Dr. Erben was publicly visible. In fact, he lists, besides Flynn, dozens of people with whom he came in contact. Proof: Erben attended a court hearing for "Errol's action against Selznick," "Cobina Wright's party at Ciro's," and "whole day on Lot 18 Footsteps in the Dark." Also listed are meetings at a yacht club, Hungarian restaurant, "steambath at Chasen's," "lunch at Brown Derby."

Higham claims that, in 1978, "Erben said that Errol drove him to the border, got him through immigration and customs with a Mexican transit card, and embraced him in friendly farewell." Erben's diary makes numerous references to Errol Flynn during the months of October and November, but not for the last two days he was in America.

The entries for the last three days read:

November 13	go to Errol, lunch with Alva Johnson of Saturday Evening Post, call Gloria.
November 14	arrive Phoenix at Midnight, sleep in car.
November 15	arrive in Tucson 1 noon. Indian village and parade in Tucson. Go to Nogales, arrive 5:15. Go across border 6 p.m.

Dr. Erben informed me that, as he recalled their farewell, it was in Burbank, at Warner Brothers studio. Indeed, this is undoubtedly the accurate version. Proof: Flynn was in the midst of *Footsteps in the Dark,* and Warner's "Daily Production and Progress Notes," meticulously kept by the studio, verify Flynn's presence on November 13, 14, and 15.

It is apparent that Flynn never felt he was harboring a fugitive, as Higham desperately tries to color the situation. Would Flynn bring a fugitive to parties or to Warner Brothers studio?

When Dr. Erben left America, he was doing exactly what the U.S. government intended to do with him when his citizenship was revoked. This is why a subpoena was issued—to insure that Erben was in court, so the government could immediately deport him. After Judge Welsh stripped him of his American citizenship, the *San Francisco Examiner* precisely explained the situation: "The doctor has ten days in which to appeal. If no appeal is made, he must leave the country. And if he fails to depart, deportation proceedings will be instigated, Government officials said."

Dr. Erben told me that he and Flynn never saw each other again after November 1940.

In Oct. 1946. Dr. Erben was a participant in the Shanghai War Crimes Trials. He testified that he had gone to Mexico to await the decision of his pending citizenship investigation. He stated that he began intelligence work in Mexico City in January of 1941. He worked for German Military Intelligence, "Particularly Naval Intelligence, due to my naval background."

He had arrived in Shanghai on March 5, 1941. "I was to cover the waterfront to approach in my capacity as a physician former shipmates to invite myself aboard ship, to get their detailed course from the ship's map. . ." Dr. Erben had worked for the Bureau Siefken, which later became the Bureau Ehrhardt. He denied ever working for the Gestapo. He had watched American ships until December 8, 1941. He had been interned in the Pootung Civil

Assembly Center from May 2, 1943, to August 17, 1945. While imprisoned, he had been a camp spy, regularly reporting to his superiors. He denied ever being a traitor, "I never went out wholeheartedly for the Germans. . ."

The Judge Advocate's Office asked him to testify against the German Officials who had employed him.

Foreign Service Report #1672, September 15, 1947, to the Secretary of State, contains the comments: "Following the V-J Day Erben was of invaluable assistance to American authorities in supplying material for the trial of the Ehrhardt members. . . ."

Interview with Dr. Hermann F. Erben, September 1980

As I stood before the massive apartment building, a disembodied voice suddenly crackled through the intercom and, with a heavy Viennese accent, authoritatively told me, "Come up, top floor." A buzzer released the electronic latch. I entered the darkened lobby and stepped into an ancient ornate elevator. As the elevator creaked to a stop, I saw before me the man I had come to know through hundreds of U.S. surveillance files.

It was hard to imagine that the frail, white-haired figure who stood before me was the focal point of world-wide notoriety concerning Errol Flynn. He leaned on a cane for a moment, then stiffly lurched his body forward. Dr. Erben extended a hand, gnarled and swollen from arthritis. He wore his hair close-cropped, and there was a distinct dueling scar on his cheek, from his university days. He led me through a dim hall, cluttered with weathered trunks, suitcases, and cardboard boxes. On both sides of the hall were large rooms filled with old furniture and additional boxes stacked to the ceiling. In his musty bedroom, he offered me a chair near a window with a view of the Vienna skyline.

From an old desk he carefully withdrew a sheaf of letters, suddenly turned, and—trembling with emotion—thrust a faded letter at me. "This was the cause of all my trouble with Uncle Sam!" he said loudly. It was a 1938 letter from Mr. Bulkley of the U.S. Treasury Department, Narcotic Enforcement Division. It stated that Erben's name had been removed from the government list of suspected narcotic smugglers. "Uncle Sam started to spy on me because of a suspicion that I was illegally selling drugs. I was a ship's surgeon. I had to always carry something for a possible emergency. I was finally cleared . . . , but all the unnecessary trouble this caused me."

He seated himself at his desk.

"I know about that letter. I've read the files on you," I told him. I reached into my briefcase and placed a mountainous pile of documents on his desk. He stared at it.

"Those are all the secret papers on me?"

"You haven't seen any of them?"

"No. What a waste of taxpayer's money. All those G-men being paid to spy on me."

I showed him the FBI letter that exonerated Flynn.

"Of course, that's just what I said on the ABC television program."

"Did you see the program, Dr. Erben?"

"No."

"You were on camera about two minutes."

"I spoke to that lady producer for an hour and half!" he bellowed.

"You said you had never brainwashed Errol Flynn to become a Nazi agent."

He nodded his head, then exclaimed: "It is so utterly preposterous to claim that this man, with all that family background, that mixture of Irish, Australian, British, and French—his mother had spent most of her life in Paris—so this mixture could never bring a spy."

He picked up a surveillance document and adjusted his thick glasses. He wore a faded-gray pin-striped coat that must have fit him years ago, but now seemed to swallow him, crumpled brown pants, no socks, and an antique pair of high-topped leather shoes. He tossed the document on the desk.

"Was Flynn fair to you in *My Wicked Wicked Ways?*"

He smiled, then shrugged.

"Some of it was true. Some of it was imaginary. When he describes our parting at Marseilles, not knowing if we would ever meet again, that was very accurate."

"Did he ever mention to you the incident in the Higham biography, where Flynn was supposedly charged with manslaughter in New Guinea, due to his lugger capsizing and three crew members drowning?"

"Well, it's true that he had lost his lugger, which an Australian wealthy widow had given him to do some self-supporting, because to just be with the territorial New Guinea Police wasn't a life-fulfilling position. He would go occasionally, as a government inspector, to see if the natives were trying to build cesspools instead of just soiling the bush.

"So, if he did have a lugger with which, as he told me, he was engaged in doing everything the government frowned on—and on the other hand liked—such as indenture . . . . Now, I know Errol too well. He would have risked his life and been smashed on the coral reef to save any one of these crew members. No, I don't think they were. He would have mentioned it. He never did.

"After we met, we traveled together for six months. We became close friends, although I was old enough to be his eldest brother. I wasn't old enough to be his father, but the age that was between us made me a senior friend, so that I was not blinded by the brilliant physique he had. To see that man in action when we were boxing together! The tiger-like movement he had was something that made me very enthusiastic about the friendship of this fellow. Because, also, his brain was so that I could admire him."

"You knew Flynn when he was merely Errol Flynn, unknown Australian, rather than Flynn the legend. Did he tell you that he wanted to become an actor?"

"Yes, sure. He wanted to get to the Old Vic and become an actor. As a matter of fact, he told me time and time again, as I saw him after he had become a star . . . . He told me, 'Doc, I don't know, I'd rather give that up and get on the legitimate stage. I feel I could do something there. But here, under the harness of a man like Curtiz . . . . ' He hated him. 'I am handicapped, but I have to do what that bastard wants me to do. I have to move the way that bastard wants me to move. I want the freedom and the interpretation of my own being on the legitimate stage.' "

"Did he change much after success?"

"I had a comparison. He hadn't changed a bit. As a matter of fact, he was even more self-critical than before success. When he tried to get to the legitimate stage, he said, 'Well, Doc, I don't know if I'm good enough. I really don't know. I wished I was, but I'm not sure.' And later on, when he was a star already, he never changed. He was also putting his achievement down. He said, 'Well, I'm not anything special; the people like my mug, and why I don't know. I can only look into the picture and see I don't have leprosy . . . , but somehow I'd be a fool it I didn't make the best of it and cooperate.' "

"In the autobiography, Flynn describes you as being somewhat tight with a dollar."

He smiled. "I never liked to waste money. When these G-men spied on old Doc Erben, they must have cursed me, because they had to eat a hot dog at the Seaman's Mission. Look at this."

From his desk drawer he removed an enormous leather-bound book. "This is my journal for 1937. For nearly sixty years, I have kept a journal whenever possible. My father always told me to keep an account of how much money I spend." He pointed to a page.

"Were you bringing money into Spain?"

"There was no money. We intended—and Errol intended—to go on the Duke of Alba's side, just to get in Spain, and that would have been Franco. That did not come off.

"I don't know why, although the Duke invited Errol personally and said, 'If you've got a friend, bring him. Any friend of Errol Flynn is my friend.' So we were sitting around in Paris . . . , and Errol said, 'Now, goddammit, I'm spending a lot of money on guys I don't even know. Why don't you stay with me at the Plaza Athenee?' I said, 'Because I'm not going to be sponging. That's why I'm staying at the Seaman's Home.' And he said, 'My God, why don't I do that! I'd love to do that.' 'No, Errol . . . .'

"And so, by not staying at one of the big hotels in Paris, I was able to meet Jorge. He was on the Loyalist side and was coming to Barcelona and staying there and visiting his folks and so on. I told him, 'I'm here with Errol Flynn, and we are both interested in going to Spain, and I have now an opportunity to go to work for the Blood Transfusion—"Transfusion de Sangre"—and do some medial work for you people on the Loyalist side.' 'Well, certainly, come along, and I'll take you to Port Bou, and we'll go then—with one of the camions—right on to Barcelona. This is still our country, thank God.' And so we went."

"Was the incident of the dead priest true, as told by Flynn?"

"Yes . . . . If you have been hungry all your life and your wife gave birth, and ten children are hungry and starve to death, and then you have a fat priest, fat as a pig . . . . A lot of hatred accumulates in you when you were so hungry throughout the years, and they remember that. So now they say, 'Cross here on this beam,' and he had to cross over, and there is some sewer, and he is to crawl over this board. A lot of fun—for the people who watched it."

"The recent biography of Flynn states that Flynn had affairs with men."

"He definitely was not a homosexual. We doctors are trained to investigate. So, in many diseases, the diagnosis is made only after a careful examination. So, we are trained to be interested—what's behind that, why does he get like that? Why does he react like that? I made four years of psychiatric studies, but it never entered my mind to find out why a homosexual is a homosexual. It is allegedly a missing of the so-called 'zietic cells' in the scrotum, in the testes, and for that reason, the homosexual is stigmatized in a way of internal glandular dysfunction; therefore, nothing to be said against the poor bastards."

Judging from his threadbare appearance, one would never have taken Erben for the medical man that he was—a surgeon and a specialist in tropical diseases. The only son of a wealthy Viennese attorney who grew up in a home with nine servants, he learned English from a British governess at the age of ten.

"The State Department and FBI files attribute anti-Semitic statements to you. Are you anti-Semitic?"

"I am a fanatic non-racist! I helped Dr. Gertrude Kary escape from Austria in 1938. I walked into the American Consulate one day in Vienna, and there were all these Jewish people, frantically looking in phone books for the names of relatives in the States, or at least someone with the last name the same. I saw this pretty girl. We started talking, and I invited her to go swimming. She said, 'You know, Jews aren't allowed there.' I said, 'Let's go anyway. We'll take a chance.' We became friends. I helped her to escape by signing her on the ship as my nurse. She later became a resident of Bryn Mawr in Pennsylvania. Look at this . . . " He reached into a drawer of his desk and pulled out a card.

"This is a letter from a Jewish lady whose family were friends of mine. She used to live here, in this building where I was born.

She writes me, thanking me for helping her mother also."

"Flynn tried to help you with your naturalization difficulties, didn't he?"

"Yes, he spoke to Eleanor Roosevelt, and when my ship called the next time—again we were sitting in his studio at Burbank— and I said, 'Errol, have you had a chance to see Mrs. Roosevelt?' He said, 'Yes, and I'm going to call her up right now.' And he picked up the receiver, and he dialed that special number that connected with the President and Eleanor Roosevelt. And as we are sitting here, I heard him say, 'Eleanor, this is Errol talking. I'm calling you up, I hope you don't mind, about my old friend. I mentioned him to you, about Dr. Erben.' And she said, 'I have seen Ma Perkins about that, and Ma Perkins said, 'Hands off; that case is dynamite.' I'm sorry, Errol, I know how you're going to feel about it, but that's the best I could do. If Ma Perkins says hands off, that's dynamite. After all, she's the immigration chief.'

"So she must have been completely snowed under by the reports of fanatic men who had staked their reputations on running me out of the country. Since they couldn't run me down with facts, they chose the next possible chance, and that was to run me out of the country."

"Was Flynn a Nazi sympathizer?"

"Of course not. He was loyal to the British."

"You gave information to the U.S. government in South America."

"Yes, I had taken photographs of the damaged *Graf Spee* in Montevideo, and later gave these to Mr. English, who passed them on to Naval Intelligence."

"How did you become involved with German Intelligence?"

"Chauncey Tramutolo, my lawyer, told me in his years of being a lawyer in San Francisco, this had never happened with a judge like Judge Welsh of the U.S. District Court, who had reserved decision on an immigration naturalization case for so long. He had decided that his decision would be given in writing. And now I waited all along until November, and no decision was rendered. Chauncey Tramutolo told me, 'Well, Doc, we still don't know the possibility of losing your citizenship in a written statement, for which we have been waiting now for so many months, for you'll be stateless, not an American, and also not a German and not an

Austrian, because you can't be naturalized against the enemy, so you'll be interned for the duration. So the only question is, you go to Mexico, apply down there, and wait, and I'm going to try to needle Judge Welsh to say yes or no, for chrissake.'

"Well, he wasn't a success in that, because, after three months, here I was. My form permitting me to stay for three months had expired, and I had to leave."

"This is when German Consul Baron Wallenberg contacted you? While you were in Mexico at the end of 1940?"

"Yes. He said, 'Your situation is such that I want you to consider the fact that blood is thicker than ink. Your citizenship hasn't brought you much happiness in America, has it?' So they had the German Intelligence there, taking stock of the few Americans who could be used, and I told him this was a decision I couldn't make overnight. 'I have to think it over. I'll have to let you know before I leave.' And I thought about it, and I realized here is perhaps a chance to regain my citizenship, showing them that I'm even willing to risk my life with high treason. It was a gamble, and I risked it."

"So when you left for your mission in China, you still didn't know if you were a U.S. citizen or not?"

"I didn't know until 1943 that I was no longer a U.S. citizen."

"Who did you work for when you arrived in Shanghai?"

"I worked for the Siefken Bureau . . . , Naval Intelligence. My trouble was that I had to do something; otherwise I would have been liquidated—life is very cheap. So I had the one and only thing which I could do, without doing real and dangerous damage to the United States—report what I heard from American crews, about such things as when they were surrounded by enemy submarines they would start to pump oil on the ocean, so that the submarine could not get any shot done properly with their periscopes. That report saved me for a long time, and Siefken said, 'Doctor, I know that you have a spot in your heart for pretty Chinese girls, but after all, you can't live on that oil. After all, you might slip on that oil report of yours, because it has been the only report for a long time . . . .' "

"You were interned as a U.S. citizen, and after your release from the Japanese prison camp, you were eventually arrested by American officials."

"I was in death-row, together with the Japanese who were executed. I could hear the trap door shut. As a doctor, I was requested to disentangle the corpse and wheel him into the morgue. This is not in addition to cheering you up. Out of the clear sky, after several months in death-row, I was told there is a Captain Farrell who wants to see you. He said, 'Well, Doc, you have been a naturalized American citizen, I understand. How do you feel about America now?' 'Well, it hasn't changed any. I want to go back. I never stopped trying.' 'We could use you, with your local knowledge. How do you feel about accepting a position as investigator for the OSS, of which I'm a member.' 'Yes, but under one condition only—that I'm not buying my freedom out of death-row . . . . If you accept my bona fide statement that I was never against America with the intention of harming as much. I worked for German Intelligence, and the reason was given, but I still insist on standing trial as an American, whether or not I have ever been naturalized legally, and therefore could never have committed high treason as an American . . . ."

Dr. Erben claimed he had gone to Shanghai as a "self-styled agent." Dr. Erben testified at the China War Crimes Trials in October of 1946. He worked with the OSS for nearly eighteen months. The Chinese eventually issued a deportation order against "Obnoxious Nazis" in the summer of 1947. Dr. Erben was surprised to learn that his name was on the list.

"You were deported, along with the men you had helped convict. You went to Ludwigsburg Prison in Germany, and you never had a trial?"

"No. Figure for yourself how you feel, when you worked really with all your heart for your reentry into the United States and for your helping America . . . , but I'm not bitter. Every nickel I ever made, I owe to America."

"There is one document in the files—a letter addressed by you to the American Consulate in Indonesia, in 1950, I believe. You say in this letter that you risked your life to enter Soviet China to regain American classified documents and personal belongings. Were you trying to obtain Flynn's supposedly 'incriminating letters,' as the Flynn biography claims?"

"I deposited sixteen trunks with the Austrian Consulate before I left China. These trunks disappeared. I also had one suitcase I gave to the OSS. This had in it all my personal American documents, medical licenses, my complete Contax equipment, and $4,800, my salary from the OSS."

"You think that the suitcase you handed over to the OSS is still around?"

"I'm not sure, but there is a curious incident concerning a photograph in the Higham book on Flynn. It is a picture of me and Abbot Chao Kung. This negative was in my suitcase. A copy of this photograph was mysteriously returned to me, but nothing else .... There were no incriminating letters from Errol."

Dr. Erben was a man who made powerful connections. He was a friend of King Saud of Arabia and President Sukarno of Indonesia. His adopted Chinese daughter was related to the Chiang-Kai-Shek family. Another close friend was the former director of the American Atomic Commission in Vienna.

Dr. Erben attempted to enter the U.S. several times, but was always refused a visa. He even had two bills introduced to attempt to return his citizenship. He believed that these efforts were unsuccessful due to the ex-OSS men with whom he worked in China.

"Why?"

"Because I know too much."

We returned through the hall. I stopped and peered in one of the rooms that was crammed with boxes.

"I'm a collector. I have more rooms down in the basement," he said proudly.

"Years of hard traveling?"

His face brightened. "Yes, I'm desperate to leave the cold climate of Vienna. Maybe I'll return to the Philippines . . . , maybe to Soweto, in South Africa . . . , maybe to California."

Uncovering The Untold Truth

During my two weeks in Vienna, I interviewed Dr. Erben several times. While admitting his own culpability, he adamantly maintained that Flynn was never involved in any type of espionage activity. Nor do the declassified government files attribute pro-Nazi sentiments to Errol Flynn. The true nature of

Flynn's political beliefs are evident in his tour of South America in 1940, especially, his visit to Brazil.

Stanley Hilton's authoritative *Hitler's Secret War In South America* (Ballantine, 1981) reveals how President Vargas of Brazil was being courted by Germany, the Reich's leading trade partner. The Roosevelt administration was greatly alarmed, since Brazil possessed strategic raw materials in abundance, and establishment of military bases in the northeastern section was vital to American security. Both America and Britain were trying to sway the shrewd and opportunistic Vargas away from Berlin's influence.

Writes Hilton: "Washington conducted intense propaganda warfare against Germany, sounding the theme of the Nazi threat to the Hemisphere."

Flynn was a very popular film star in South America, important enough to meet with the Brazilian head of state. What transpired at their meeting is unknown. What did take place was a radio broadcast by Flynn, promoting Pan-American unity.

Brazilian Broadcast of Errol Flynn in Rio, June 14, 1940:

> Boa noite!
> The Department of Press and Propaganda has been kind enough to invite me to address the people of Brazil. This I consider a great honor and a wonderful opportunity for me to express a little of the very deep and sincere emotion that you people have inspired in me by your extraordinarily kind reception.
>
> There I was at the airport—a stranger who can't even speak your language, but when I arrived and saw all around me hundreds of happy, smiling friendly faces— somehow I didn't feel like a stranger any longer. So I had to come and thank you, and I would like to take this opportunity to speak to you of one other thing— something that is very close to my heart.
>
> I like to feel that perhaps my visit down here had helped in a very small way to forge one more link in the great chain that binds South America and North America.
>
> If this is so, no matter the link, I could not possibly be

more happy. For in these days, when the world is resounding to the tramp of armies, when the weak no longer seem to have any security, when might surmounts right, for the world's future may lie in Pan Americanism.

North and South America stand united, strongly bound together by a sense of right—perhaps this union will show a light—that will shine like a blazing beacon to guide back the rest of mankind towards the principles of our continents. I personally would not want to live in a world ruled by other principles than these. Brazilians, please forgive me for being so serious. But if sincerity means speaking of those things closest to a man's heart, then I have been sincere.

Perhaps I will have another opportunity to speak to you—next time I hope not so seriously. Perhaps then I shall be able to tell you about our country in the North, of Hollywood, and what we are doing in the picture world. Once more—let me thank you from the bottom of my heart.

Terei Saudades (I will have great longings to return)

The speech seems to have been made at the request of Washington, for Flynn immediately sent a copy to President Roosevelt:

June 15, 1940

Errol Flynn to President Franklin D. Roosevelt

Dear Mr. President:

I thought you might be interested in this copy of a radio address which I made last night at the invitation of the Brazilian Government over the "Hora do Brazil" hookup.

This broadcast followed an interview I had in the afternoon with President Getulio Vargas, and I hope coincides with your ideas of Pan-American unity and friendship.

I trust you are enjoying the best of health, and with

kindest regards to Mrs. Roosevelt and yourself, I remain,

Cordially yours,
Errol Flynn

President Roosevelt sent the following response:

June 26, 1940

Dear Errol Flynn:

Please accept my thanks for your kind letter of June fifteenth from Rio de Janeiro. I am delighted to have the copy of the radio address which you delivered at the invitation of the Brazilian Government over the "Hora do Brazil" hookup.

Very sincerely yours,
Franklin D. Roosevelt

Flynn was a great admirer of President Roosevelt, as verified by the letter he sent to Marguerite Lehand, the President's secretary.

April 29, 1942

Dear Miss LeHand,

A couple of years ago the President and Mrs. Roosevelt very kindly sent me pictures of themselves.

Not long ago these were burnt in a fire caused in my study by a careless friend who had gone to sleep there with a drink in one hand and a cigarette in the other— presumably I only escaped a similar fate by having tired of this friend's conversation and gone to sleep in another part of the house.

The pictures, of course, were highly prized possessions—so do you think it would be too much trouble to have two more inscribed to me?

Kindest personal regards.

Sincerely
Errol Flynn

The White House response:

May 20, 1942

My dear Mr. Flynn:

In accordance with the request contained in your letter of April twenty-ninth to Miss LeHand, the President has been very glad to sign one of his photographs to replace the one which was destroyed. It comes to you with his best wishes.

Very sincerely yours,
Grace G. Tully

Higham claims that Flynn was also involved with other individuals, besides Dr. Erben, who were supposedly pro-Nazi collaborators. These were: Countess Dorothy Dentice di Frasso, Freddy McEvoy, Axel Wenner-Gren, Sir Harry Oakes, and Gertrude Anderson. An examination of the FBI files reveals information to the contrary.

Countess di Frasso was an American socialite who had lived in Italy for many years. She regained her American citizenship in 1941, and her home in Los Angeles became a center for celebrity gatherings. The FBI conducted an investigation of Countess di Frasso because of suspicion that her years of living in Italy had been due to Fascist sympathies. According to Higham, she was "a pro-Nazi operator" who had offered to finance an elaborate explosive device for use by the Axis. Once again, Charles Higham has the facts in error. Dorothy di Frasso had made clear her anti-Axis sentiments in FBI interviews. The FBI had been suspicious of her frequent trips to Mexico; however, the true reasons for trips to Mexico were patriotic, rather than sinister. She was developing explosives for the U.S. military.

FBI Memorandum, Sept. 25, 1942, Edward A. Tamm to Mr. Ladd:

Joe Keenan called with reference to the Countess di Frasso who he is representing. He advised that she is doing some work with a Dr. Bonato who is in Mexico but who is an American citizen of Italian extraction. The two have been working in close harmony with the Army's Ordinance Department on explosives and have been working with Colonel Weeks, Military Attache to the American Embassy in Mexico City. The War Department has been sending these people TNT for experimental purposes, and the finished product, their own composition, is sent back to the United States for the Government . . . .

Freddy McEvoy was a close friend of Flynn. Usually characterized as a playboy and sportsman who married wealthy women, he was supposedly "pro-Nazi." Higham claims that his special virtue for the Nazis was that he could bring socialites into Hitler's orbit.

Freddy McEvoy had been investigated by the FBI, because he had been issued an exit visa from the French Government during the German occupation while still a British subject of military age. In the course of the FBI's investigation, an anonymous individual reported that McEvoy was pro-German, yet the official FBI "synopsis of facts" states: "these allegations were not confirmed." The following conclusions were reached concerning the FBI's investigation of Freddy McEvoy:

> FBI File No. 100-12556 FAC Frederick G. McEvoy
> August 25, 1942
> (excerpt)
>
> A review of the investigation to date fails to indicate that subject is pro-Nazi in his sympathies, or that he is engaged in any subversive activities . . . .

Higham writes of Freddy McEvoy being involved in setting up German U-boat refueling bases in Mexico and Central America, and those charges can only be termed as preposterous and without factual reference.

Axel Wenner-Gren was an extremely wealthy Swedish industrialist who, writes Higham, "was one of Errol's closest friends. Tall, magnificently built, he looked like a Viking, but had the soul of a rattlesnake . . . ." A *Washington Times-Herald* photo of March 25, 1945, shows Wenner-Gren to be a paunchy, white-haired man in his sixties. There is no foundation to Higham's claim that he was a close friend of Flynn. Wenner-Gren was the founder and major stockholder of the international Electrolux Corporation. Numerous stories circulated about Wenner-Gren, due to his enormous wealth and connections with world leaders. On January 15, 1942, Wenner-Gren's name had been placed on the Proclaimed List at the suggestion of the State Department. His assets in the U.S. were frozen.

According to Higham, part of his fabulous wealth came from his sale of munitions and other strategic materials to Hitler.

An in-depth interview by representatives of the FBI and the Attorney General's Office was conducted in March 1945, in Mexico. Wenner-Gren was at a loss to understand why he had been placed on the Proclaimed List. Reference was made to Wenner-Gren's book, *Call To Reason,* published in 1938. In this book, he had extolled democracy and denounced fascism and nazism. He explained his connection with the Swedish munitions firm known as Bofors: "He stated that he was selected as Chairman of the Board of the company and in this capacity he installed a program of refusing to sell armaments to Japan, Germany, or Russia . . . . " Wenner-Gren had been scrutinized by U.S. officials because he had met with Hermann Goering, in an intermediary capacity, to prevent war between Germany and Britain. After all, Wenner-Gren was Swedish, a citizen of a neutral country.

But, he told the U.S. officials that "he has no sympathy with the Nazi cause . . . ."

Yet, writes Higham, "Wenner-Gren introduced Errol to the multi-millionaire Canadian Sir Harry Oakes and the Duke and Duchess of Windsor. Since they shared his admiration for Hitler, Errol was in ideal company." The declassified FBI files of Sir Harry Oakes, who was mysteriously murdered, make no reference to Errol Flynn at all. The meeting, like Flynn's "admiration for Hitler," is unsubstantiated in the Higham biography, leaving no credibility for the author's sensational claim.

Gertrude Anderson was, writes Higham, a Swedish "Nazi singer," who was Flynn's mistress and on the American government's list of wanted Nazi agents. Flynn had supposedly dated other Nazi beauties, such as "Tara Marsh." In Hawaii, he supposedly was enamored with a Nazi agent named "Erna Bauer," and the FBI had been intercepting her telegrams to him—which mentioned the sinking of Allied ships.

The U.S. Department of Justice, Office of the Associate Attorney General, informed me that a search had been initiated by the FBI, and "the Bureau has been unable to locate any records which are identifiable with those named individuals . . . ." The conclusion must be drawn that these Nazi dream girls are fictitious.

The same can be said of Flynn's alleged connection with German Consul, *George Gyssling.* The declassified FBI file of Gyssling makes no reference to Flynn whatsoever.

However, the Department of the Army intelligence file on Gyssling reveals an interesting letter. It is from Julius Klein, National Commander of the Jewish Veterans to Military Intelligence of the War Department (Dec. 18, 1947).

> If you will look through the confidential files, at the time when I conducted investigations against subversive elements, you will find that Dr. Gyssling had been of immense help to us in giving me important information. I do not hesitate to say that he was always against his superiors, and without his aid I could not have secured the information which was so necessary to get a complete dossier on subversive activities.

In examining the "documentary excerpts" in the appendix of *The Untold Story,* there appears, under No. 27, a document that has not been published in its entirety and is consequently misleading. It is a Department of State memo of a telephone intercept concerning Errol Flynn.

The document, as printed by Higham, has *blank spaces* where names actually appear. The true memo is released to the public, with the names clearly visible.

Jan. 18, 1943
VD-Mr. Alexander:

Your particular attention is invited to attached telephone intercept SATP 9891 from Errol E. Flynn to

Linda P. Welter. FC understands that Flynn was recently in Mexico at which time he associated with *Hilda Kruger,* (alias Militza Korjus?) German national and suspected enemy agent.

VD may desire to consider most carefully the visa application of *Linda P. Welter.*

W.H.A. Coleman

The impression conveyed by the Higham version is that Flynn was definitely consorting with a "suspected enemy agent." Once the actual names of the women mentioned in the memo are inserted, the situation is made clearer.

Linda P. Welter came to the U.S. as Flynn's protege. She became the actress Linda Christian and later married Tyrone Power. Miliza Korjus was an opera singer who had appeared in the MGM film, *The Great Waltz.* Korjus was in Mexico during this period, working in Mexican films.

Hilda Kruger was a German actress who had made several films at the UFA Studio in Germany. She had come to America in September of 1939, with the intention of making films. For several months, she had met with important Hollywood figures to advance her career. In May of 1940, she had accompanied German consul Fritz Wiedemann to a nightclub, thereby incurring the curiosity of many, including FBI agents, that she was involved in suspicious activities.

In February of 1941, she entered Mexico, where she subsequently made four motion pictures. It is apparent from the surveillance files that American intelligence agents in Mexico had difficulty distinguishing between Kruger and Korjus. Many documents actually state that Kruger/Korjus was one person, as is apparent in the January 18, 1943, Department of State document. Consequently, it is unclear with whom Flynn supposedly associated in Mexico.

Kruger was a woman who moved in prominent social circles and claimed to have known Anthony Eden, Churchill's Secretary of State for War. In Los Angeles, she met numerous producers, actors, and wealthy men. She denied any involvement with German espionage and was never charged with such activity.

In addition to analyzing U.S. surveillance files and materials in the Warner Archives, I contacted numerous individuals to discover the facts about Flynn. Was he a fascist or anti-Semitic? When Flynn arrived in Britain in 1933 to commence his acting career, he supposedly immersed himself in an English aristocratic set, who were admirers of fascism. "Errol's hatred of Jews," writes Higham, "endeared him to the admirers of Hitler in the 'Fascist Mayfair set.' "

In May of 1940, police had seized the membership list of the British Union of Fascists. Prominent leaders, such as Oswald Mosley, were eventually imprisoned during World War II. If Flynn had been a sympathizer of Mosley or fascism, the information would have undoubtedly surfaced during the intense British crackdown of fascist collaborators. One of the foremost authorities on British fascism is Professor Robert Skidelsky. His authoritative biography, *Oswald Mosley,* is an excellently researched book about Mosley and other aristocrats who believed that fascism would benefit England. Professor Skidelsky informed me, "I have no knowledge of Errol Flynn's involvement with Mayfair fascists" (letter, June 24, 1981).

Another glaring historical error—and preposterous claim—is Higham's statement that Erben may have been present—or possibly planned—the assassination of Austrian Chancellor Dollfuss. Higham's appalling lack of historical accuracy is evident when he writes: "Hundreds of Gestapo men burst into the Chancellery and cornered the anti-Nazi Chancellor." Even second-rate historians know that the Gestapo was the German Secret State Police. Dollfuss had been murdered by members of the Viennese SS Standarte. It is apparent how far afield Higham has wandered from his realm of Hollywood gossip. Claims that Erben was involved in the Dollfuss murder lack, to say the least, historical credibility.

The Warner Archives

The University of Southern California was given invaluable motion picture material by Warner Brothers. The Warner Archives contain stills, scripts, pressbooks, and numerous memos relating to motion pictures made by Warner Brothers. Scholars and researchers may examine the material, with explicit guidelines explained by archivists responsible for administering use of the collection. Each individual examining material is informed that copyright clearance remains with Warner Brothers, and that *nothing may be quoted* unless permission is granted by the Warner Brothers Legal Dept. A major portion of *The Untold Story* was based on numerous documents in the Warner Archives. Clearance is a very time-consuming procedure. It took me one year to obtain permission to quote from the Warner Archives. The following comparison illustrates "the Higham technique" of senationalizing primary source material to unfairly blacken Flynn. During the shooting of *Another Dawn,* a contract dispute occurred between Warner Brothers and Flynn. Flynn's agent, Myron Selznick, attempted to resolve the trouble.

The Higham Account:

> One afternoon, Errol had to shoot a crucial scene with Kay Francis. Errol refused to come out of his dressing room. He had been told not to do so until the letter of agreement arrived in Selznick's office. The production manager, Tenny Wright, beat on Errol's door and screamed, "What the fuck do you think you're doing?" Errol shouted back a stream of abuse. Tenny Wright called Jack Warner. Warner called Selznick. Selznick yelled down the line, "Yes, I did tell him to wait there, and he'll go on waiting there until you send me that letter you promised." The battle went on all afternoon. Finally, Warner was forced to rush a telegram to Selznick so that the scene could be shot that night.

The Actual Memo by Tenny Wright (in the Flynn Legal File, Warner Archives):

November 10, 1936

> The following incident occurred today about 2:30 p.m.; Mr. Jack Warner telephoned me at my office and asked me if I knew that Errol Flynn was not on the set. I told him I did know it; that Flynn was in his dressing room; that I understood from him that Mr. Warner had

told him to wait in his dressing room for a call from Mr. Warner to Myron Selznick. Mr. Warner denied asking Flynn to wait in his dressing room, but admitted that he had an appointment with Myron Selznick at 2:30 p.m. in his office. Mr. Warner instructed me to go to Flynn's dressing room and find out why Flynn had not reported on the set to the call of the production office, as the whole company, including Miss Francis, was waiting on the stage, and was being held up and not able to do anything until Flynn arrived.

As I was going toward the dressing room, I saw Mr. Flynn entering Stage 8, where the production company was shooting. I went up to him and asked why he had been waiting in his dressing room, and he replied that he had waited there because Mr. Myron Selznick instructed him to do so. I asked Flynn if he didn't know he was working for Warner Brothers and was holding up the company. He said he knew that, but he was taking instructions from his personal representative, Mr. Myron Selznick, who had told him to wait there with him for a call from Mr. Warner. I told him that he had had orders from the company assistant to report on the stage at a certain time, and that Mr. Selznick had no right to tell him to do otherwise. Mr. Flynn replied, "I don't want to have any trouble with you, Tenny," and I told him that I wasn't looking for trouble, but that he was to take orders from the company assistant instead of Myron Selznick. I also asked him, "Are you going on?" meaning, was he going on with his part, and he replied, "That's what I came down for," and he walked on the stage. I then returned to Projection Room #4, where Mr. Warner, Mr. Wallis, Mr. McCord, Mr. Lord, and Mr. Arnow were looking at rushes, and reported to Mr. Warner what had occurred, the telephone rang, and Mr. Selznick was on the phone and wanted to know when he could see Mr. Warner. Mr. Warner told him that he could not see him today, and would not be able to see him until the early part of next week. Mr. Warner also asked Mr. Selznick why he had instructed an actor to wait in his dressing room and hold up a production company. I could not hear what Mr. Selznick answered, but Mr. Warner said, "Yes, you did, because Flynn just told our Production Manager, Mr. Wright, that you had ordered him to wait there." Then Mr. Selznick said, "Yes, all right, I'll admit it. I did tell him to wait there," and he said it in such a loud voice over the phone that all of the above mentioned gentlemen could hear him.

Mr. Warner then told me to go to Mr. Obringer's office and dictate the above facts.

T.C. Wright

"The above facts" make no mention whatsoever of Flynn or Tenny Wright shouting abuse. Higham's biography of Bette Davis also leaned heavily on the Warner Archives. He refers to an incident that took place while Bette Davis was working with Flynn in *The Sisters*. Higham's version claims that Jack Sullivan, the assistant director, wrote an acid memorandum to his superior, Tenny Wright, saying, "I don't know whether she's sick or getting too much social life." Higham claims this was a sly reference to the persistent rumors that Davis had been dating Howard Hughes.

The actual memo is:

Jack Sullivan to T.C. Wright

July 12, 1938 (excerpt)

Anita Louise tells me that when she started this picture she had an acute attack of appendicitis, and she was afraid this was a re-attack. She was continually complaining of how bad she was feeling when she went into this picture. She said she was very tired. My personal opinion is: I don't know whether she is sick, or if it is too much social life.

Jack Sullivan

It is amazing that Higham has not only misapplied this comment about Anita Louise, but has also conjured up the deduction that this confirmed the rumor that Better Davis had been dating Howard Hughes! Davis denounced the Higham biography about her. She termed the author a "literary crook who, until the end of time can wreck, not only our lives, but those of our families and friends . . . " (letter, Aug. 10, 1982).

A research analysis of the Warner Archives material regarding Flynn reveals many other instances of Charles Higham inventing scenes that never happened. One such situation concerns a story that pertains to Flynn's work in the film, *The Case of the Curious Bride.* Higham says, in one scene, Flynn hit Margaret Lindsay over the head with a poker, then she fell "bleeding and unconscious" and was rushed to the hospital. A week later, she came out with eleven stitches in her head and did the scene again.

The "Daily Production and Progress Report" for February 20, 1935, states: "cast started today—Errol Flynn." The records show that Flynn worked with Margaret Lindsay on the 20th and 21st. Miss Lindsay worked with other cast members on the 22nd and 23rd, while Flynn was off. The entire cast was off February 24, a Sunday. On the 25th, Miss Lindsay worked. On the 26th, Flynn and Miss Lindsay worked together, and the report reads: "cast closed today—Lindsay-Woods-Flynn." There is no mention whatsoever of Margaret Lindsay being struck in the head by Flynn, nor of her stay in any hospital. That a virtual unknown, such as Flynn, could have injured a major star and continued to work at Warner's strains credibility. Certainly, something so eventful would have been noted, for even minor problems were mentioned. One memo during production states that Hal Wallis wanted to get a new cameramen, because three shots had been out of focus.

The production material of *Dive Bomber* directly refutes another tale that Higham writes about. The "late Robert Lord," producer of the film, supposedly revealed to Higham that a "special, semi-documentary" advance print had been sent to Japan. This print included scenes of Pearl Harbor that were included at Flynn's suggestion. In reality, the film was closely supervised by Naval Intelligence officials while being shot at the San Diego Naval Station. That there was never any such "special, semi-documentary" advance print is made clear by Robert Lord's own statement, which shows explicitly the meticulous review procedure regarding any film made with the assistance of the Navy.

Robert Lord directed a July 8, 1941, memo to Mr. W.J.McCord of the Film Editing Department (Warner Archives):

Dear Mac:

I know we are in a great rush to get DIVE BOMBER finished and so I want to remind you of a routine that has to be gone through with the Navy. Before we can show this picture to a public audience—even to a preview audience—the picture must be passed by the Naval Board of Review in Washington. I believe this is provided for in a contract that Warner Brothers signed with the Navy before getting naval co-operation. As soon as we get a complete color print from Technicolor, Commander Warner, George Amy and I should fly to Washington—having previously shipped a print of the picture air-express. The picture must be run for the Naval Board and any changes made as demanded by them before it can be shown to a public audience. This is especially true now since the United States is in a state of national emergency and the Navy is triply careful . . . "

That Warner Brothers would have possibly shipped a film print to Japan without Naval authorization is another preposterous piece of fiction invented by Charles Higham.

For a demonstration of Higham's technique of inventing quotations where none exist, the following passage is presented. It concerns a memo written during *Objective Burma*.

The Higham Version:

He told producer Frank Mattison, "Mattie, I'm just walking through this goddamn picture. Or wading, if you like. Not a bloody thing has happened since this picture started except routine dialogue and walking, walking, walking."

The Actual Memo:

June 19, 1944

Frank Mattison
to T.C. Wright
(excerpt)

> As you know, MR. FLYNN says he had been waiting for
> changes to come through and they came through
> SATURDAY apparently unchanged from the previous
> script. MR. FLYNN has told me that he is still walking
> through the picture and not a damn thing has happened
> since the picture started where anything other than
> routine dialogue and walking has been photographed.

To invent quotations where none exist displays a blatant
disregard for journalistic integrity.

According to Higham, the Warner Archives "disclose Flynn's
evasion of the draft and refusal to sell bonds or subscribe to the
USO drive." *(Los Angeles Times* March 2, 1980.)

Contrary to the Higham assertions, Errol Flynn participated in
a USO tour to Alaska, bond drives in Louisiana and Missouri, and
numerous patriotic fund-raising events in Los Angeles, including
the following parade, described in the *Los Angeles Times* (Nov. 19,
1944). The headline proclaims "350,000 Cheer Parade for War Loan
Campaign." Then: "First to appear was Errol Flynn, swashbuckler
turned cowboy, who was greeted by squeals of delight and warm
applause . . . ."

Higham never misses an opportunity in accusing Flynn of
being a compulsive liar. He claims that Flynn even lied to his most
intimate friends about the reason he was rejected for military
service: "Like most liars, he made mistakes. He told Jim Fleming
and Buster Wiles he had spots on his lungs." The veracity of
Flynn's statement is verified in this Warner memo.

> Frank Mattison to T.C. Wright, July 16, 1942 (Warner
> Archives):
>
> It is 11:20 a.m. and I have just finished talking to Dr.
> Leland Chapman concerning Errol Flynn, who is still in
> the Good Samaritan Hospital . . . He told me that they
> had checked Mr. Flynn over very thoroughly yesterday,
> and he says that Mr. Flynn's lungs are, as you know,
> spotted, and that the man was in a state of collapse . . . .

The Untold Story contains so many sensationalistic tales that,
since Higham fails to document their source, curious readers or

scholars who wish to verify their accuracy are at a loss. Upon close scrutiny, the eye-opening fables evaporate like puffs of smoke.

Example: Charles Higham writes of an incident that supposedly took place in Miami, in early 1950. According to the tale, Flynn and Freddy McEvoy "hired a girl," whom they shared. In the morning, after they had left the Nautilus Hotel, the woman was found dead. States Higham: "The police questioned them closely, but a bribe silenced an investigating officer." In response to my query regarding this incident, Captain Konrad VonEiff of the Miami Beach Police Department informed me that "most of our files go back as far as 1950, particularly important files such as homicide. In addition, our Central Index goes back to 1930."

The police files do not reflect *any records whatsoever* of this story. As Captain VonEiff puts it: "There was no Nautilus Hotel in the year 1950, so either the date in the book is wrong or the incident did not take place in this city" (letter, June 12, 1980). Since Higham provides no name of the victim, source, or pertinent facts, little credibility can be attached to such a tale. Indeed, the Miami vice story seems to be in the realm of Higham's claim that Flynn, as a boy, had glued the eyelids of a mad dog together. *A mad dog!*

But what should a reader expect when, on the very first page of *The Untold Story*, Charles Higham actually quotes Errol Flynn's ghost! How many serious biographers quote the deceased? Only Charles Higham.

The biased attitude that prevails throughout the book reaches a pinnacle when Higham belittles Flynn for the name of his yacht:

Errol left a final joke. For years, he told people 'Zaca' was the Samoan word for peace. But the Samoan alphabet does not contain the letters Z and C. The word comes from no known language. It means nothing.

If Flynn gave the explanation of "Zaca" as "peace" he was merely quoting its original owner. In *The Cruise of the Zaca* by former owner Templeton Crocker (Harper, 1933) appears the following passages: "Zaca is an Indian word meaning 'peace.'"

Higham's imagination flies off the page when he writes that Flynn aided an IRA gunman in an attempt to assassinate King

George and Queen Elizabeth in 1939. Claims Higham: "Scotland Yard and FBI agents seized Russell, who admitted the Flynn connection." Of course, neither nation prosecuted Flynn. Why not? No reason is put forth by the author. How does Higham explain the fact that Flynn met Queen Elizabeth in 1949. Higham purports that these tales are in Britain's Ministry of Defence files. As previously noted, this agency termed the spy allegations a "lot of nonsense."

Individuals with whom I spoke are especially resentful about seeing their name in the "acknowledgments" section. It gives the impression that they had actually participated in damning Flynn. The actual extent of this type of involvement in the book may be judged by examining the participation of Chauncey Tramutolo who was Dr. Erben's attorney during his denaturalization trial. He undoubtedly would know a lot about Dr. Erben during the period before he went to Mexico. I eventually located Chauncey Tramutolo's daughter, Ann Van Sicklen. She was surprised that her father was listed in the acknowledgments of the book, since he is unfortunately senile and has been in this condition for a number of years. The impression given by listing his name is that he had been interviewed by Higham.

The most vocal critic of *The Untold Story* was Flynn's second wife, Nora Eddington. She recounted her life with Flynn in her own book, *Errol and Me*. This is one of the primary sources about the life of Errol Flynn. Although she experienced considerable anguish as Flynn's wife, Nora Eddington still comes to Flynn's defense when Higham writes of Flynn being a Nazi and worse. She terms the book "vile lies" and regrets that she and her daughters ever spoke to Higham. Her daughter, Rory Flynn, says that Higham came to them explaining how he was going to write "a tribute" to their father.

Patrice Wymore, Flynn's third wife, termed the book "libelous, scandalous, ridiculous, and preposterous." Acclaimed actress Ida Lupino was equally vehement in her comments: "I am outraged, and so are others, about the sick and evil lies regarding Errol Flynn. For years, he was one of the finest friends I ever had, and we both hated Nazis." Olivia de Havilland, Flynn's co-star in many motion pictures, termed the book "reprehensible allegations."

Paul McWilliams, Jr., actor and stuntman, is one of the many individuals who knew Flynn personally and felt betrayed and used after they helped Higham and were then confronted with a biography stating Flynn was a Nazi spy. Says an incensed McWilliams, "Errol was a wonderful guy. Higham is nothing but a liar." Charles Higham informed Eddie Albert that he was "a historian" investigating Flynn's Nazi connections. "By then," says Albert, "word had spread about the type of book he was doing. I said, 'You? A historian? What a joke!' I hung up in his face."

Veteran actor Robert Douglas related information "off the record" and was shocked to see that Higham had used the stories anyway. Director Irving Rapper was also treated in a similar fashion. Rapper admittedly found Flynn "rather tinsel," but was startled to see that Higham had "twisted" his comments, to Flynn's detriment.

Teddy Stauffer, the man who is known as "Mr. Acapulco," was a lifelong friend of Flynn, beginning with the early forties. When Flynn traveled to Mexico, he usually relaxed at one of Stauffer's hotels or nightspots. Says Stauffer, "All the fag stuff about Errol being homosexual with Tyrone Power, all that stuff is so poor. It's so cheap. I never saw Flynn with any boys in Mexico." Stauffer was especially incredulous about Higham's claim that Flynn had some type of affair with Apolonio Castillo, one of the first divers to plunge from Acapulco's steep Quebrada cliffs. Continues Stauffer: "The champion swimmer, Apolonio Castillo—Higham calls him Apolonio Diaz—was married and had children. A girl I tried to make and loved very much, he got her before I got her, and she was in love with him. She figured like his second wife."

Nina Quirol, a model in Mexico in the forties, knew both Flynn and Castillo. She also scoffs at Higham's homosexual fantasy: "Apolonio was a man's man."

Jerry Courneya, still photographer for Errol Flynn Productions during the forties, was equally adamant in his assertions that Flynn had no attraction to men. Says Courneya, "I was a young guy, practically a kid, when I went to work for Flynn. We spent hours together on his last yacht, the *Zaca*. I even sailed with him to Jamaica. He never approached me or anyone else with some type of homosexual advance. In all the years I knew him, I never even heard the slightest rumor about such a thing. The homosexual allegation, like the rest of the book, is pure bullshit."

British actress Freda Jackson worked with Flynn in the Northampton Repertory Theater during this period and could not recall anything anti-Semitic in his attitude (*Chronicle and Echo,* Jan. 8, 1980).

The comments of Vincent Sherman, director of *The Adventures of Don Juan* and other classic films:

> As for Errol being a Nazi spy, I have my doubts. He was completely apolitical . . . . I found him a perfectly delightful and charming human being, with a fantastic sense of humor and most talented in the field that he best demonstrated . . . .
>
> He certainly knew I was Jewish and he could not have been more pleasant and friendly to me. At the end of Don Juan he gave me a gold cigar clipper, which some said was unusual since he was supposed to be tight with money.

The writer who helped Flynn with *My Wicked Wicked Ways,* Earl Conrad, says "Flynn knew I was Jewish on the day we started work together. We became good friends." Conrad was furious over *The Untold Story.* He had graciously loaned Higham rare photographs of Flynn as a child in Australia, but prohibited reproduction of the photographs in the paperback version of *The Untold Story.* Conrad studied Flynn's private papers, including early diaries and letters. He never derived the least impression that Flynn was an anti-Semite or Nazi sympathizer. He described the book as "Shades of Joe McCarthy and guilt by association . . . literary ghoulism."

Phyllis Searles, former wife of artist John Decker, was appalled by *The Untold Story:* "Flynn was the most charming person you'd ever want to meet in your life. Everyone who knew him was aware what the real man was like. The book is such a lie, not only about Errol but John Decker too. John was one of the best artists in the country, but to hear Higham tell it, he was only a caricaturist or cartoonist."

At one time, Searles had been married to Jim Fleming, Flynn's stand-in. It was Fleming who had arranged her interview with Higham. Says Searles: "Jim was a very tragic man. He didn't really care about anybody. He was the biggest liar in the world. The story Higham printed about John Decker's death, where John's body supposedly sat up during the cremation and Errol acting so silly and so on, it's untrue. That came from Fleming. The actual incident had happened to John Decker. A bartender friend had died, and John was asked to be a witness at the cremation. Of course, the body's contractions made it sit up. John always said, 'God, it was terrible to watch.' How the story ever came to be about Flynn is an amazing distortion, really ridiculous."

Buster Wiles, Flynn's stunt double and close friend, was also incredulous as to Fleming's purported statement that Flynn had admitted to him that he was guilty of sexual relations with Peggy Satterlee and Betty Hansen. Says Wiles: "At no time, during the trial or in later years, did Errol make such a statement to me or any other close friend. If he had, the information would have gotten around to me. As for Peggy Satterlee, I was on the *Sirocco* the weekend she was supposedly attacked. I shared the cabin with Flynn and *know for a fact* he did not have relations with her. Jim Fleming obviously did not know what he was talking about."

Fleming's lack of credibility is apparent, even in 1970, when he told Higham: "I had conclusive evidence from somebody who was very close to Errol at the end that he deliberately killed himself with morphine." That Fleming would make such an erroneous statement is beyond belief. The truth is in the scientific evidence of the coroner's report: "Exhaustive Toxicological Examination has disclosed no poison or foreign substance which could be directly associated in any way with his death."

Nadia Gardiner, wife of the late actor Reginald Gardiner, agreed to Higham's pleas for an interview, but was astonished at his questions: "I knew he was out to make Errol look bad. Errol was a wonderful man, so I didn't say much."

Other friends of Errol Flynn wish they had done the same thing.

The true source of the controversy, Dr. Erben, died in January 1985. Prior to his death, I interviewed his British-born wife, Joan Erben. They had met aboard a ship in 1939, but did not marry until after the war, in 1950. Their marriage was destined to be a stormy one. When I spoke with Joan Erben she was living in London, separated from her husband. Mrs. Erben characterized her husband as an enigma, a strange mixture of brilliance and stupidity. In their years together, they lived in distant lands: Iran, Saudi Arabia, and Indonesia.

Joan Erben didn't learn of her husband's controversial past until after they were wed. She finally decided to leave him after he failed to fulfill a promise made years earlier. Said Mrs. Erben: "He always promised me a home, a real house, but he never purchased one." But she describes with pride how Dr. Erben's profound knowledge of tropical diseases led to the quarantine laws of Indonesia, which are still in effect, just as his medical work with lepers was admired. Yet, his strange personality brought about continuous quarrels.

As she explained, "Money was always a source of friction between us. He was very stingy. He didn't even wear socks or underwear, to save money. He—actually a doctor, mind you— would beg bread from ships and then resell it, just to make money. He was always ready to blame someone else for his own mistakes."

During our conversation in Joan Erben's home, her elderly mother brightened on learning that Dr. Erben suffered from arthritis: "He stole my daughter's inheritance. I wish I could be there to see him die, not just die, but suffer." Joan Erben later wrote to me about her curious husband:

> It seems to me a great tragedy that he always used his undoubted talents for unworthy objectives. I believe he could have become anything he would have chosen— a Nobel prize winner, a minister in the Government, but he is a very secretive man and lacks a total commitment to anything. He works with superhuman energy for short periods of time; then comes a complete change of direction . . . He was born a Jew, became a Protestant, then a Muslim, and finally worked for the Catholic Mission in Lewoleba, Indonesia . . . . When we lived in Bali we had some half-dozen monkeys which were his special pets and spent a great deal of time in the house. On a trip to the outlying islands we saw a very tiny monkey, not more than six inches tall but with a face as old as Time. He made no secret of the fact that he wanted

to acquire this animal, but I did not feel I could cope with yet another monkey. He swore the strongest oath he could swear on his mother's life that he would not buy the monkey. I believed him. When our ship was ready for sailing the next day, he came along with this small monkey perched on his shoulder. I was very distressed at seeing this and reminded him of his promise. He sneered and, I shall never forget it, said, "I only promised you I would not buy it! I did not promise you I would not get it in any other way! I did not buy it, so I have not broken my promise. If you didn't want me to have it you should have made sure what sort of promise you were dragging out of me!"

I recall once in 1939, I asked him what he would do were Germany and America to go to war on opposite sides. He was then claiming to be a U.S. citizen but with strong ties to Austria. He was furious and said that "the good old USA would never fight Great Britain's war this time against Germany!"

I realize how he is frightened to make a decision in case the decision he makes will not be the one that brings him maximum reward all the time. He wants all of everything, all the time and even then he is not sure in his own mind that he has really got the very best deal . . . Politically, I do not believe he thought America would enter the war and that Germany would be the victor. Nonetheless, in characteristic fashion, he wanted to hedge his bet and work for both sides, so that he could claim a reward no matter who won (letters, Dec. 1, 1980, May 14, 1981).

Such is the essence of a strange man, an opportunist who would use anyone, including Errol Flynn, to protect himself.

Flynn made a serious misjudgment in trying to help Erben while the latter was in trouble over his citizenship dispute with the U.S. government. However, it is clear from Flynn's comments that he did not believe that Erben was a German agent, merely an oddball who often got in trouble. Reminiscing about Flynn, Erben often told his wife: "He was weak. Errol was easily bamboozled."

Amidst the many unsupported claims of Charles Higham's is the accusation that, during World War II, while Erben was in China, Flynn sent incriminating letters to him. As Higham puts it, "Detailed research into the records of the period show us clearly now that those letters were ultimately seized by the OSS. They are still under lock and key in the CIA files of OSS material."

After a wait of four-and-a-half years, the CIA sent me the declassified OSS file. The lengthy file, all of which pertains to Dr. Erben, contains *no incriminating letters* or otherwise, between Flynn and Erben. Once again, Higham's wishful thinking invents what he cannot prove. In fact, the OSS papers sum up Dr. Erben exactly as his wife described him, "He was an American when it was in his interests to be one, and a Nazi German on other occasions. He tried to play both sides against the middle but at last reports had failed ignominiously."

Dr. Erben always tried to whitewash his own espionage activities but even by his own admission in 1946 at the China War Crimes Trials he was a German spy in China. He betrayed his adopted country by spying on American seamen and internees in truly reprehensible actions. In 1938, he admitted to a U.S. official that *he* had spied in Spain.

There is no question that Flynn liked Erben but an individual must be judged *by his own actions,* not those of his friend. It is Dr. Erben who took photographs to Berlin and it is Dr. Erben who spied in China. The contention that Errol Flynn was a "subagent" is farfetched. In the mountainous pile of declassified files there is not even *one document* attributing pro-Nazi sentiments or actions to Errol Flynn. Analyzing the declassified documents Erben emerges as a political schizophrenic, often appearing as a rabid Nazi who professed admiration for Hitler, yet, othertimes appearing as an apolitical physician. Even in 1980 when I spoke to him he readily admitted that he had admired Hitler: "Oh, yes, he rebuilt the German economy and I admired Roosevelt too, because he did the same in America."

I enjoyed hearing Erben discuss his adventurous life but I knew the details of his betrayal of America and the Loyalist forces in Spain. Had Flynn ever read the lengthy transcript of Erben's testimony at the China War Crimes Trials he may not have been so kind to him in his memoirs. But calling Flynn a Nazi collaborator is no more valid than terming Erben's lawyer the same thing, simply because both men tried to assist Erben.

Whenever asked about the veracity of *The Untold Story*, Charles Higham indignantly referred the curious to the thousands of documents in Washington; yet, when the opportunity arose to substantiate his claims in the paperback version of his biography, he altered a critical FBI document and offered the fabrication to the unsuspecting who purchased his book. Any reporter guilty of such an action would be immediately dismissed from a newspaper. Any book, especially a biography, is only as valid as the author's credibility.

Charles Higham describes himself as a serious writer and a scholar; yet, in the academic realm the worst sin is falsifying primary source material to prove one's thesis. Deceitful, pseudoscholarship degrades information and distorts the truth. Anytime a biographer or historian does not present specific documentation, especially in controversial books, the accuracy of the text is immediately suspect.

Declassified surveillance documents are the proper realm of an objective, competent historian. Simply because an FBI file exists does not signify that the subject is guilty of anything; in fact, it has been established that the FBI under J. Edgar Hoover kept dossiers on one hundred-fifty of America's most distinguished writers, including William Faulkner, Katherine Anne Porter, John Steinbeck, and others.

As for Errol Flynn, the FBI provides a clear statement: "No information was developed to indicate that he had been a Nazi agent . . . ."

After carefully analyzing the declassified surveillance documents which supposedly form the basis of *Errol Flynn: The Untold Story*, the true nature of the book is apparent. It is a wild concoction, an abject travesty of serious literary technique. How much credence can be given to "a prominent director," "Anne C." or other anonymous sources who provide sensational, yet unverifiable stories? It is merely the author's word that these tales are true.

The biography was advertised as "the entire truth—long hidden in British and American classified files . . . ." Can a book with a fake surveillance document be regarded as true? Readers purchased the biography, fully expecting "the untold story;" instead, they received "the untrue story." Would not a refund be appropriate? "The Gestapo's most glamorous agent" exists only in the pages of an atrocious biography.

Mr. Higham's *American Swastika* (Doubleday 1985) is another book designed for sensational reading, rather than precise historical information. Chapter Fifteen, "The Man Who Used Cary Grant," returns to the subject of Carlos Vejarano y Cassina. Vejarano is featured as a dangerous agent: ". . . he learned of the secret arrangements between Roosevelt and Churchill for a U.S.-German war . . . . " And, claims the author: "One of his contacts was Errol Flynn."

In the extensive investigation concerning Vejarano there is no mention, not even one surveillance page, stating that Vejarano and Flynn had ever met. FBI agents questioned dozens of individuals and even traced Los Angeles telephone calls Vejarano had made. The subject met many famous people but there is no documentation that they knew one another. Once again, the author conveys the illusion of proof rather than the truth.

Neither is there any documentation in the declassified files, listed as source material for the chapter, that Vejarano had learned of "secret arrangements" between Roosevelt and Churchill. The latter information simply pumps up Vejarano to give the impression that he was a big-time spy, when actually he was virtually nothing. The FBI report of Special Agent L.L. Laughlin (July 4, 1944) documents the agency position: "Intensive investigation failed to develop any affirmative indications that Vejarano actually endeavored to gather information of an espionage character in the sense of being a real spy, although, as mentioned, he did report some impressions gained from conversations with prominent persons in the United States during the first few weeks after his arrival here. His falling in love with and subsequent marriage to a professional model in New York City, coupled with generous gifts from some of his more affluent friends, which enabled him to do considerable traveling in the United States, apparently resulted in imbueing Vejarano with a desire to remain here. In correspondence written around this time to his father, which was voluntarily turned over to the FBI, Vejarano mentioned how happy he was with his new-found life and expressed a desire to discontinue further association with the Captain in France."

An FBI radio script, prepared for public transmission, describes Vejarano as "The Playboy Spy."

Higham makes a surprising mistake concerning Vejarano's German handler: "Wurmann's right-hand man, Captain Richard Weiss . . . ." Weiss-Wurmann was the same person as verified in the FBI report of January 4, 1944: "Captain Richard Weiss who is also known as Major Richard Wurmann." Another glaring error is the author's claim that Vejarano went to prison for "a trifling two years." An FBI document of January 27, 1944, confirms: "Subject sentenced this morning by Federal Judge John Clancy to serve one year and one day in a Federal Penitentiary."

The chapter ends with another shot at Flynn. This time "proof" of Flynn's spy activities is based on "the internal evidence of Erben's diaries and letters." Claims Higham: "Flynn himself took thirteen reels of film of the Loyalist installations and handed them over to the Fascist spy Bradish Johnson in Paris." This is another misinterpretation of source material. Josef Fegerl was allowed access to Dr. Erben's personal papers. Fegerl wrote me:

> I have in my possession photocopies of his diary . . . documents and photos . . . . Erben wrote in his 1937 diary: 'Give Errol 13 reels exposed film.' In his 1938 diary: 'Errol return to me 10 reels film from Spain, 3 he keep.'

The reels were obviously given to Flynn for his *Photoplay* article. Higham claims that they were "handed over" to a spy but the diaries confirm that the 13 reels remained in Flynn's possession for a year. And, most logically, had they been of any significance they would have gone with Erben to Berlin. Higham invents the fact that these specific reels were of military installations. Josef Fegerl reproduces many of the photos from these reels in his 1985 book. They show Flynn as a journalist, meeting officials and common Spaniards alike. Flynn was in Spain from March 26 to April 4, 1937; however, Erben remained until May 8.

Dr. Erben later told A.J. Nicholas of the Department of State Passport Division (April 26, 1938) that "he had gone into the portion of Spain held by the Loyalist forces for the purpose of spying upon them . . . ." This is a strange thing for a trained spy to say; yet, once again, even in 1938 Erben admitted his own spy work but there is no mention of Errol Flynn being involved. After all, the true source of the controversy was always Dr. Hermann F. Erben.